'I Did It'
Mathematics
CCE Edition

Sudha Mahesh

CAMBRIDGE
UNIVERSITY PRESS

CAMBRIDGE UNIVERSITY PRESS
Cambridge, New York, Melbourne, Madrid, Cape Town,
Singapore, São Paulo, Delhi, Mexico City

Cambridge University Press
4381/4 Ansari Road, Daryaganj, Delhi 110002, India

www.cambridge.org
Information on this title: www.cambridge.org/9781107654051 Paperback
www.cambridge.org/9781107645127 Paperback with CD-ROM

© Cambridge University Press 2013

This publication is in copyright. Subject to statutory exception
and to the provisions of relevant collective licensing agreements,
no reproduction of any part may take place without the written
permission of Cambridge University Press.

First published 2013

Printed in India at Sanat Printers, Kundli

A catalogue for this publication is available from the British Library

ISBN 978-1-107-65405-1   Paperback
ISBN 978-1-107-64512-7   Paperback with CD-ROM

Additional resources for this publication at www.cambridgeindia.org

Cambridge University Press has no responsibility for the persistence or
accuracy of URLs for external or third-party internet websites referred to in
this publication, and does not guarantee that any content on such websites is,
or will remain, accurate or appropriate.

Every effort has been made to trace the owners of copyright material included in this
book. The publishers would be grateful for any omissions to be brought to their notice for
acknowledgement in future editions of the book.

Contents

	Overview	iv
	Preface	viii
1.	Patterns	1
2.	Numbers	9
3.	Numbers in Operation	23
4.	Roman Numerals	38
	Summative Assessment 1	**44**
5.	Test of Divisibility	46
6.	Factors and Multiples	52
7.	H.C.F and L.C.M	67
	Summative Assessment 2	**76**
8.	Fractions	77
9.	Decimals	106
10.	Profit and Loss	124
11.	Metric Measures	129
12.	Angles, Circles and Nets	140
	Summative Assessment 3	**155**
13.	Time	157
14.	Perimeter and Area	166
15.	Graphs	177
16.	Money	185
	Summative Assessment 4	**195**

Overview

Chapter	Chapter Name	Time Allotted	Content
1	Patterns	1 week	• Patterns in other spheres such as Mathematics, language, music, etc. • Patterns as being infinite • Vertical, horizontal and symmetrical patterns • Natural and man-made patterns
2	Numbers	2 weeks	• Comparison of numbers up to 6 digits • Numbers rounding off to the nearest ten, hundred and thousand • Numbers in Hindu Arabic and International systems • Regrouping numbers • Place value and face value • Number skills to solve word problems related to real-life situations
3	Numbers in Operation	2 weeks	• Exercises involving the four arithmetic operations • Terms related to each operation
4	Roman Numerals	1 week	• Different ancient number systems • Comparison between Hindu Arabic and other systems • Introduction to Roman numerals • Rules applied in writing Roman numerals • Conversion of Hindu Arabic numerals into Roman numerals and vice versa
5	Test of Divisibility	1 week	• Rules for dividing • Test of divisibility for numbers 2 to 9 • Completion of numbers to make them divisible by the given
6	Factors and Multiples	2 weeks	• Prime and composite numbers • Twin and coprime numbers • Methods to find factors, multiples, common factors
7	H.C.F and L.C.M	1 week	• Methods to find H.C.F. and L.C.M.
8	Fractions	4 weeks	• A fraction as part of one whole unit • A fraction as part of a set taken as one whole unit • Like and unlike fractions • Proper and improper fractions • Equivalent fractions • Addition and subtraction of fractions

Overview

Objectives	Outcome
- To help students look at patterns, beyond their natural environment - To help them appreciate patterns in music, language and Mathematics - To recognise patterns as being infinite - To understand that patterns can be natural, as that on a butterfly's body, or man-made - Music can be created through vocal and instrumental sounds	The students will be able to appreciate patterns in nature and use their creativity to make patterns on their own by using different media. As patterns in sound and music connect easily to students, it will be greatly enjoyed and can be used to teach concepts. Patterns will also help them in problem solving.
- To help student look at big numbers and express their numerical form - To help apply their understanding in real life situations - To compare two or more 6-digit numbers and arrange them in ascending and descending orders - To help change numbers from standard form to number names and vice versa	The students will be able to recognise big numbers and apply them in appropriate places. They will be able to quantify objects in real life.
- To help students develop an understanding of numbers - To develop understanding of arithmatic operations and techniques - To help them explore the relationship between operations - To learn estimation in problem solving and checking the results - To help the students memorise the process	The students will develop an understanding of the four arithmetic operations and the link between them. They will be able to visualise a variety of methods, useful for approaching problems.
- To learn about the ancient numeral systems - To help the students understand the usage of Roman numerals by everyone around the world - To see the similarities in the patterns used for numbers - To learn to convert from one system into the other	The students will be able to recognise, understand and apply the Roman numerals in their day-to-day activities. They will be able to use them in appropriate places.
- To learn the rules of divisibility - To determine if the test based on the rules works	The students will be able to apply the skill learnt, while dividing big numbers. They will also be able to use the appropriate divisor, based on the rules learnt.
- To help identify numbers as prime and composite using the sieve of Eratosthenes - To understand the relationship between factors and multiples - To quickly identify divisors of numbers	While recognising numbers as prime or composite the students learn about the divisibility rules of such numbers. Students will be able to identify divisors of numbers quickly and easily.
- To find H.C.F. and L.C.M. of numbers	Students will learn different methods of finding H.C.F and L.C.M.
- To help students understand that fractions can be derived from numbers as well - To understand what a numerator and a denominator mean - To recognise the fraction of a set - To read, write and identify fractions - To learn to use fractions in real-life situations	The students will understand fractions and use them to solve their day-to-day problems. They will be able to read and write fractions and make comparisons using the formulae.

Overview

Chapter	Chapter Name	Time Allotted	Content
9	Decimals	3 weeks	<ul><li>Decimals as part of a whole</li><li>Similarities and differences between decimals and fractions</li><li>Identification of place value of decimals</li><li>Application-based problems</li><li>Comparison of decimal numbers</li><li>Addition and subtraction of decimal numbers up to 3 places</li></ul>
10	Profit and Loss	1 week	<ul><li>Definitions of profit and loss</li><li>Rules involving profit and loss</li><li>Problem solving exercises to determine profit/loss</li></ul>
11	Metric Measures	3 or 4 weeks	<ul><li>Conversion of units</li><li>Measurement using customary units</li><li>Solving problems using appropriate measuring units and tools</li><li>Estimating and resolving</li></ul>
12	Angles, Circles and Nets	4 weeks	<ul><li>Point, line, line segment and ray</li><li>Definitions for different types of angles</li><li>Estimating, describing and constructing angles</li><li>Definition and ways of using a protractor</li></ul>
13	Time	2 weeks	<ul><li>Revision of different ways of finding out the passage of time</li><li>Time as shown by the clock, the seasons calendar and day and night</li><li>Conversion of time into lower units and from one unit into another</li></ul>
14	Perimeter and Area	3 weeks	<ul><li>Perimeter as the boundary of closed figures with straight sides</li><li>Area as the space occupied inside a closed figure</li><li>Methods to find area and perimeter</li><li>Perimeter and area of given figures</li></ul>
15	Graphs	2 weeks	<ul><li>Locating points on a grid using ordered pairs</li><li>Making different kinds of graphs</li><li>Graphs to gather information and answer questions</li></ul>
16	Money	2 weeks	<ul><li>Conversions – changing rupees to paise and vice versa</li><li>Different denominations of rupees and coins</li><li>Addition and subtraction involving money</li></ul>

Overview

Objectives	Outcome
- To help students understand the meaning of decimals - To help them see the similarities and differences between fractions and decimals - To help them apply their whole number skills for decimals - To help identify place value of decimals - To help solve problems involving decimals	The students will be able to learn that 'decimals' are yet another way of looking at parts of a number. They will be able to relate to it through fractions and find similarities and differences between the two. They will be able to create and solve problems in real-life situations using decimals.
- To understand the meaning of profit and loss - To interpret the given data and solve problems to find profit or loss	The students will be able to apply the concepts learnt in real-life situations that involve money transactions.
- To help students measure length, weight and capacity using the appropriate tools for measurement - To solve problems by using correct units and tools - To learn to convert from one unit to the other within the metric system - To help make inferences and select the right measuring tools - To apply the learnt skills in day-to-day life situations	The students will be able to see the importance and value of the metric units of measurement in their daily life. They will be able to use the appropriate tool for solving problems related to metric system.
- To learn to integrate measurement into Geometry - To estimate and measure angles - To construct different angles, using the available information - To apply spatial reasoning while constructing angles	The students will be able to understand, how angles are formed and apply their spatial reasoning while constructing angles. They will also learn the use of a protractor.
- To teach students to read time, using different measuring units - To reinforce telling time to 5 minutes intervals - To solve problems relating to elapse of time - To select the appropriate tool to solve real-life problems related to time - To teach how to determine time - To help students recognise the importance and value of time	The students will be able to read a clock to the minute. They will be able to see how different tools are used to measure time in different ways. They will be able to add or subtract time in hours, minutes and seconds.
- To understand Geometry and measurement as a branch of Mathematics - To develop visual and spatial skills - To learn to differentiate between perimeter and area - To understand that same perimeter can have different areas - To learn to estimate and measure perimeter and area using formulae	The students will be able to identify, describe, compare and classify properties of geometrical shapes, using spatial reasoning. They will be able to determine formulae and procedures needed to solve measurement problems and convert units within the metric system.
- To locate points on a grid, based on the available information - To learn to present information on a graph - To learn to make different kinds of graphs - To read a graph and gather information about any given topic	The students will be able to learn about different topics using graphs. They will be able to explore, read and interpret graphs of different kinds outside the class as well.
- To learn about the role of money in our day-to-day living - To learn about the different uses of money (earning, spending and saving) - Use of money is universal though it called by different names and has different values - To perform arithmetic operations involving money	The students will learn to value money and its usage. They will be able to handle cash and carry out age-appropriate transactions.

Preface to the new CCE edition

'I Did It' Mathematics has been prepared in conformity with the latest NCERT syllabus and the National Curriculum Framework (2005). The thoroughly revised edition of the series

'I Did It' Mathematics has been redesigned to make the learning of mathematical concepts an active process, which is an important curriculum need. It provides plenty of opportunities to 'Do and discover' through individual and co-operative work and at the same time paves the path for advanced learning through simple explanations and information.

A **Continuous and Comprehensive Evaluation (CCE)** Process is a good methodology adopted in the field of education. It is not only stress free, but it also strives to give children a good quality of learning. It facilitates linking learning with application. The main purpose of learning lies in the usage of knowledge gained and CCE aims to fill this vacuum.

CCE is broadly classified into **Formative Assessment (FA)** and **Summative Assessment (SA)**. While the first stage deals with the process, the second stage deals with the end result.

While tools such as Mid-term Examinations, Terminal Examinations and Annual Examinations for SA are essential to check students' holistic understanding, it has become necessary to concentrate more on the missing link, the FA to improve upon the quality of learning in a comprehensive manner. There are several scientific approaches for this, such as Diagnostic Approach, Observation Approach, Pop Questions Approach, Journal Approach and Worksheet Approach. In our series, these have taken the form of *You Know*, *Maths Lab Activity*, *True or False Questions*, *Multiple-Choice Questions*, *Mental Math questions*.

As learners require concrete examples as against abstract thinking, care has been taken to bring in as much of hands-on experience into the book as possible. A variety of activities also helps sustain the interest and enthusiasm of the learner. Adequate ascendancy from standard formats to developing **Higher Order Thinking Skills (HOTS)** has been provided. Thus, the series turns out to be comprehensive in all respects.

It is not ideal to start CCE at an advanced level of formal education and as such the same is taken through different stages of intensity, through various class levels. This helps the student to stride into the system gradually and confidently.

Sudha Mahesh

Patterns

You know ...
- patterns repeat
- patterns can be man-made or natural
- patterns can be seen both on living and non-living things
- patterns can be created using a variety of things.

Maths Lab Activity 1

Materials required
- A pack of cards with a different numerical pattern drawn on each one of them
- Different types of objects or simple instruments that can produce different sounds

Method (Note for the Teacher)

Give one card to a student to see the pattern. Suppose the pattern on the card is 1, 2, 3, 1, 2, 3. Ask the student to take any three objects or instruments and beat them in the same pattern to produce a sound in sequence. The next card may have the pattern 1, 2, 3, 11, 22, 33, 111, 222, 333. So the sounds should be produced in the same pattern.

This game develops concentration and helps the students to follow a rhythm. The students can exchange the cards and play the game again.

Patterns, as you know, play a very important role in our lives. They are seen everywhere.

When an object shows the same pattern, colour, size and shape on its left and right side or on top and at the bottom, we say it shows a **symmetrical pattern**. The butterfly is an excellent example of symmetrical pattern. If you observe its colour, shape and size carefully, you will notice an identical pattern on both the wings.

This is a natural pattern, not man-made.

Have you seen a beehive?

It is not man-made. It has a beautiful shape. What is the shape of its cells?

Each cell is a **hexagon**. A hexagon has six sides.

Man-made patterns are created by people. They can be formed in any way keeping in mind the rules of patterns.

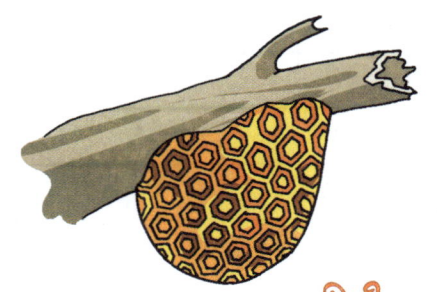

Exercise 1

Tick (✓) the natural patterns in the boxes given below the picture.

Patterns are noticed not only in designs but also in numbers, language, music and stories. When you start looking for patterns, they help you to think systematically and solve problems.

Mathematical Patterns

Look at this number sequence.

2, 4, 6, 8, 10, 12, 14, ...

The pattern you see here is a sequence of numbers being counted in twos. Here it is easy to continue this pattern by predicting the numbers to be written.

Think of any four patterns that can be predicted. They need not be related to Mathematics. One has been done for you.

a. Seasons are patterns that can be predicted.

b. _____

c. _____

d. _____

e. _____

We could also say that patterns are infinite. This means that they can continue without ending.

Think of any three patterns that are infinite. They need not be related to Mathematics. One has been done for you.

a. All odd numbers are infinite, for example, 1, 3, 5, 7, 9, ...

b. _____

c. _____

d. _____

e. _____

Pattern in Table of 9

Let us look at some patterns in multiplication.

9 × 1 =
9 × 2 =
9 × 3 =
9 × 4 =
9 × 5 =
9 × 6 =
9 × 7 =
9 × 8 =
9 × 9 =
9 × 10 =

Look at the answers that you have arrived at for the table of 9. The tens' digit is increasing by one and the ones' digit is decreasing by one. This is a pattern. In fact, all the multiplication tables have patterns, though not as simple as this.

Pattern in Multiples of 10

Look at this pattern.

$$2 \times 10 = 20, \quad 2 \times 100 = 200, \quad 2 \times 1000 = 2000, \ldots$$

What do you notice here? We are actually multiplying the given number (2) by 1 and adding as many zeroes as there are after 1 in the multiplier.

MENTAL MATH

Now complete this table.

×	10	100	1000	10000
3		300		
12				120000
25		2500		
37				
68			68000	

Language Patterns

Exercise 2

Circle the last word in each line of the poem.

One, two,
Buckle my shoe.
Three, four,
Shut the door...

What is the pattern you see in this poem?

_____
_____
_____
_____

Complete the poem.

_____
_____
_____
_____
_____

Here, every two lines are ending with rhyming words. So, this is a pattern in language.

Exercise 3

Eight words are given here. Write a small poem ending each line with a word given below.
(school, cool, stool, pool, bend, mend, send, spend)

_____
_____
_____
_____
_____
_____
_____

Patterns can be circular, linear or symmetrical.
In a circular pattern, the pattern will go round and come back to the starting point.
Here is an interesting old song which is a good example of circular patterns in language.

There's a Hole in the Bucket

There's a hole in the bucket, dear Liza, dear Liza
There's a hole in the bucket, dear Liza, there's a hole.
Then fix it, dear Henry, dear Henry, dear Henry

    Then fix it, dear Henry, dear Henry, fix it.
    With what shall I fix it, dear Liza, dear Liza?
    With what shall I fix it, dear Liza, with what?

With a straw, dear Henry, dear Henry, dear Henry
With a straw, dear Henry, dear Henry, with a straw.
But the straw is too long, dear Liza, dear Liza
But the straw is too long, dear Liza, too long

Then cut it, dear Henry, dear Henry, dear Henry
Then cut it, dear Henry, dear Henry, cut it.
With what shall I cut it, dear Liza, dear Liza?
With what shall I cut it, dear Liza, with what?

With an axe, dear Henry, dear Henry, dear Henry
With an axe, dear Henry, dear Henry, an axe.
The axe is too blunt, dear Liza, dear Liza
The axe is too blunt, dear Liza, too dull

    Then sharpen it, dear Henry, dear Henry, dear Henry
    Then sharpen it, dear Henry, dear Henry, sharpen it.
    With what shall I sharpen it, dear Liza, dear Liza?
    With what shall I sharpen it, dear Liza, with what?

With a stone, dear Henry, dear Henry, dear Henry
With a stone, dear Henry, dear Henry, a stone.
The stone is too dry, dear Liza, dear Liza
The stone is too dry, dear Liza, too dry

    Then wet it, dear Henry, dear Henry, dear Henry
    Then wet it, dear Henry, dear Henry, wet it.
    With what shall I wet it, dear Liza, dear Liza?
    With what shall I wet it, dear Liza, with what?

With water, dear Henry, dear Henry, dear Henry
With water, dear Henry, dear Henry, with water.
How shall I get it, dear Liza, dear Liza,
  How shall I get it, dear Liza, how shall I?

    In the bucket, dear Henry, dear Henry, dear Henry
    In the bucket, dear Henry, dear Henry, in the bucket.

There's a hole in the bucket.

Linear patterns can be vertical or horizontal.

Exercise 4

Draw a linear pattern on the bookmarks. Make a nice pattern that repeats itself and colour it.

a.

b.

Exercise 5

Here are two incomplete patterns. Complete them to make them look symmetrical.

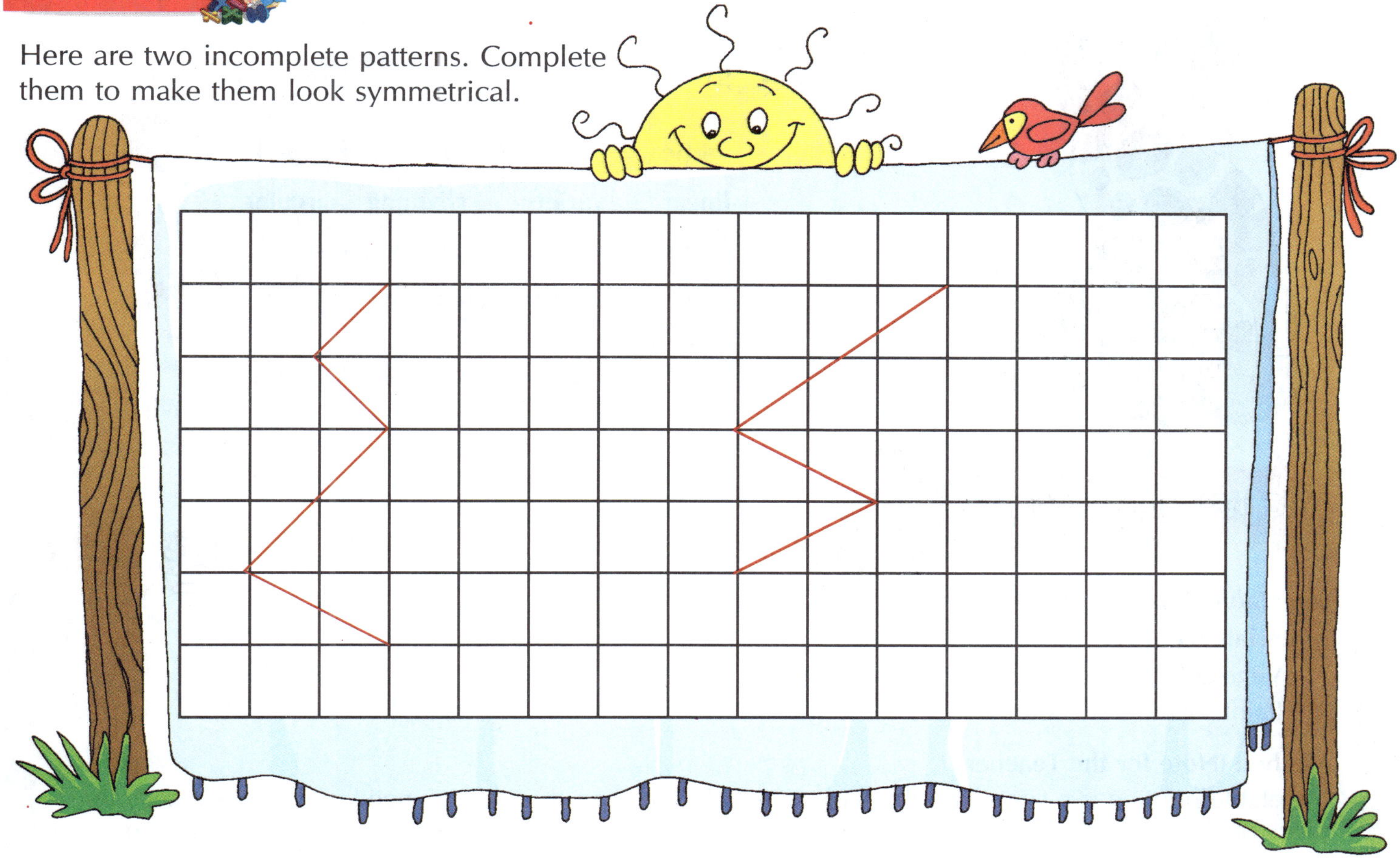

Exercise 6 HOTS

Draw the other side of each shape to make it look symmetrical.

Vocabulary Learnt

vertical   symmetrical   horizontal
linear   variety   rhyming   circular
infinite   natural   man-made
numerical   instruments

Maths Lab Activity 2

Vegetable Print Patterns

Materials required
- Vegetable like potatoes, lady's finger, onions, beetroots, capsicums
- Paints of different colours
- A knife

Method (Note for the Teacher)

Vegetable printing is a simple art that even small children can try out. You need only some vegetables, a piece of cloth and fabric paints to make the print. Vegetables can be cut lengthwise or breadth wise to make beautiful patterns of flowers, leaves, etc. Here is an example for you.

Take one capsicum and cut it into two pieces. Ask the children to apply fabric paint of their choice carefully on the brim of the capsicum piece. Then ask them to punch the painted capsicum on the cloth to make petals of a flower. Cut the ladies finger lengthwise to make leaves and breadth wise to make small flower designs. Ask them to punch with the small flower design in the centre of the flowers.

If they want to make the design more attractive they can punch the small flower designs in the corners of the cloth. Ask them to choose contrast colour paints for effect.

2 Numbers

You know ...
- numbers up to four digits
- place value up to four digits
- how to regroup when the value is more than nine in ones' place
- how to arrange numbers in ascending and descending orders
- big and small numbers.

Maths Lab Activity 1

Materials required
- A set of ten cards having digits 0 to 9 for each student. Only one digit should be written on a card.

Method (Note for the Teacher)
Let all the students sit in a circle. Ask them to keep their number cards, face down, in front of them. When you say 'ready', every student should pick up six cards at random and place them face up. Then ask everyone to make the following numbers using their cards.

a. The greatest number   b. The greatest even number   c. The greatest odd number
d. The smallest number   e. The smallest even number   f. The smallest odd number

Exercise 1

a. What is the number?

i. 4 after 116

ii. 8 after 824

iii. 9 after 401

iv. 7 after 372

v. 11 after 291

vi. 13 after 562

vii. 98 after 530

viii. 63 after 786

ix. 29 after 932

x. 101 after 674

xi. 83 after 198 xii. 75 after 532

xiii. 100 after 874 xiv. 111 after 666

xv. 56 after 75 xvi. 23 after 323

b. What is the number?

i. 7 before 163 ii. 9 before 185

iii. 14 before 475 iv. 12 before 342

v. 16 before 479 vi. 13 before 728

vii. 68 before 475 viii. 45 before 385

ix. 23 before 236 x. 99 before 470

xi. 52 before 856 xii. 63 before 444

xiii. 59 before 282 xiv. 77 before 112

xv. 39 before 786 xvi. 21 before 193

10

Exercise 2

Use the greater than (>) or less than (<) sign between the given numbers.

a.  b.  c.

d.  e.  f.

g.  h.  i.

j.  k.  l.

Exercise 3

Read the instructions carefully and colour the numbers using the given colour code.

a. The greatest 4-digit number (dark green)
b. The smallest 2-digit number (yellow)
c. The greatest 3-digit number (purple)
d. The smallest 4-digit number (sky blue)
e. The total of the smallest 2-digit number and greatest 3-digit number (brown)
f. The difference between the greatest 4-digit number and the smallest single-digit number (orange)
g. The greatest 2-digit number (red)
h. The greatest single-digit number (pink)
i. The sum of the smallest 2-digit number and the smallest 3-digit number (grey)
j. The difference between the greatest 2-digit number and the greatest single-digit number (light green)

Exercise 4

Arrange the following numbers in ascending order.

a. 34521, 23412, 45321, 54123, 34123, 23214, 52341

b. 87502, 87250, 78052, 70825, 70528, 78025, 70258

c. 30872, 80372, 80327, 72308, 72083, 80723, 73280

d. 16384, 13658, 16483, 83641, 83416, 63148, 63441

e. 99765, 96579, 57996, 56979, 79965, 75669, 77569

Exercise 5

Arrange the following numbers in descending order.

a. 54378, 57634, 63475, 63574, 57436, 75654, 65437

b. 10032, 12030, 13002, 12300, 30012, 20013, 32100

c. 74291, 71924, 79124, 12497, 14279, 17924, 14297

d. 32673, 33762, 73326, 26733, 27363, 62373, 62337

MENTAL MATH

1. How many 10s make 9000?
2. What is the double of 3750?
3. What is next in the series: 53, 55, 59, 65, _____
4. Write 30007 in words.

Place Value

You have already learnt about the place value of a digit in a number. It is determined by the position of the digit in a number.

Look at this.

In 56432, the place value of 6 is thousands.

In 54361, the place value of 6 is tens.

There are two different systems of grouping numbers.

Remember
If there is no digit to represent a place, then write a zero.

a. The **Hindu-Arabic System**, which is used in India.
b. The **International System**, which is used in most parts of the world.

The digits are grouped together into periods of 2 or 3 digits and each is given a place value.

The Hindu-Arabic System

Crores Period		Lakhs Period		Thousands Period		Ones Period		
Ten crores	One crore	Ten lakhs	One lakh	Ten thousands	One thousand	Hundred ones	Ten ones	Ones
1	8,	4	3,	5	2,	9	2	3

You read the periods from the right but the number from the left. A comma is used to separate one period from the other.

Exercise 6

Answer the following questions.

a. How many places are there in the ones period?

b. How many places are there in the other periods?

c. Which place is missing in the other periods that is there in the ones' period?

Exercise 7

Put commas according to the Hindu-Arabic System.

a. 2 4 7 0 9 2   b. 2 6 9 7 4 2 1   c. 9 0 8 0 6 7 5   d. 5 0 2 1 8 5 8

e. 8 9 0 7   f. 5 0 8 7 4 2   g. 9 0 0 5 4 4 4   h. 6 9 0 8 4

Remember

Read the number from the right and put commas.

Exercise 8

a. Expand the following numbers.

Example

4,39,867 = 400000 + 30000 + 9000 + 800 + 60 + 7

i. 5,08,792 =	ii. 3,17,654 =
iii. 1,20,985 =	iv. 9,87,706 =
v. 8,97,653 =	vi. 2,00,670 =
vii. 9,08,087 =	viii. 1,23,004 =
ix. 7,05,080 =	x. 4,67,897 =

b. Write the standard numeral.

Example

One crore, thirteen lakh, forty-three thousand two hundred seven — 1,13,43,207

i. Five crores, three thousand sixteen

ii. Eight lakhs, nine thousand, six hundred twenty-one

iii. Forty-nine thousand, one hundred thirty-five

iv. Seven crores, eighty-four lakhs, one thousand eleven

v. Six lakh, six thousand thirty-three

Exercise 9

Some number names are given on the next page. Write the place values in the top row of the boxes. Write the number in the boxes in the second row. Do not forget to put commas at the correct places. Colour the ones' period in red, the thousands' period in green, the lakhs' period in yellow and the crores' period in blue. Do not colour the boxes where a zero comes.

a. Twenty-three crore forty-six thousand one hundred eighty-two

b. Three crore seven lakh five thousand thirty-five

c. Twenty crore nine lakh one hundred four

d. Sixty-two crore thirty-nine lakh seventy-five thousand three hundred fifty-three

Large numbers can also be represented on an abacus.
Look at this number.

5136523

Exercise 10

Represent the following numbers on an abacus.

a. 3098703

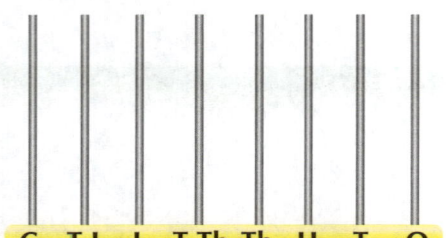

b. 5009321

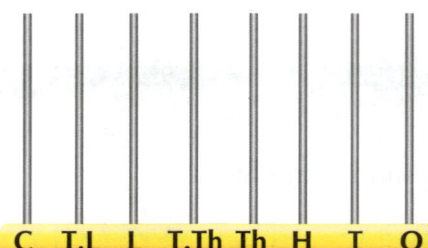

c. 71123908

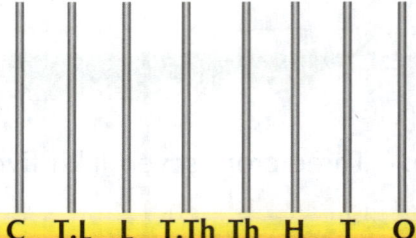

d. 80600054

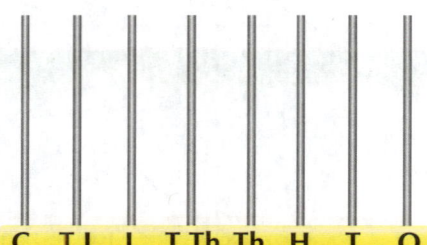

e. 67098541

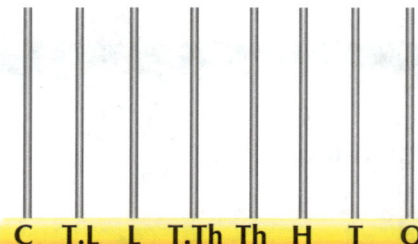

f. 12308700

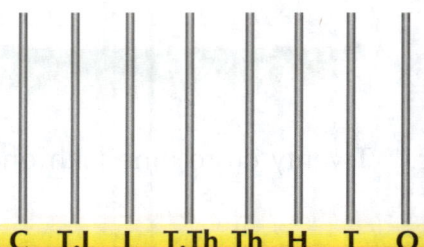

Exercise 11 HOTS

Each box given below represents a place value. Look at the patterns in the boxes carefully. See what each box represents.

- Ten crores
- One lakh
- Hundred ones
- One crore
- Ten thousands
- Ten ones
- Ten lakhs
- One thousand
- Ones

Now count the boxes of each type. Write the digits in the correct place to find the hidden number.

a.

b.
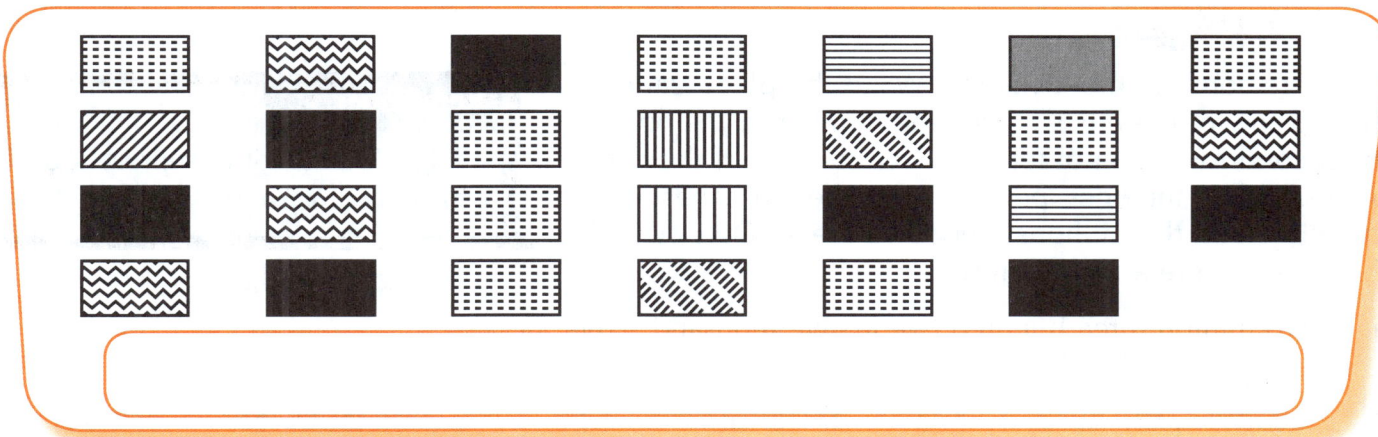

c.
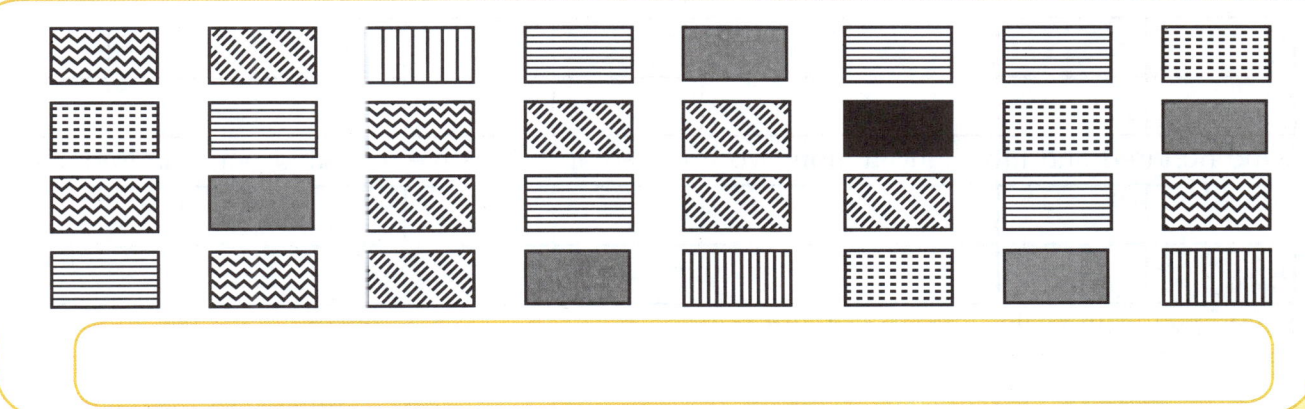

The International System

In the International System, the digits are grouped in a different way.
Look at this.

Millions Period			Thousands Period			Ones Period		
Hundred millions	Ten millions	One million	Hundred thousands	Ten thousands	One thousands	Hundred ones	Ten ones	Ones
1	8	4,	3	5	2,	9	2	3

Here, there are three places in a period. So, we put a comma after every three digits, unlike in the Hindu-Arabic System. Here again, the commas start from the right.

Exercise 12

Put commas for the following numbers according to the International System.

a. 7 6 9 8 4 5
b. 9 0 0 8 6 5
c. 8 0 0 4 3 2 7 6
d. 1 2 9 4 0 3 9
e. 9 4 0 6 0 0 3 2 8
f. 9 8 7 0
g. 2 8 1 0 3 8 1 2
h. 4 8 3 5 6

Exercise 13

Here are some number names. Write the place values in the top row of the boxes. Write the number in the boxes in the second row. Do not forget to put commas at the correct places. Colour the ones' period in red, the thousands' period in yellow and the millions' period in green. Do not colour the boxes where a zero comes.

Remember

If there is no digit to represent a place, then write a zero.

a. Two million three hundred twenty-five thousand sixty-four

b. Sixty-two million five hundred and one thousand seventy-three

c. Nine hundred and fifty-eight million two hundred and forty-five thousand one hundred and twelve

d. Eighty-two million three thousand and four

Exercise 14 HOTS

Each box given below represents a place value. Look at the patterns in the boxes carefully. See what each box represents.

- Hundred millions
- Hundred thousands
- Hundred ones
- Ten millions
- Ten thousands
- Ten ones
- One million
- One thousand
- Ones

Now, count the boxes of each type. Write the digits in the correct place to find the hidden number.

a.

b.
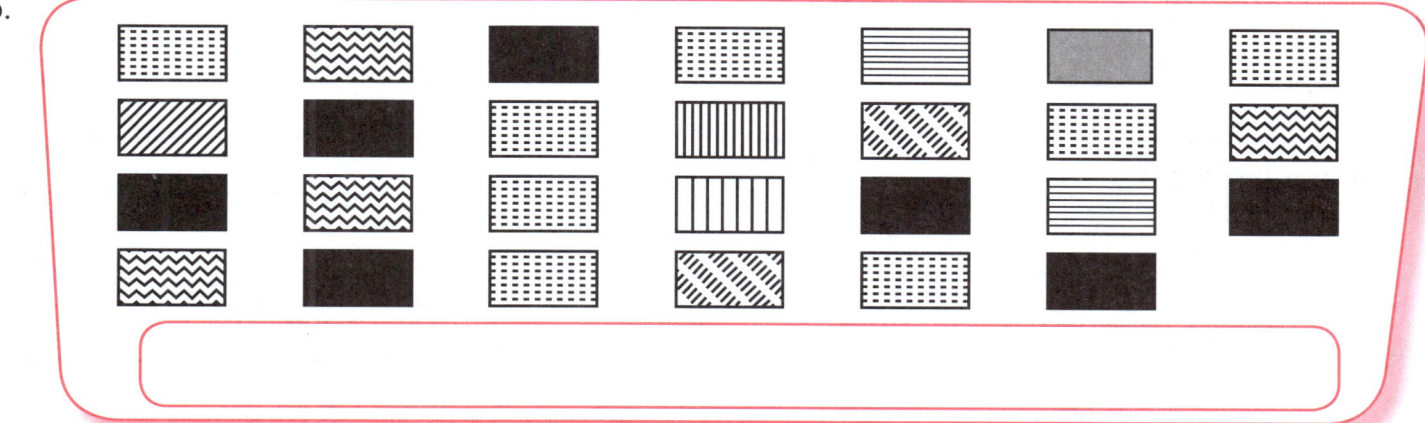

c.

Exercise 15

Put commas and write the number names for the following numbers both in the Hindu-Arabic System and the International System.

Example

3 6 9 7 5 0 3 2

Hindu-Arabic System

3, 6 9, 7 5, 0 3 2

Three crore, sixty-nine lakh, seventy-five thousand thirty-two.

a. 4 8 7 6 0 0 9 4 2

_____

_____

b. 5 5 6 6 0 8 0 4 3

_____

_____

International System

3 6, 9 7 5, 0 3 2

Thirty-six million, nine hundred seventy-five thousand thirty-two.

4 8 7 6 0 0 9 4 2

_____

_____

5 5 6 6 0 8 0 4 3

_____

_____

c. 1 9 3 0 4 0 5 3 2 _____
_____
_____

d. 6 0 8 0 0 7 3 3 3 _____
_____
_____

e. 1 0 2 0 3 9 4 8 6 _____
_____
_____

1 9 3 0 4 0 5 3 2 _____
_____
_____

6 0 8 0 0 7 3 3 3 _____
_____
_____

1 0 2 0 3 9 4 8 6 _____
_____
_____

Exercise 16

Find the 4-digit numbers by using the clues given below.

a. 3 is not next to 4
    1 is not next to 2
    2 is next to 4
    1 is in hundreds' place

b. 1 is not next to 3
    3 is not next to 2
    2 is not next to 4
    2 is in ones' place

c. 3 is just to the left of 2
    4 is not next to 2
    1 is not next to 3
    4 is in thousands' place

d. 1 is after 4
    2 is before 4
    3 is next to 1

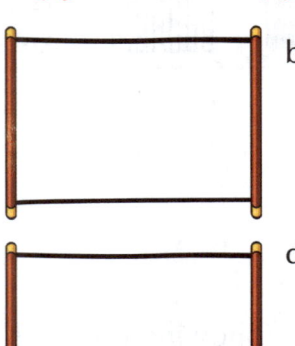
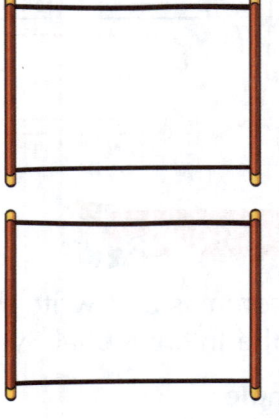

Exercise 17

Find the 5-digit numbers by using the clues given below.

a. 3 is not next to 5
    2 is not next to 3
    2 is not next to 4
    1 is not next to 4
    1 is in hundreds place'

b. 1 is not next to 3
    2 is not next to 3
    4 is just to the right of 5
    2 is in ones' place
    1 is to the left of 2

c. 4 is first in the number and just before 5
    5 is not next to 2 or 1
    3 is after 5 and not next to 1

Exercise 18

Find the 6-digit number by using the clues given below.

6 is last in the race

5 is before 2

2 is before 3

1 is ahead of 3

4 is four steps before 1

Exercise 19

Find the 7-digit number by using the clues given below.

4 is last in the race

5 is not next to 7 and not next to 1

7 is not next to 4 and 3

6 is before 5 and next to 7

2 is after of 5 and before 3

Now find out if it works with a number of your choice. Write down the steps in your notebook.

Math Magic

Do you like magic? Do you want to perform like a magician? Here is a simple magic trick. Learn it and demonstrate it before your friends and surprise them. Give your friend a pen or a pencil and a piece of paper. Now ask him/her to do the following:
- Choose any number between 1 and 10.
- Double it.
- Add the number chosen first.
- Add 6 to the answer.
- Divide the answer by 3.
- Take away the number chosen first from the answer.
- Multiply the answer by 5.
- Again Multiply the answer by 5.
- Now without looking at the paper, you can say what the final number is.

Isn't is interesting?

Clue: The answer will always be 100.

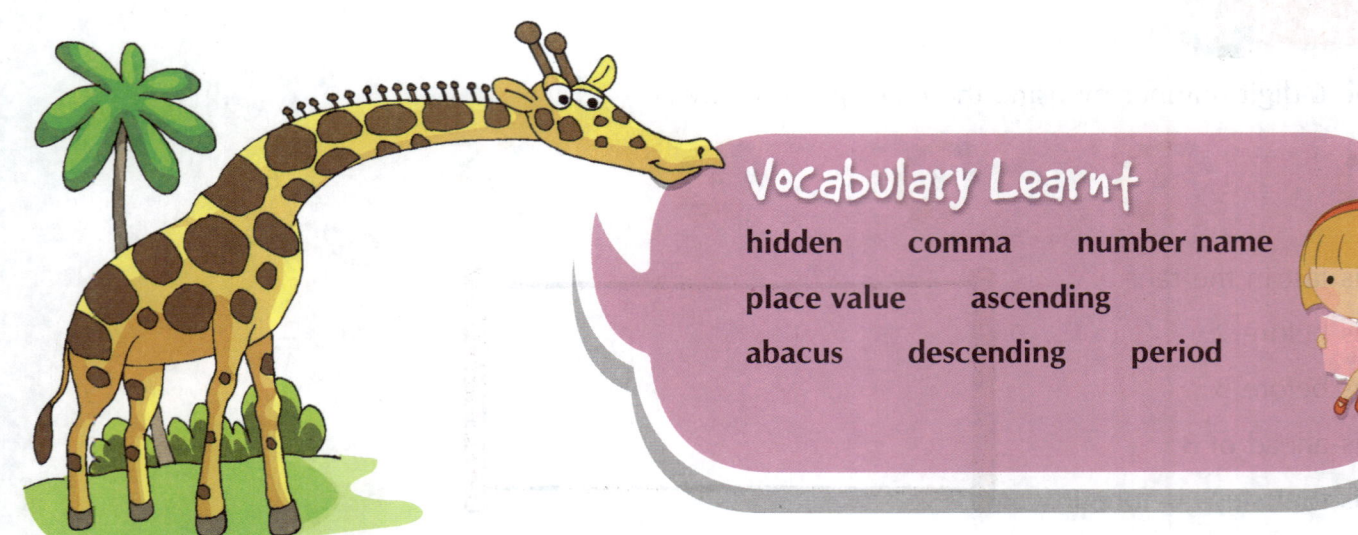

Vocabulary Learnt

hidden   comma   number name
place value   ascending
abacus   descending   period

Maths Lab Activity 2

FA

Number collage

Materials required
- Old newspapers and magazines
- Black chart paper
- Glue
- Scissors

Method (Note for the Teacher)

Divide students into groups. Ask each group to look through the papers and cut out numbers ending with a zero. Ask them to draw the outline of a large simple picture and stick the numbers on it like a collage, close to one another without leaving gaps. The numbers can overlap. Ask them to leave a border on all four sides like a photo and hang the collage in the class.

3 Numbers in Operation

> **You know ...**
> - the four operations and their special properties
> - how to apply the four operations in real-life situations
> - how to solve a problem by using the correct operation, after analysing and understanding the problem.

Maths Lab Activity 1

Materials required
- Big flash cards of words related to the four operations (add, multiply, leftover, product, remainder, etc.)

Method (Note for the Teacher)
Ask the students to sit in a circle. Place all the cards face down in the centre. Ask one student at a time to get up and pick up any one card. He/she should say what operation it is related to and also frame a simple word problem using the card.

Addition

Combining two or more numbers together is called **addition**. Addition of numbers can be done with and without renaming. The numbers that are added are called **addends** and the answer is called the **sum**. The term used for addition is **plus** and the symbol for addition is **+**.

```
    4 8 3 6 5 1 0
  + 2 0 3 1 2 1 5
    ───────────────
    6 8 6 7 7 2 5
```

Remember
When the sum of the two digits to be added is 9 or less, then there is no need for renaming.

MENTAL MATH

Where will you be?

1. Start at 34. Move 5 steps forward. Hop back 3 steps.
2. Start at 32. Move back 8 steps. Hop forward 11 steps.
3. Start at 75. Move 2 steps back. Hop back 6 steps.
4. Start at 63. Hop back 10 steps. Move 10 steps forward.
5. Start at 87. Hop back 2 stops. Move forward 12 steps.

Exercise 1

Add without renaming or carrying over.

a. 3 742 001
  + 3 125 672

b. 58 314 920
  + 11 341 038

c. 75 123 452
  + 13 564 427

d. 12 345 125
  + 85 240 162

e. 93 521 156
  + 5 200 142

f.   1 723 159
  + 3 246 120

g. 30 309 522
  + 26 180 143

h. 12 569 132
  + 36 120 116

i. 76 531 021
  + 12 225 427

Exercise 2

Add by renaming or carrying over.

a. 2 365 137
  + 1 263 953

b. 1 361 259
  + 5 231 686

c. 2 365 918
  + 9 534 928

d. 7 329 819
  + 9 361 298

e. 3 659 123
  + 5 832 911

f. 2 361 398
  + 9 523 187

g. 632583 + 698252

h. 8362197 + 1913582

i. 2981262 + 9763749

j. 4563871 + 2987458

k. 63547028 + 13597658

l. 75438641 + 25786493

Exercise 3

Copy the sums given below vertically and add.

Write the digits at their correct place value, otherwise the answer obtained will be wrong.

Write the greatest number on top, then the second greatest and so on. Remember every number must have the ones' place.

Example

a. 4950 + 56781 + 32 + 9 + 5600783

T.L	L	T.Th	Th	H	T	O
5	6	0	0	7	8	3
		5	6	7	8	1
			4	9	5	0
					3	2
+						9
5	6	6	2	5	5	5

b. 331555 + 44 + 267541 + 5 + 4325312

T.L	L	T.Th	Th	H	T	O
4	3	2	5	3	1	2
3	3	1	5	5	5	5
	2	6	7	5	4	1
					4	4
+						5
4	9	2	4	4	5	7

a. 3651 + 48300 + 75 + 9368154 + 27
b. 2 + 4963 + 580 + 7300591 + 38912
c. 452 + 63 + 9 + 245678 + 5100
d. 7849563 + 26752 + 5419 + 3 + 27
e. 8145093 + 65481 + 352 + 41
f. 249056 + 29411231 + 451 + 83

Commutative Property of Addition

Two numbers added in any order give the same answer. Observe the following.

4963 + 2785 = 7748
2785 + 4963 = 7748

Exercise 4

Add the following by using the commutative property of addition.

a. 7643 + 8251 b. 6581 + 7802 c. 4961 + 2594
d. 7845 + 2111 e. 6581 + 1045 f. 2963 + 1812

Associative Property of Addition

Three numbers added in any order give the same answer.

Observe the following.

5839 + 2653 + 1259

(5839 + 2653) + 1259 = 9751

(2653 + 1259) + 5839 = 9751

(5839 + 1259) + 2653 = 9751

Exercise 5

Add the following using the associative property.

a. 7068 + 4321 + 5963 b. 8521 + 1009 + 2786
c. 4789 + 2436 + 1080 d. 3481 + 3102 + 2697
e. 5912 + 6375 + 1121 f. 7496 + 1234 + 5076

Addition by Rearranging

Addition can also be done by rearranging the numbers in a suitable way.

Example   23 + 14 + 6 + 7

= (23 + 7) + (14 + 6)

= 30 + 20 = 50

Exercise 6

Rearrange and add the following.

a. 51 + 7 + 63 + 9   b. 25 + 8 + 25 + 92   c. 99 + 63 + 1 + 27
d. 146 + 153 + 47 + 54   e. 18 + 102 + 8 + 12   f. 63 + 74 + 6 + 17
g. 72 + 11 + 59 + 18   h. 65 + 4 + 35 + 96   i. 43 + 18 + 37 + 62
j. 223 + 541 + 77 + 59

Zero Property of Addition

Adding zero to a number is like adding nothing to the number.

Example   0 + 2561 = 2561
              2561 + 0 = 2561

The number remains unchanged when zero is added to a number or the number is added to zero.

Exercise 7

Now complete the following.

a. 0 + 2583 = ☐   b. 76493 + ☐ = 76493

c. ☐ + 0 = 9611   d. 0 + ☐ = 28111

Subtraction

Taking away a number from a greater number is called **subtraction**. The term used for subtraction is minus and the symbol for minus is —. The number which is subtracted is called **subtrahend** and the number from which you subtract is called **minuend**. The number left after subtraction is called the **remainder** or **difference**.

Subtraction does not have any special properties like addition.

A number can be subtracted from the other with and without renaming.

Without Renaming or Borrowing

Example
```
   9 8 4 3 2 7
 – 6 1 2 1 1 4
   ─────────
   3 7 2 2 1 3
```

Remember
To subtract, you borrow only when the minuend is smaller than the subtrahend.

Exercise 8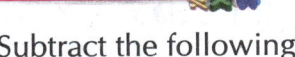

Subtract the following.

a.
```
   7 5 0 3 8 7 4
 – 2 1 0 2 6 4 2
```

b.
```
   9 8 0 7 6 4 3
 – 4 4 0 3 4 1 2
```

c.
```
   7 6 5 8 9 4 4
 – 4 2 3 4 5 0 0
```

With Renaming or Borrowing

Example

T.L	L	T.Th	Th	H	T	O
④	⑰	⑫	⑩	⑮	⑯	⑫
5	8	3	1	6	7	2
– 2	9	4	7	8	9	5
2	8	8	3	7	7	7

T.L	L	T.Th	Th	H	T	O
⑧	②	⑫	⑥	⑧	⓪	10
8	3	2	6	8	1	0
– 3	1	7	5	7	0	7
5	1	5	1	1	0	3

Exercise 9

Subtract the following.

T	L	T.Th	Th	H	T	O		T.L	L	T.Th	Th	H	T	O		T.L	L	T.Th	Th	H	T	O
5	8	3	1	0	0	8		8	4	1	2	3	1	6		9	5	1	3	6	5	1
− 1	3	1	2	7	5	9	−	2	9	9	0	8	7	5	−	3	9	8	7	5	1	0

Exercise 10

Copy vertically and subtract.

a. 59783 − 241

b. 796895 − 4831

c. 943651 − 23

d. 896532 − 4079

e. 184754 − 5903

f. 784632 − 195

g. 4090601 − 5800

h. 847562 − 1486

i. 942678 − 4387

Subtraction with Zero

When zero is subtracted from a number, the answer is always the number itself, as nothing really has been taken away.

Example 5892 − 0 = 5892

Exercise 11

Complete the following.

a. 51492 − 0 = _____

b. 6310 − _____ = 6310

c. _____ − 0 = 1119

d. _____ − 0 = 8432

Exercise 12

Find the missing digit. **HOTS**

a.
```
   7 □ 9 2 5
 − □ 1 □ 8 4
   2 3 8 4 1
```

b.
```
   9 8 □ 4 2 0
 − 2 4 5 □ 9 4
   □ 3 6 2 □ 6
```

Subtracting from a Number with Zeroes

Example

Exercise 13

Subtract the following.

a.
```
  9 0 0 0 0 0
- 2 7 4 8 9 6
```

b.
```
  6 0 0 0 0 0
- 2 3 4 5 7 2
```

c.
```
  8 0 0 0 0 0
- 6 9 4 7 6 2
```

d.
```
  5 0 0 0 0 0
- 1 2 3 4 5 7
```

Multiplication

Multiplication is repeated addition of the same number. It is a quick way of finding the answer where you have to add the same number successively, several times. However, the multiplication tables have to be memorised.

The numbers that you multiply together are called the **multiplicand**s and the answer you get is called the **product**. Multiplication has the same properties as addition.

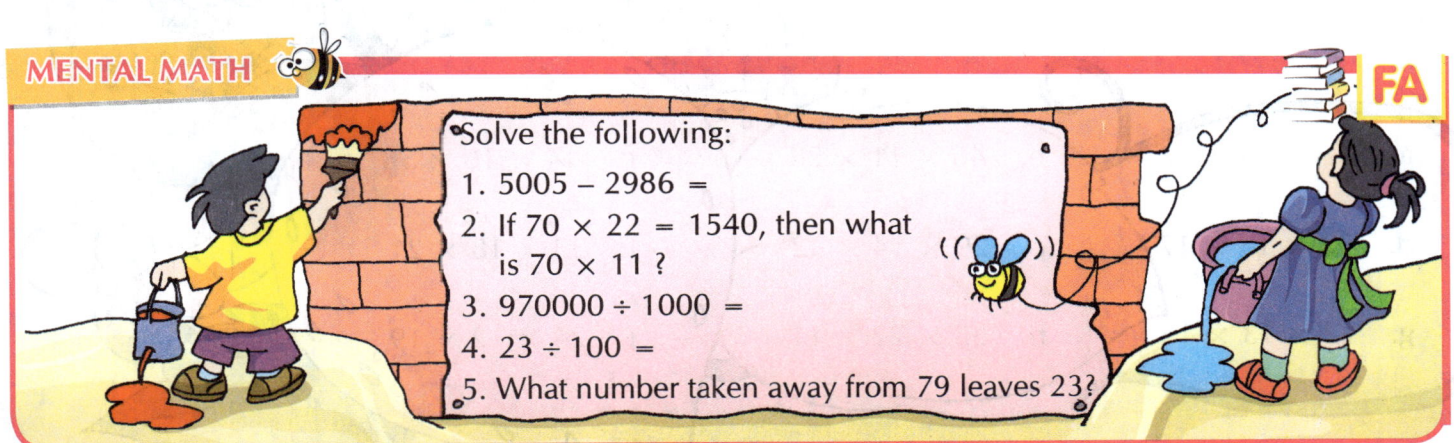

MENTAL MATH

Solve the following:
1. 5005 − 2986 =
2. If 70 × 22 = 1540, then what is 70 × 11 ?
3. 970000 ÷ 1000 =
4. 23 ÷ 100 =
5. What number taken away from 79 leaves 23?

Commutative Property of Multiplication

Two numbers multiplied in any order give the same product.

Example   41 × 23 = 943
23 × 41 = 943

Exercise 14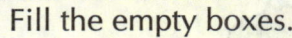

Fill the empty boxes.

a. 93 × ☐ = 41 × 93   b. 78 × 34 = ☐ × 78

c. ☐ × 67 = 67 × 29   d. 12 × 70 = 70 × ☐

Associative Property of Multiplication

Three numbers multiplied in any order give the same product.

Example   45 × 36 × 21   25 × 26 × 20

(45 × 36) × 21 = 34020   (25 × 26) × 20 = 13000

(45 × 21) × 36 = 34020   (25 × 20) × 26 = 13000

(36 × 21) × 45 = 34020   (26 × 20) × 25 = 13000

Exercise 15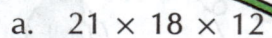

Multiply the following.

a. 21 × 18 × 12   b. 46 × 11 × 28   c. 14 × 16 × 56

d. 13 × 15 × 17   e. 29 × 14 × 32   f. 33 × 18 × 21

g. 12 × 13 × 15   h. 33 × 22 × 11   i. 24 × 12 × 19

Distributive Property of Multiplication

Multiplication too can be done by breaking up the greater number. Round off the number to the nearest multiple of 10. Use addition if the second multiplicand is more than 100 and subtraction if it is less than 100.

Example 29×99

$(29 \times 100) - (29 \times 1)$

$2900 - 29 = 2871$

34×103

$(34 \times 100) + (34 \times 3)$

$3400 + 102 = 3502$

Exercise 16

Solve the following using the distributive property.

a. 45×103
b. 62×91
c. 19×101
d. 55×98
e. 88×99
f. 21×111
g. 26×111
h. 38×94

Zero Property of Multiplication

A number multiplied by zero or a zero multiplied by a number will give only zero as the product. This means multiplication of any number with zero reduces the number to zero.

Example $2461 \times 0 = 0$

$0 \times 2461 = 0$

Exercise 17

Solve the following.

a. $0 \times 2409 =$ ☐
b. ☐ $\times 4532 = 0$
c. $0 \times 2097 =$ ☐

Property of One for Multiplication

Any number multiplied by 1 will always give the number itself as the product.

Example $2508 \times 1 = 2508$

$1 \times 2508 = 2508$

Exercise 18

Multiply the following.

a. $5734 \times 1 =$ ☐
b. $1 \times 6757 =$ ☐
c. $8858 \times$ ☐ $= 8858$
d. ☐ $\times 1 = 5320$

Multiplication of Large Numbers

Example

C	T.L	L	T.Th	Th	H	T	O
		6	4	5	2	1	9
					×	2	4
	2	5	8	0	8	7	6
1	2	9	0	4	3	8	×
1	5	4	8	5	2	5	6

T.C	C	T.L	L	T.Th	Th	H	T	O
		5	6	7	8	1	3
					×	4	7	2
		1	1	3	5	6	2	6
	3	9	7	4	6	9	1	×
2	2	7	1	2	5	2	×	×
2	6	8	0	0	7	7	3	6

Exercise 19

Multiply the following.

a. ☐ ☐ ☐
    2 4 6 2
        × 8
─────────

b. ☐ ☐ ☐
    3 6 5 7
        × 5
─────────

c. ☐ ☐ ☐
    7 7 3 7
        × 8
─────────

d. ☐ ☐ ☐
    3 1 2 4
       × 2 3
─────────

e. ☐ ☐ ☐
    9 7 8 8
       × 6 1
─────────

f. ☐ ☐ ☐
    5 3 2 3
       × 2 9
─────────

g. ☐ ☐ ☐
    3 6 9 7
       × 3 5
─────────

h. ☐ ☐ ☐
    7 7 3 7
       × 1 2
─────────

i. ☐ ☐ ☐
    9 0 0 7
       × 7 2
─────────

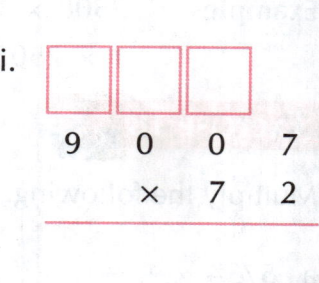

j.
```
    3 1 2 5
  ×     9 6
  ─────────
```

k.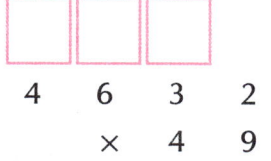
```
    4 6 3 2
  ×     4 9
  ─────────
```

l.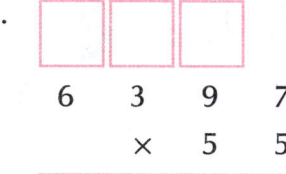
```
    6 3 9 7
  ×     5 5
  ─────────
```

m.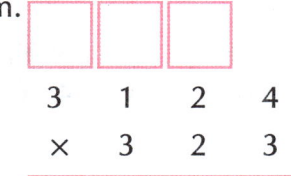
```
    3 1 2 4
  ×   3 2 3
  ─────────
```

n.
```
    9 7 8 8
  ×   6 1 1
  ─────────
```

o.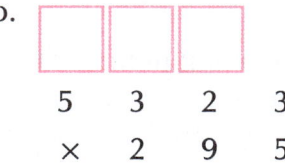
```
    5 3 2 3
  ×   2 9 5
  ─────────
```

p.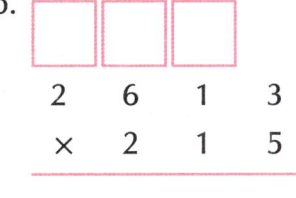
```
    2 6 1 3
  ×   2 1 5
  ─────────
```

q.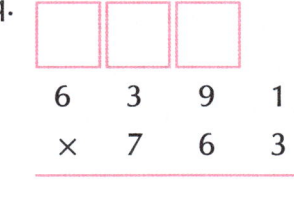
```
    6 3 9 1
  ×   7 6 3
  ─────────
```

r.
```
    4 3 2 1
  ×   3 2 7
  ─────────
```

Division

Division is repeated subtraction of the same number. It also means 'sharing equally'. The number to be divided is called **dividend**. The number used for carrying out division is called **divisor**. The number of groups you get is the **quotient**. The leftover is called the **remainder**.

Example

```
           9 9 6 7
       ┌─────────
    5 )  4 9 8 3 5
       - 4 5
       ─────
           4 8
         - 4 5
         ─────
             3 3
           - 3 0
           ─────
               3 5
             - 3 5
             ─────
                 0
```

Quotient, Q = 9967
Remainder, R = 0

Exercise 20

Solve the following division operations.

a. 3)76593   b. 9)84367   c. 5)43085   d. 4)28648

e. 7)85961   f. 8)49586   g. 2)96531   h. 3)75126

i. 9)54132   j. 5)64100   k. 7)6749   l. 8)8956

Rounding Numbers

Rounding numbers to the nearest 10, 100 or 1000, when dividing by big numbers, helps in estimating the quotient. Finding the multiples of 20, 400 or 6000 is just as easy as finding the multiples of 2, 4 or 6. So, let us learn how to round numbers to the nearest 10, 100 or 1000 on the number line.

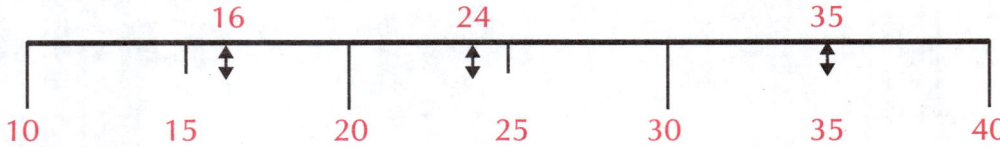

While trying to round numbers, we choose the number closer to the given number and round it to the number on that side.

A number like 16 is closer to 20 than to 10. So it can be rounded to 20.

A number like 24 is closer to 20 than to 30. So it should be rounded to 20.

A number like 35 is midway between 30 and 40. In such a case, it should always be rounded to the higher number, which is 40.

Exercise 21

Round the following to the nearest 10.

a. 34   b. 67   c. 23

d. 79   e. 65   f. 91

g. 21   h. 53   i. 86

Look at this.

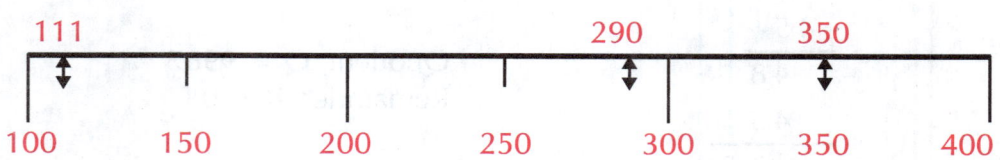

A number like 111 is closer to 100. So it should be rounded to 100. A number like 290 is closer to 300. So it should be rounded to 300. A number like 350 is midway between 300 and 400, so it should be rounded to the higher number, which is 400.

Exercise 22

Round the following to the nearest 100.

a. 451
b. 786
c. 345

d. 803
e. 632
f. 885

g. 411
h. 912
i. 542

Now, look at this.

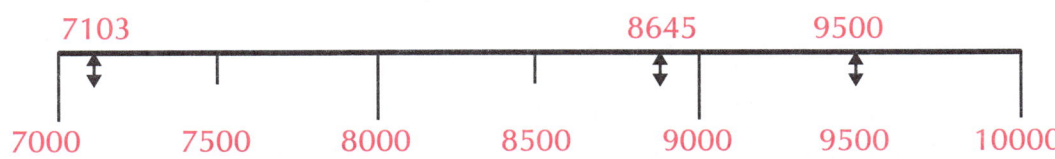

A number like 7103 is closer to 7000, so it should be rounded to 7000. Similarly, the number 8645, being closer to 9000, should be rounded to 9000. The number 9500, which is half way between 9000 and 10,000, should be rounded to 10,000.

Exercise 23

Round the following to the nearest 1000.

a. 4567
b. 7832
c. 9085

d. 2311
e. 6750
f. 2500

g. 9765
h. 7899
i. 7183

Now, that you know how to round numbers, you can learn how to estimate and find the quotient for a number. Look at this.

$$45378 \div 34$$

Here, you may not know the table of 34. So, first round 34 to the nearest 10. 30 is the nearest ten.

Steps

a. Find out how many 30s you can get in 45. It is like testing with the table of 3. You can get one. Now find out if you can get one 34. (Yes) Subtract 34 from 45 and find the remainder. It is 11. Bring down the 3. You have 113 now.

b. Find out how many 30s you can get in 113. You can get three 30s. Now find out if you can get three 34s in 113. (Yes) Subtract 102 (34 × 3 = 102) from 113 and find the remainder. It is 11. Now bring down 7 and you have 117.

c. Find out how many 30s you can get in 117. You can get three 30s. Now, find out if you can get three 34s in 117. (Yes). Subtract 102 (34 × 3 = 102) from 117 and find the remainder. It is 15. Bring down the last digit 8 and you have 158.

d. Find out how many 30s you can get in 158. You can get five 30s. Now find out if you can get five 34s in 158. (No) So go back one step. Find out if you can get four 34s. (Yes) Subtract 136 (34 × 4 = 136) from 158 and get the remainder. (158 − 136 = 22).

e. Since you have no more numbers to bring down, 22 becomes your remainder and 1334 is your quotient.

45378 ÷ 34 (30)

```
        1 3 3 4
    34 ) 4 5 3 7 8
       − 3 4
         1 1 3
       − 1 0 2
           1 1 7
         − 1 0 2
             1 5 8
           − 1 3 6
               2 2
```

Quotient, Q = 1334
Remainder, R = 22

Remember to round the divisor each time before starting a problem. Also, remember that the rounded number is only to help you estimate and work faster and it is not the actual divisor.

Exercise 24

Divide the following.

a. 23)34572   b. 46)60987   c. 74)78632   d. 17)90065

e. 56)86587   f. 34)67890   g. 42)64006   h. 87)56008

i. 33)96014   j. 29)81499   k. 62)69140   l. 52)87452

Exercise 25

Match the following. Show by colouring the two boxes that match alike.

The sum of the smallest 2-digit number and the biggest 3-digit number	98901
The difference between the biggest 4-digit number and the smallest 4-digit number	10018
The product of the biggest 2-digit number and the biggest 3-digit number	11111
The difference between the smallest 3-digit number and the smallest 5-digit number	1009
The total of the greatest 1-digit number, smallest 2-digit number and the greatest 4-digit number	999000
The quotient of the greatest 5-digit number divided by the greatest 1-digit number	8999
The product of the smallest 4-digit number and the biggest 3-digit number	9900

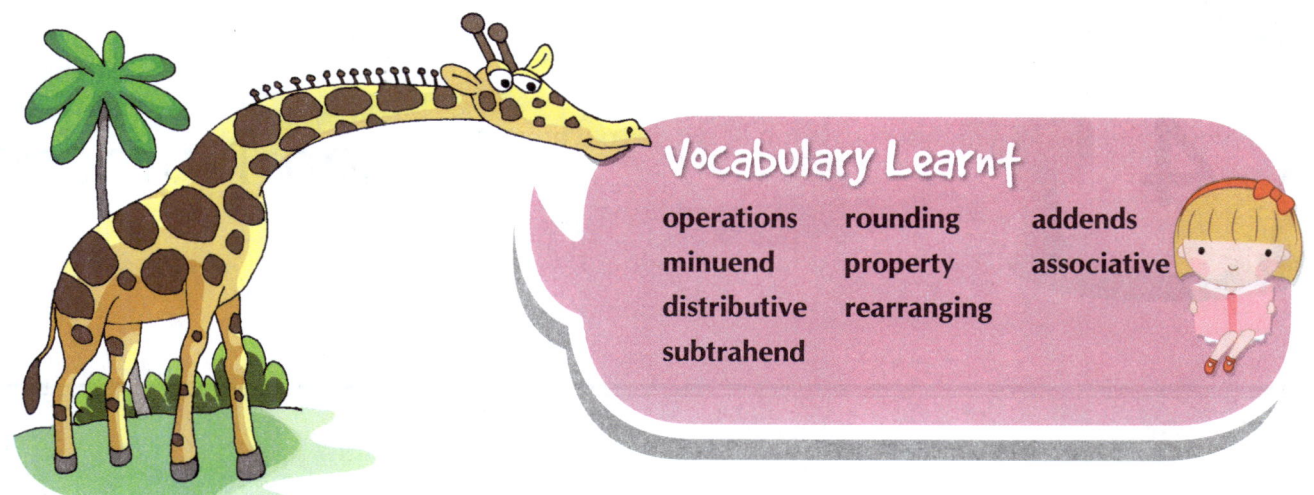

Vocabulary Learnt

operations rounding addends
minuend property associative
distributive rearranging
subtrahend

Maths Lab Activity 2

Given below are 4 stars with 4 different patterns in them, each standing for one operation and words related to all the operations are given. Read the words carefully in the clouds to check the operation to which they belong and draw the respective patterns in the clouds.

Addition	Subtraction	Multiplication	Division
★ (diagonal stripes)	★ (dots)	★ (crosshatch)	★ (zigzag)

- add
- more than
- times
- take away
- product
- sum
- total
- in all
- remainder
- minus
- subtract
- quotient
- both
- altogether
- difference
- multiplied by
- less than
- part
- decreased by
- each part
- shared equally
- increased by
- put together
- leftover
- more than
- plus
- divided by

Roman Numerals

> **You know ...**
> - we use numerals in daily life.

A numeral is a symbol used to write a number. The numerals 0, 1, 2, 3, 4, 5, 6, ... that we use all over the world today are called the Hindu-Arabic Numerals. These were used by the Hindus during the ancient times and later by the Arabians.

Here is a chart showing some ancient number systems belonging to different regions. See how they differ from the Hindu-Arabic Numerals.

Hindu-Arabic	Egyptian	Roman	Mayan	Hebrew	Babylonian
1	I	I	•	א	V
2	II	II	••	ב	V V
3	III	III	•••	ג	V V V
4	IIII	IV	••••	ד	V V V V
5	IIIII	V	――	ה	V V V V V
6	IIIIII	VI	•	ו	V V V V V V
7	IIIIIII	VII	••	ז	V V V V V V V
8	IIIIIIII	VIII	•••	ח	V V V V V V V V
9	IIIIIIIII	IX	••••	ט	V V V V V V V V V
10	∩	X	――	י	V V V V V V V V V V

Now, write the numerals in the following systems.

Digit	Hindu-Arabic	Roman	Babylonian	Mayan	Egyptian	Hebrew
5						
2						
7						
10						

The Roman Numerals were created 2000 years ago, but they are still in use. You can find them on the faces of clocks and watches, in inscriptions on buildings (where dates are also given), magazines and books.

- The Roman Numeral System uses only seven letters to represent all numbers. You might have seen them.

  I, V, X, L, C, D and M are the seven letters which are used in this system.

- These seven letters are used in different ways to make all the numbers.

Look at this.

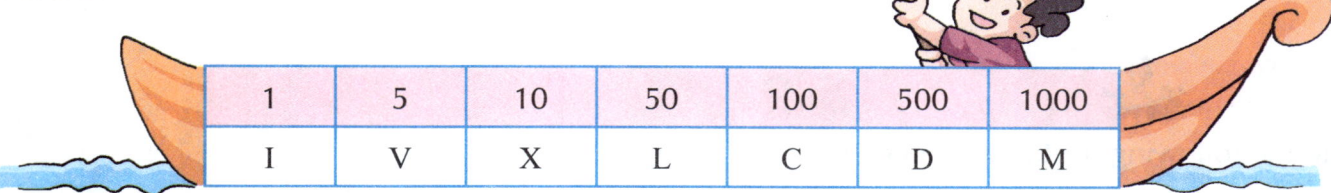

1	5	10	50	100	500	1000
I	V	X	L	C	D	M

However, writing Roman Numerals is not that simple. It follows several rules. They are as follows.

a. There are no symbols for 4 and 9.
b. There is no zero in this system.
c. When a symbol is repeated, add to find the numbers.
   Example III = 1 + 1 + 1 = 3. Only symbols for 1, 10, 100 and 1000 can be repeated.
d. When a symbol is followed by a symbol of a smaller number, add to get the number.
   Example VI = 5 + 1 = 6
e. No symbol can be repeated more than three times.
f. When a symbol is preceded by a symbol of a smaller number, then subtract to get the number.
   Example IV = 5 – 1 = 4
g. When a symbol of a smaller number is placed between two symbols of greater value, then subtract from the number represented by the symbol that follows it immediately.
   Example

I can be subtracted from V and X.
X can be subtracted from L and C.
C can be subtracted from D and M.

A Table of Roman numerals up to 20

1	2	3	4	5	6	7	8	9	10
I	II	III	IV	V	VI	VII	VIII	IX	X
11	12	13	14	15	16	17	18	19	20
XI	XII	XIII	XIV	XV	XVI	XVII	XVIII	IX	XX

Exercise 1

Rewrite the following sentences by changing the Roman numerals to Hindu-Arabic numerals.

a. There are XVI students in Class V in our school.
_____

b. I was born IX years ago.
_____

c. Gita's birthday is on the VII of December.
_____

d. XX children from Class VIII went on a picnic.
_____

Exercise 2

Write the following in Roman numerals.

a. 5   b. 7   c. 10   d. 14

e. 19   f. 11   g. 3   h. 20

i. 13   j. 4   k. 8   l. 2

Exercise 3

Write the following in Hindu-Arabic numerals.

a. VII   b. XX   c. XIII   d. XVI

e. VIII   f. IV   g. V   h. XII

Exercise 4

a. Colour the boxes that match across the three columns alike.

5	eighteen	XX
9	seven	IX
13	nineteen	VII
18	twelve	II
7	twenty	IV
19	four	XII
12	two	V
4	nine	XVIII
20	five	XIII
2	thirteen	XIX

b. Complete the crossword with the Hindu-Arabic numerals.

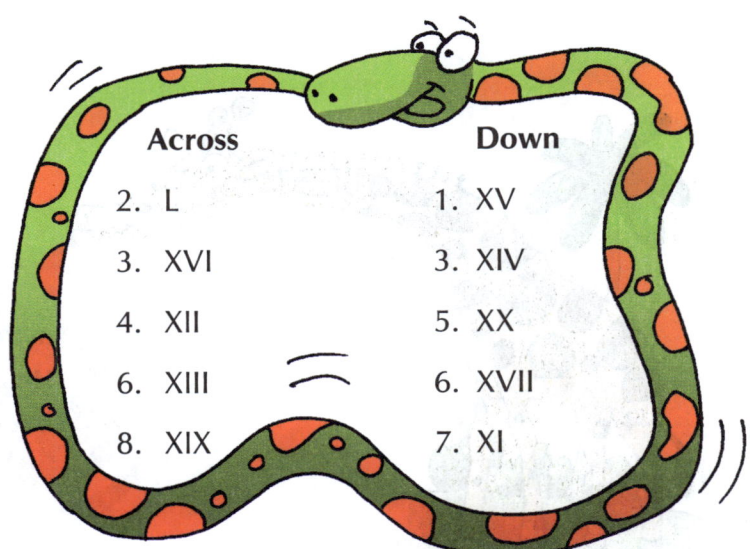

Across
2. L
3. XVI
4. XII
6. XIII
8. XIX

Down
1. XV
3. XIV
5. XX
6. XVII
7. XI

Exercise 5

1. Sita and Rama wrote 540 in Roman numerals. Sita wrote DXL. Rama wrote DLX. Who wrote it correctly?
   _____

2. Rewrite the following sentences using Roman numerals.

   a. There are 330 trees in the garden.
   _____

   b. Ram scored 950 points in a video game.

3. Simran had 840 pencils. She shared the pencils equally into 15 boxes. How many pencils were there in each box? (Rewrite this problem using Roman numerals.)
   _____

4. The population of a town is 620. If there are 410 men, find out the number of women in the town. Write down the answer using Roman numerals.
   _____

5. My sister is 5 years younger than me. If I am 30 years old, how old is my sister? Write the answer as a Roman numeral.
   _____

6. 190 people visited Appu Ghar on Monday and 400 people visited the place on Tuesday. How many people visited Appu Ghar in all, on both the days? Write down the answer as a Roman numeral.
   _____

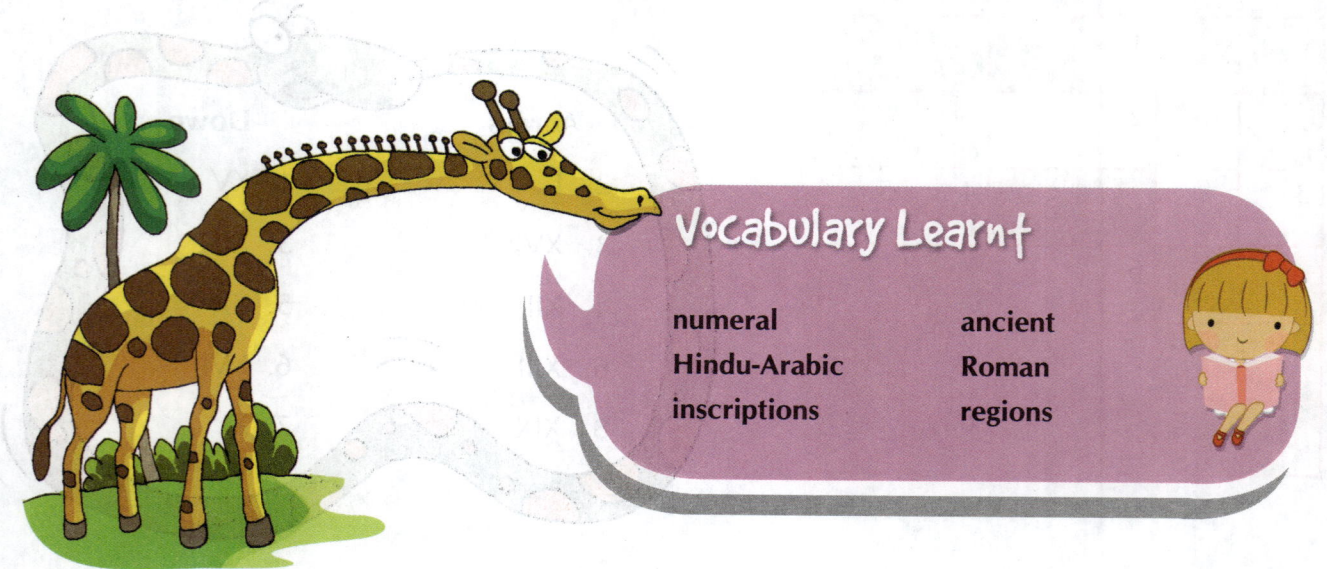

Vocabulary Learnt

numeral   ancient
Hindu-Arabic   Roman
inscriptions   regions

Maths Lab Activity 1

Materials required
- 10 boxes of matchsticks or toothpicks
- Glue
- Sheet of chart paper

Method (Note for the Teacher)

Divide students into small groups. Give each group a box of sticks. Ask them to make as many Roman numerals as they can using the matchsticks and paste on a sheet of chart paper. Go around to see what they are doing and periodically ask them to name the number they are making.

Summative Assessment 1
(For chapters 1 to 4)

1. State whether the following sentences are true or false.

   a. Patterns repeat.　　　　　　　　　b. Patterns are made using designs only.

   c. Patterns are finite.　　　　　　　　d. 1, 3, 5, 7, . . . is an even number pattern.

2. Draw lines of symmetry for / in the following letters.

   A　　B　　C　　D　　H　　M　　U

3. Match by colouring alike.

Largest single-digit number	99	Largest 3-digit number	10	1000
999	Smallest 4-digit number	Smallest 2-digit number	9	Largest 2-digit number

4. Arrange the following in ascending order:

   49675, 46975, 96475, 94765, 79465, 76594

5. Write the following numbers both in the Hindu-Arabic System and the International System.

   a. 49600125　　　　　　　　b. 39010802

6. Find a 4-digit number using the following clues:

   a. 3 is not next to 5　　　　b. 8 is to the right of 5　　　　c. 1 is before 5

7. Circle the correct answer.

   　　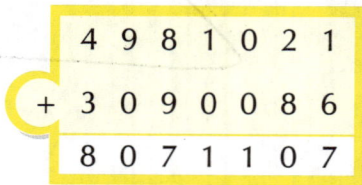

8. Arrange the following in vertical order and add.

   a. 598 + 3471 + 6 + 58003　　　　b. 32 + 5965 + 420 + 3

9. Find the missing digits.

   a.　　　　　　　　　　　b.

   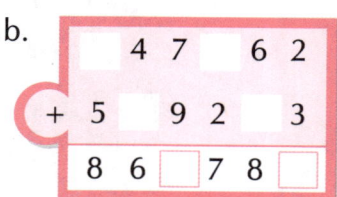

10. Circle the correct answer.

 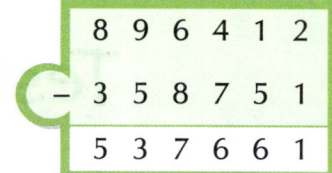 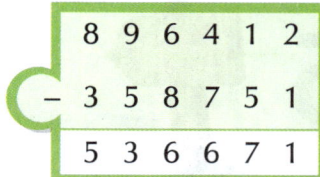

11. Find the missing digits.

    a.
    ```
        7   6 3
    -   2 5   4
        3 6 □ 3 5
    ```

    b.
    ```
          4     3
    -   5 1 7   8
        4 □ 2 2 6
    ```

12. Multiply the following using distributive property.

    a. 59 × 101   b. 46 × 98   c. 23 × 109

13. Multiply the following:

    a. 4 9 6 8
        ×   7

    b. 5 8 3 1
        ×   1 4

    c. 2 4 6 9
        × 3 5 8

14. Round the following numbers to the nearest 10, 100 and 1000.

    a. 4 3 8 1   b. 6 9 1 8

15. Divide the following:

    a. 12) 4 9 8 7 6   b. 23) 9 0 4 3 8 5

16. Arrange the following in descending order:

    83012, 80132, 13820, 13280, 21308

17. Add the following:

    a. 49 + 83 + 1 + 27   b. 63 + 72 + 17 + 18
    c. 146 + 153 + 47 + 54   d. 16 + 18 + 12 + 44

5 Test of Divisibility

> **You know ...**
> - how to divide numbers
> - all numbers are not divisible by every other number.

You all know that there are four operations in Arithmetic, namely, addition, subtraction, multiplication and division. Every operation has its own set of rules. Now we will learn about the rules of division.

The number you divide is the **dividend**. The number you divide by is the **divisor**. The answer you get is the **quotient**. The number left is the **remainder**.

Every number cannot be divided by every other number exactly. Also, it is difficult to find out whether a number is divisible by another number just by looking at it unless it is a small number. So, to find out whether a number is a divisor of a given number, we follow certain rules. These are called the **tests of divisibility**.

Test of Divisibility by 2

- All even numbers are divisible by 2.
- Even numbers end in 0, 2, 4, 6 and 8. So, all the numbers ending in 0, 2, 4, 6 and 8 are divisible by 2.
- However large a number is, you can say whether it is divisible by 2 or not, by just looking at the last digit. For example, 2472 is divisible by 2, because 2472 is an even number as its last digit is 2.

Test of Divisibility by 3

A number is divisible by 3 if the sum of the digits of that number is divisible by 3.

Example   2421

Here sum of the digits of the number is 2 + 4 + 2 + 1 = 9.

This number is divisible by 3 because the sum of the digits of this number is 9, which is divisible by 3.

Test of Divisibility by 4

A number is divisible by 4 if the last two digits are both 0 or the number formed by the last two digits is divisible by 4.

Example   3800 and 1448

In the first number, the last two digits are zero, so the number is divisible by 4.

In the second number, the last two digits make 48, which is divisible by 4. So the whole number is divisible by 4.

Test of Divisibility by 5

A number is divisible by 5 if the last digit is 0 or 5.

Example   1405 and 3100

In the first number, the last digit is 5. So the number is divisible by 5.

In the second number, the last digit is 0. So this number also is divisible by 5.

Test of Divisibility by 6

A number is divisible by 6 if it is divisible by both 2 and 3.

Example   342

342 is divisible by 2 because it is an even number. 342 is divisible by 3 because the sum of the digits is equal to 9, which is divisible by 3. So 342 is also divisible by 6.

Test of Divisibility by 9

A number is divisible by 9 if the sum of all the digits is divisible by 9.

This rule is very similar to that of 3, but you must remember that all numbers divisible by 3 are not divisible by 9. However, all numbers divisible by 9 are divisible by 3.

Example   1755

Here 1 + 7 + 5 + 5 = 18 = 1 + 8 = 9. Since the sum of all the digits in 1755 is 9, it is divisible by 9.

Test of Divisibility by 10

A number is divisible by 10 if the last digit of the number is 0.

Example   3890

This number is divisible by 10 because the last digit is 0.

Exercise 1

Tick (✓) the correct boxes.

	Numbers	Divisible by 2	Divisible by 3	Divisible by 4	Divisible by 5	Divisible by 6	Divisible by 9	Divisible by 10
a.	166							
b.	177							
c.	148							
d.	765							
e.	255							
f.	630							

The Divisibility Rules

These rules let you test if one number is divisible by another, without having to do too much calculation!

A number is divisible by:	If:	Example:
2	The last digit is even (0, 2, 4, 6, 8).	12**8** is divisible by 2. 12**9** is not.
3	The sum of the digits is divisible by 3.	381 (3+8+1 = 12, and 12 ÷ 3 = 4) **Yes** 217 (2+1+7 = 10, and 10 ÷ 3 = 3 1/3) **No**
4	The last 2 digits are divisible by 4.	13**12** is (12 ÷ 4 = 3) divisible by 4. 70**19** is not.
5	The last digit is 0 or 5.	17**5** is divisible by 5. 80**9** is not.
6	The number is divisible by both 2 and 3	114 (it is even, and 1+1+4 = 6 and 6 ÷ 3 = 2) **Yes** 308 (it is even, but 3+0+8 = 11 and 11 ÷ 3 = 3 2/3) **No**
9	The sum of the digits is divisible by 9 (Note: you can apply this role to that answer again if you want)	1629 (1+6+2+9 = 18, and again, 1+8 = 9) **Yes** 2013 (2+0+1+3+6) **No**
10	The number ends in 0	22**0** is divisible by 10. 22**1** is not.

MENTAL MATH

1. Is 344 divisible by 6?
2. What digit should be added to 2600, so it gets divided by 9?
3. What will be the quotient if 7 is divided by 2?
4. What is 29000 ÷ 10?
5. Write a number divisible by 2, 4 and 8.

Maths Lab Activity 1

Materials required
- Game boards with numbers and factors
- Counters or seeds

To play this game, the students should know:

a. the multiplication tables,
b. the rules of divisibility.

Method (Note for the Teacher)

Divide the students into groups. Give each group a board and a few seeds or counters. Ask the groups to sit around the board and start finding whether the numbers are divisible by 2, 3, 4, 5, 6, 9 and 10, using the rules of divisibility. When they find a factor, ask them to place a seed on the board under the factor, along the number.

Divisible by→ ↓Numbers	2	3	4	5	6	9	10
1436							
940							
1020							
4218							
1830							
2043							
9344							
7552							
7488							
3757							

To find out quickly whether a number is divisible by the given number or not, remember two things:

a. Multiplication tables
b. Rules of divisibility

Exercise 2

Which digit will you add at the end to make these numbers divisible

a. by 2?

i. 2341 _____   ii. 4532 _____   iii. 7863 _____   iv. 7869 _____

b. by 3?

i. 3124 _____   ii. 4531 _____   iii. 4401 _____   iv. 7090 _____

c. by 4?

i. 5677 _____   ii. 3122 _____   iii. 4531 _____   iv. 9084 _____

Exercise 3

Colour the following numbers by using the given colour code.

Numbers divisible by 2, 3 and 6	— Yellow	Numbers divisible by 2 and 4	— Orange
Numbers divisible by only 5	— Blue	Numbers divisible only by 3	— Green
Numbers divisible by 5 and 10	— Red	Numbers divisible by 3 and 9	— Pink

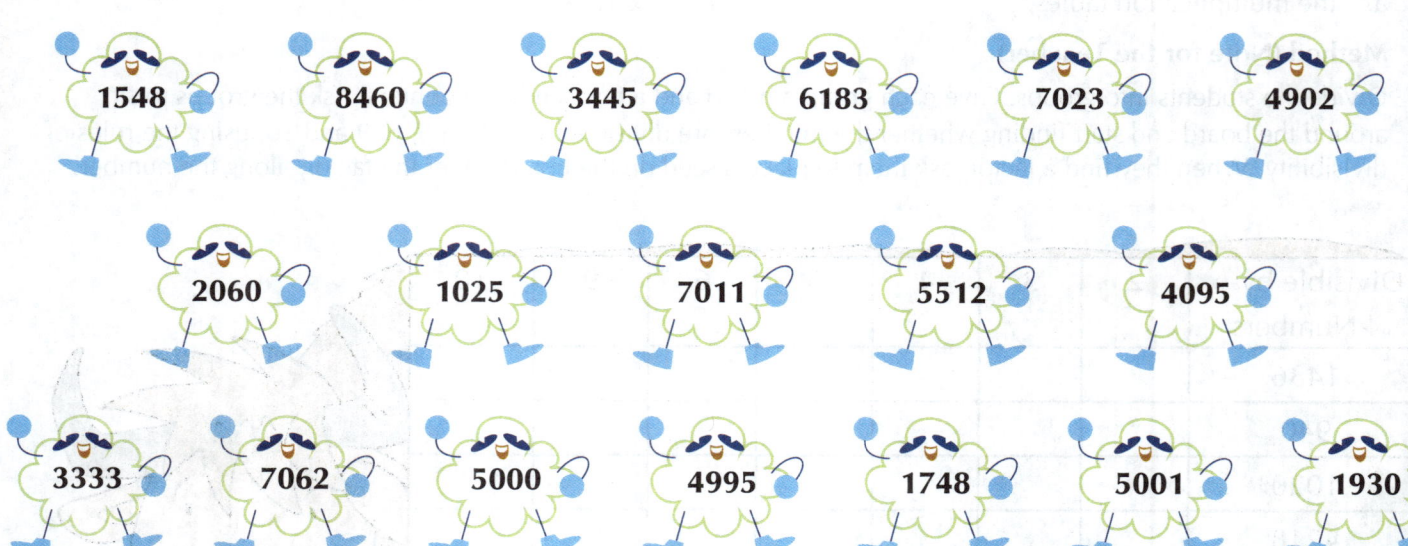

MENTAL MATH

Write **true** or **false**.

a. A number is divisible by 6 if it is divisible by 2 and not by 3.

b. A number is divisible by 5 if the last digit is "0" or "5".

c. A number is divisible by 9 if the sum of the digits is not equal to 9.

d. A number is divisible by 4 if the last 3 digits are divisible by 4.

e. Numbers ending in 0, 2, 4, 6 and 8 and divisible by 2.

f. 3 is a prime number.

g. 15 is a composite number.

h. 67 is a prime number.

i. A factor is a number that can divide another number exactly.

Vocabulary Learnt

divisible   quotient   divisor

dividend   rule   test

remainder

Maths Lab Activity 2

FA

Ask each student to follow a path of numbers divisible by 2, 3 and 5 respectively, by colouring the numbers, to take the boy to the bus. The path may go up, down or across.

44	16	49	8	10	70	11	47
24	60	21	55	68	41	71	94
44	72	49	51	37	120	8	91
28	27	45	91	150	99	126	77
63	47	36	75	180	23	200	61
88	10	8	78	17	31	6	36
45	25	12	21	40	64	54	135
59	61	19	37	99	79	39	22

6 Factors and Multiples

You know ...
- multiplication tables
- rules of divisibility of numbers.

Maths Lab Activity 1

Materials required
- A worksheet having a number and its factors, as shown below
- Crayons
- Pencil

Method (Note for the Teacher)

Give each student a number card with a number in a rectangular box as shown below and all its factors and a few other numbers written around it. Ask them to circle and colour all the numbers that are factors of the given number. Give both prime and composite numbers on the card.

1	18	2
3	7	8
4	9	6
5		12
	18	

Here, the given number is 18. The numbers that can divide 18 without leaving a remainder are 18, 9, 3, 6, 2 and 1. So only these numbers should be circled while other numbers like 5, 4, 7, 12 and 8 should not be circled.

Once all the students have completed the exercise, ask the following questions.

a. What is your number? (18)
b. How many numbers on your card can divide the given number without leaving any remainder? (1, 2, 3, 6, 9, 18)
c. How did you find out?
d. How many of you found only two factors for your number?

Once all the students have given the answers, they could be told that

a. All the numbers that divide the given number without leaving a remainder are called its factors. In the above example, 1, 2, 3, 6, 9 and 18 are the factors of 18.
b. The given number is the multiple of these factors.

52

Take 18 counters and arrange them in different rectangular patterns. In how many ways can you do this?

18 is arranged equally in 6 columns.
18 is arranged equally in 3 rows.

18 is arranged equally in 9 columns.
18 is arranged equally in 2 rows.

18 is arranged equally in 18 columns.

18 is arranged equally in 1 row.

Take the number of rows and columns from each example. They are 1, 2, 3, 6, 9 and 18.

If you divide 18 by these numbers, no remainder will be left, as 18 ÷ 1 = 18, 18 ÷ 2 = 9,

18 ÷ 3 = 6, 18 ÷ 6 = 3, 18 ÷ 9 = 2 and 18 ÷ 18 = 1

All these number 1, 2, 3, 6, 9 and 18 are called factors of 18.

The factors of a number are all the numbers that divide it exactly, without leaving a remainder

Remember
Factors of a number always include 1 and the number itself.

Exercise 1

Now find the factors of the following numbers by arranging them in rows and columns.

a. 36 b. 42 c. 40 d. 56

e. 28 f. 48 g. 54 h. 60

Factors can be found by using division also. Any number that can divide another number without leaving a remainder is a factor.

Example

Factors of 20

a. 20 ÷ 1 = 20
b. 20 ÷ 20 = 1
c. 20 ÷ 5 = 4
d. 20 ÷ 4 = 5
e. 20 ÷ 10 = 2
f. 20 ÷ 2 = 10

Hence, 20, 1, 4, 5, 2, and 10 are the factors of 20. So, factors can also be called divisors.

> **Remember**
>
> When you divide a number exactly by another number, the quotient and the divisor become factors of that number. For example, if you divide 14 by 2, then 2 (divisor) and 7 (quotient) become the factors of 14.

Exercise 2

Colour the numbers that have only two factors in green and the numbers that have more than two factors in red.

12, 24, 30, 17, 19, 20, 48, 9, 29, 42, 7, 23, 36, 50, 41, 54

Prime and Composite Numbers

Now try to arrange 7 balls in equal rows and Columns. In how many ways, you can arrange them?

   or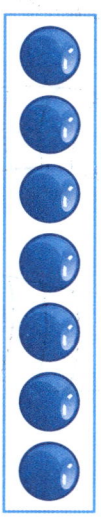

7 is arranged equally in a row. There are 7 ones.

7 is arranged equally in one colomn. There is only one 7.

So, 1, and 7 are factors of 7. Also, 7 ÷ 1 = 7 and 7 ÷ 7 = 1. Can you think of any other number which divides 7 exactly without leaving a remainder?

No numbers, other than 1 and 7, divide 7 exactly. Such numbers are called **prime numbers**.

Now, let us take the number 11. 11 ÷ 11 = 1 and 11 ÷ 1 = 11. No other number can divide 11 completely. So, like 7, 11 also has only two factors (1 and 11).

Numbers that have *only* two factors (1 and the number itself) are called **prime numbers** and numbers that have more than two factors are called **composite numbers**.

Remember

1 is neither a prime nor a composite number.

2 is the only even number that is prime, as it has only two factors.

But, how do we know which numbers are prime and which numbers are composite?

Maths Lab Activity 1

Given on the next page is a snake with its segments marked with numbers 1 to 100 and instructions as to what you should do with the numbers. Ask the students to use different colours and keep colouring the segments. Some colours may overlap. Tell them not to worry. The numbers that do not come under the multiples of any of the given numbers are called prime numbers.

This method of finding prime numbers below 100 was discovered by a mathematician called Mr. Eratosthenes. So it is called "The Sieve of Eratosthenes".

Prime Numbers *(Sieve of Eratosthenes)*

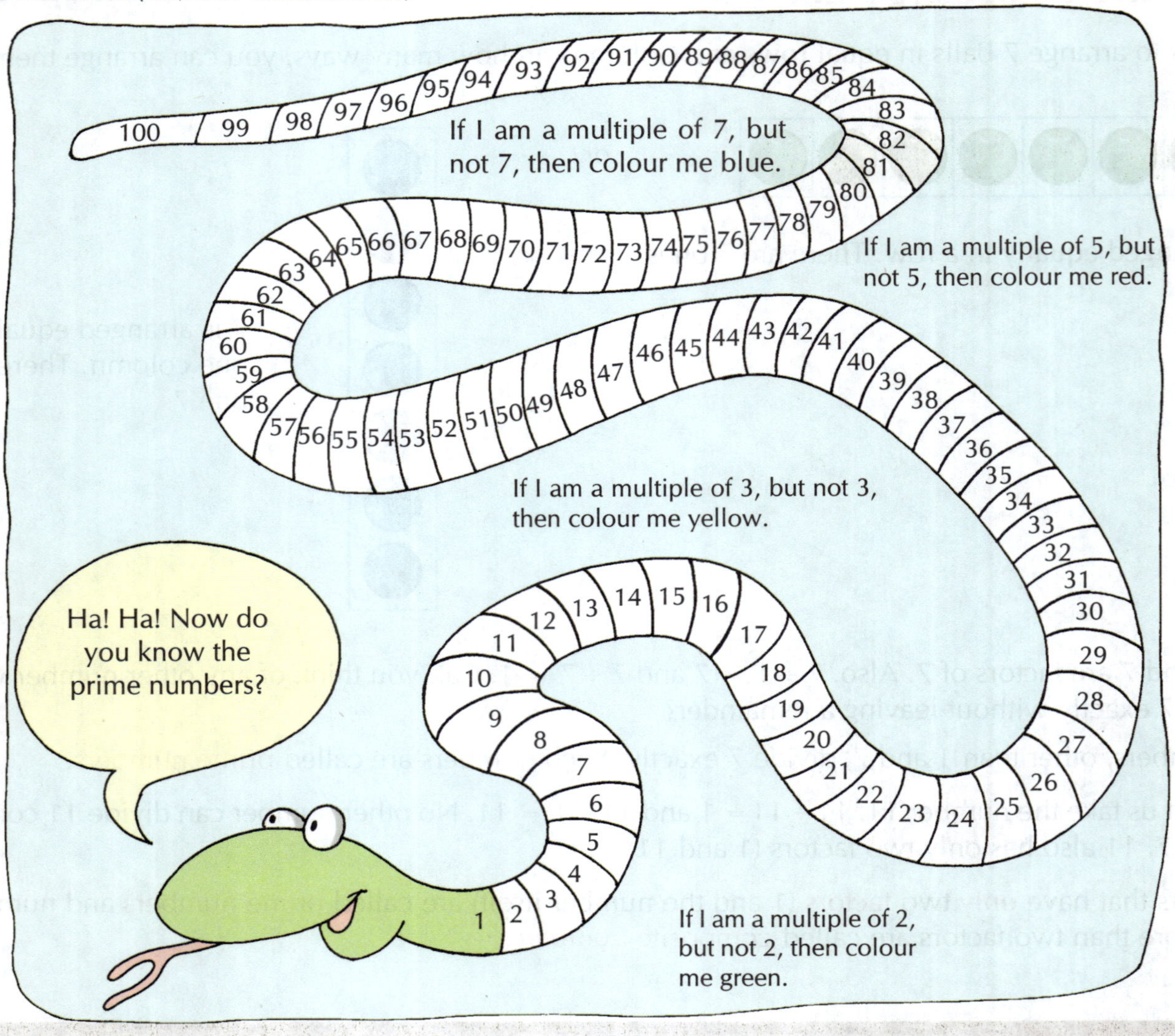

If I am a multiple of 7, but not 7, then colour me blue.
If I am a multiple of 5, but not 5, then colour me red.
If I am a multiple of 3, but not 3, then colour me yellow.
If I am a multiple of 2, but not 2, then colour me green.
Ha! Ha! Now do you know the prime numbers?
1 2 3 4 5 6 7 8 9 10 11 12 13 14 15 16 17 18 19 20 21 22 23 24 25 26 27 28 29 30 31 32 33 34 35 36 37 38 39 40 41 42 43 44 45 46 47 48 49 50 51 52 53 54 55 56 57 58 59 60 61 62 63 64 65 66 67 68 69 70 71 72 73 74 75 76 77 78 79 80 81 82 83 84 85 86 87 88 89 90 91 92 93 94 95 96 97 98 99 100

Exercise 3 HOTS

Here is a number monster. He can eat only prime numbers. Circle all the numbers that he cannot eat.

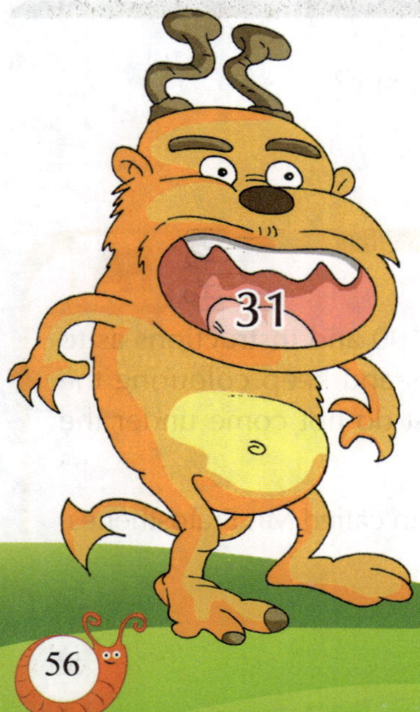

31

2	**7**	**4**	**12**	**9**	**15**
27	**44**	**32**	**58**	**27**	**11**
52	**13**	**43**	**78**	**19**	**25**
29	**68**	**97**	**51**	**83**	**60**

Write the prime numbers between 1 and 100 in the boxes given alongside.

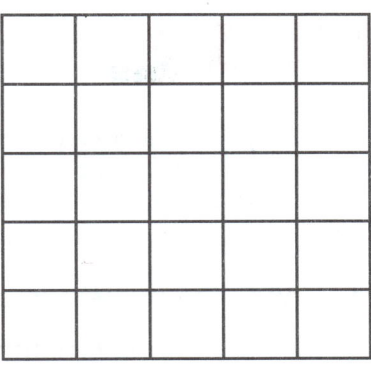

You already know that a factor is also called a divisor.

So, when you are trying to find a prime number less than 100, it is just enough if you know the divisibility rule for 2, 3, 5 and 7, because any number that is not divisible by 2, 3, 5 and 7 is a prime number.

Let us see if 41 is a prime number or not.

Is it divisible by 2? No
Is it divisible by 3? No
Is it divisible by 5? No
Is it divisible by 7? No

41 is a prime number

Exercise 4

Look at this table of factors. Say whether the given numbers are prime or composite.

Number	Factors	Prime or composite
12	1, 2, 3, 4, 6, 12	
13	1, 13	
24	1, 2, 3, 4, 6, 8, 12, 24	
15	1, 3, 5, 15	
29	1, 29	
17	1, 17	
28	1, 2, 4, 7, 14, 28	
9	1, 3, 9	
91	1, 91	

Exercise 5

a. Write the prime numbers between 10 and 20.   11, 13, 17, 19
b. Write the prime numbers between 30 and 66.   _____
c. Write the prime numbers between 56 and 99.   _____
d. Write the prime numbers between 16 and 69.   _____
e. Write the prime numbers between 25 and 100.   _____

Exercise 6

Find the factors of the following numbers. Then, write whether they are prime or composite numbers.

a. 21   Factors: 1, 3, 7, 21   Composite
b. 37   _____
c. 90   _____
d. 48   _____
e. 79   _____
f. 18   _____
g. 41   _____
h. 100   _____

Twin Prime Numbers

If two prime numbers have only one number between them, then they are called twin prime numbers.

Example   11 and 13

Find other twin prime numbers below 100 and write them in the stars.

11, 13

Fun with Factors

Perfect numbers

The factors of 6 other than 6 are 1, 2 and 3. If you add these 3 numbers you get 6. So, 6 is called a **perfect number**.

Abundant number (abundant means plenty)

The factors of 12 other than 12 are, 1, 2, 3, 4 and 6. If you add these numbers, it is more than 12. So 12 is called an **abundant number**.

Deficient Number (deficient means not enough)

The factors of 10 other than 10 are, 1, 2 and 5 and if you add these numbers, it is less than 10. So 10 is called a **deficient number**.

Exercise 7

Now, find an example of your own for each of the above-mentioned type of numbers.

Common Factors

Common factor refers to a situation when two or more things have something in common. Given below is an activity from which you can understand the meaning of common factor before you work with numbers.

Example

1. Guru likes the colour of the sky, but not the colour of the dark cloud.

2. Raghu likes the colour of the sea, but not the colour of the crabs.

3. Ismail likes the colour of the kingfisher, but not the colour of the crow.

4. Edward likes the colour of a sapphire, but not the colour of emerald.

In the above sentences, all the boys seem to like a particular colour, more than any other. If you read the sentences carefully, blue seems to be the common factor among colours that they like. So, blue is a common factor of all the four sentences.

Exercise 8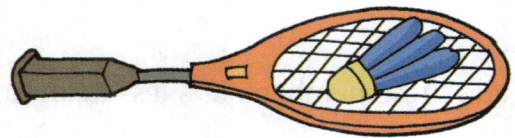

Now find the common factor in each group of sentences:

1. Ravi likes buns but not cashews.
   Geetha likes croissants but not milk.
   Robin likes cookies, but not juices.
   Payal likes cakes but not fries.

2. Meera likes lawn tennis, but not swimming.
   Nasreen likes badminton but not high jump.
   Latika likes squash but not sprint.
   Kiran likes table tennis but not volley ball.

3. Tanya likes rings but not necklaces.
   Tara likes bangles but not hairclips.
   Chandan likes hoola hoops but not fishing rods.
   Rosina likes her car's wheels but not the colour of the car.

4. Gurdeep's pup likes milk but not bread.
   Somdev's pup likes soup but not meat.
   Pranoy's pup likes water but not biscuits.
   Somayajulu's pup likes broth but not dog food.

Common Factors

Many numbers can divide more than one number, without leaving a remainder.

Example

4 can divide 20,
4 can divide 8,
4 can divide 16 and so on.

4 is a divisor and a factor of 20, 8 and 16 and many other numbers. So, 4 is a common factor of these numbers.

To find common factors, we can use 3 methods.

Method 1

By finding all the factors.

Example Common factors of 12 and 18

Factors of 12 = 1, 2, 3, 4, 6 and 12.   Factors of 18 = 1, 2, 3, 6, 9 and 18.

So, the common factors of 12 and 18 are 1, 2, 3 and 6.

Method 2

By dividing.

Example   12 and 18

12 ÷ 1 = 12	18 ÷ 1 = 18
12 ÷ 2 = 6	18 ÷ 2 = 9
12 ÷ 3 = 4	18 ÷ 3 = 6
12 ÷ 4 = 3	18 ÷ 6 = 3
12 ÷ 6 = 2	18 ÷ 9 = 2
12 ÷ 12 = 1	18 ÷ 18 = 1
Factors of 12 = 1, 2, 3, 4, 6 and 12	Factors of 18 = 1, 2, 3, 6, 9 and 18

So, the common factors of 12 and 18 are 1, 2, 3 and 6.

Method 3

By multiplying.

Example   12 and 18

1 × 12 = 12	1 × 18 = 18
3 × 4 = 12	2 × 9 = 18
6 × 2 = 12	3 × 6 = 18
Factors of 12 = 1, 2, 3, 4, 6 and 12	Factors of 18 = 1, 2, 3, 6, 9 and 18

So, the common factors of 12 and 18 are 1, 2, 3 and 6.

MENTAL MATH FA

What is common to all?

1. Jayath likes law coats.
2. Sonal likes ravens better than sparrows.
3. Bagath likes rain bearing clouds more than white clouds.
4. Shiva likes a police man's shoes better than his sports shoes.
5. Pamela likes crows better than pigeons as they dirty her balcony a lot.

Exercise 9

Find the common factors by finding out all the factors.

a. 20, 24

b. 16, 20

c. 24, 30

d. 30, 50

e. 12, 18   f. 20, 25

g. 14, 21   h. 15, 12

i. 24, 28   j. 35, 42

Remember
The divisor and the quotient are factors of a number.

Exercise 10

Find the common factors by the division method.

a. 12, 15   b. 20, 25

c. 21, 27   d. 15, 18

e. 18, 27   f. 18, 36

Remember
Both the multiplier and the multiplicand are factors of a number.

g. 30, 35   h. 35, 50

i. 10, 35   j. 24, 36

Exercise 11

Find the common factors by the multiplication method.

a. 32, 36   b. 40, 25

c. 28, 30   d. 18, 21

e. 32, 48   f. 28, 42

g. 30, 75

h. 48, 64

i. 36, 42

j. 49, 56

MENTAL MATH

1. Change one digit in the number so it becomes divisible by 5. 408543
2. Change one digit in the number so it becomes divisible by 8. 859321
3. Change one digit in the number so it becomes divisible by 2. 459287
4. Change one digit in the number so it becomes divisible by 4. 564791
5. Change one digit in the number so it bocomes divisible by 6. 904815

Coprime Numbers

When two numbers have only 1 as their common factor, they are called coprime numbers. One or both can be composite numbers and still be coprime.

Example   4 and 9

Find other coprime numbers below 100 and write them on the sheeps.

Prime Factors

You have already learnt what prime numbers are. So it is easy to find prime factors.

Example

Take 20 and find all its factors.

20 = 1, 2, 4, 5, 10 and 20

Factor Tree Method is another method to find prime factors.

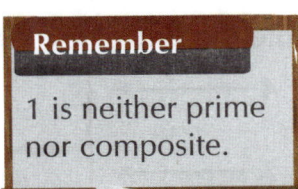

Remember

1 is neither prime nor composite.

Step 1: Start with any two factors of 20 and continue till you get all factors as prime factors.

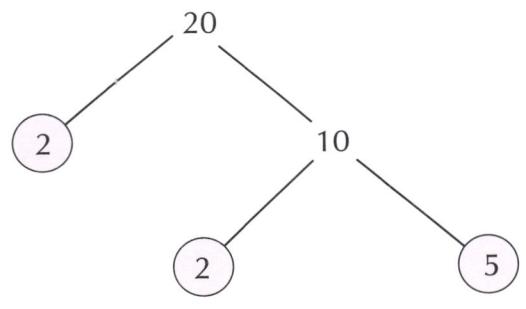

Step 2: Again take any two factors that give you the other number as the product. Again, circle the prime numbers.

Here 20 can be expressed as the product of its prime factors (2, 5), but one of them has to be taken twice (2). So, 20 = 2 × 2 × 5.

Keep converting all composite numbers into prime numbers. Here you have three prime numbers that are circled and they give the product of 20 when multiplied.

So, prime factors of 20 are 2 × 2 × 5. Do not write it as 2 and 5.

Exercise 12

Use the Factor Tree Method to find the prime factors of the following.

a. 30	b. 45	c. 19
d. 25	e. 36	f. 42
g. 48	h. 56	i. 18
j. 55	k. 24	l. 63

Multiples

You have already learnt the multiplication tables of many numbers.

Look at this.

Table of 5 = 5, 10, 15, 20, 25, 30, 35, 40, 45, 50, ...

All the numbers that come in the table of 5 are its multiples. Multiples are never ending. So they are called infinite. You cannot find the last multiple of any number. You can only find the least multiple of a number.

When you are learning about multiples, you should remember the following.

a. Every number is a multiple of itself.

b. Every number is a multiple of one.

c. Multiples are infinite.

Write the first nine multiples of the following numbers.

4 ⟶
7 ⟶
9 ⟶
8 ⟶
6 ⟶
3 ⟶

Common Multiples

Two or more numbers can have a common multiple. Since multiples are never ending, you should specify the number of multiples you are going to look at to find some common multiples.

Let us find the common multiples of 2 and 4, within their first 10 multiples.

Multiples of 2 = 2, 4, 6, 8, 10, 12, 14, 16, 18, 20

Multiples of 4 = 4, 8, 12, 16, 20, 24, 28, 32, 36, 40

When you compare the first 10 multiples of 2 and 4, you will find that they have five common multiples, i.e. 4, 8, 12, 16 and 20. There will be more if you continue to look for more multiples.

Exercise 13

Look at the first 10 multiples of the two given numbers and find the common multiples.

a. 2, 3

b. 3, 5

c. 4, 6

d. 2, 8

e. 5, 10

f. 4, 8

g. 8, 6

h. 7, 6

i. 3, 9

Exercise 14

Choose the correct answer.

1. Which of these is a perfect number?

   (a) 26 (b) 27 (c) 28 (d) 29

2. Which out of these is a deficient number?

   (a) 6 (b) 28 (c) 12 (d) 8

3. Identify the abundant number among these.

   (a) 15 (b) 18 (c) 16 (d) 10

4. Which among these is a pair of coprime numbers?

   (a) 14 and 15 (b) 14 and 21 (c) 14 and 28 (d) 14 and 7

5. Which of these is a pair of twin prime numbers?

   (a) 11 and 17 (b) 7 and 17 (c) 5 and 11 (d) 17 and 19

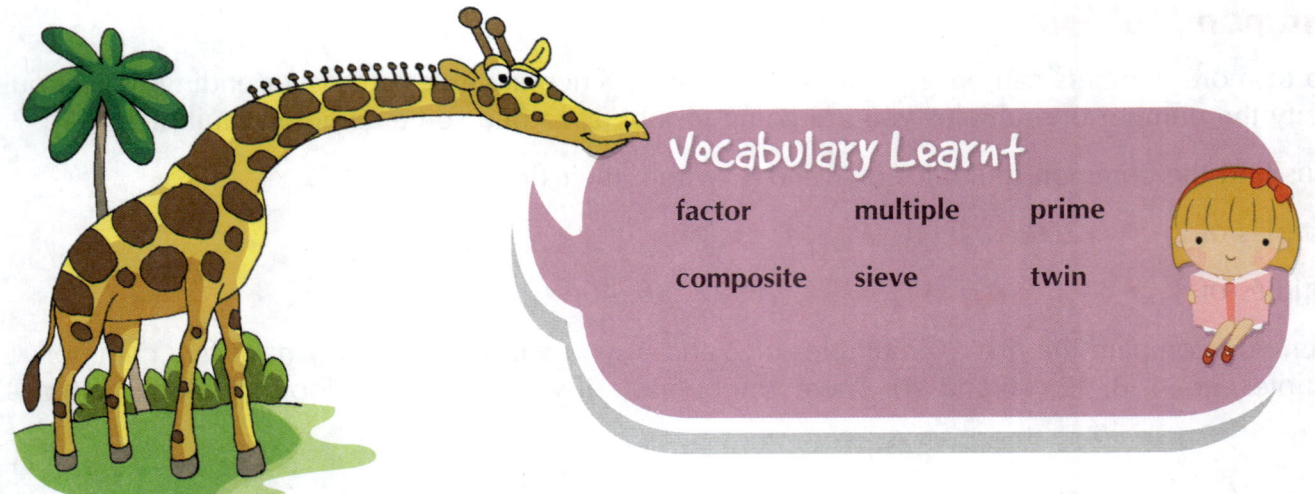

Factors and Multiples Crossword

Solve the crossword puzzle with the help of the clues given below.

Across

2. 6 is called a _____ number.

3. 48 is a _____ number.

4. 2 is both even and _____ number.

5. 12 is an _____ number.

Down

1. 10 is a _____ number.

7

H.C.F. and L.C.M.

You know ...
- what are prime and composite numbers
- what are factors and multiples.

Maths Lab Activity 1

Materials required
- Cards for writing numbers

Method (Note for the Teacher)

Write any two composite numbers on the blackboard (for example, 24, 30). Divide the class into two groups. Ask the students of the first group to come one by one and write the factors of the first number written on the blackboard on the cards. Once all the factors have been written, ask one child from the first group to arrange the numbers in ascending order. Now repeat this with the second group for the second number written on the blackboard. Now ask one child from that group to come and arrange the factors in ascending order. Once this is done, write the factors on the blackboard. Now ask one child from the first group to take out all the factors that are common for both the numbers. Then ask one child from the second group to come and pick up the highest number among the common factors. Ask the child to show this to the entire class.

Now repeat this activity for different pairs on numbers and then explain what HCF is.

Highest Common Factor (H.C.F.)

When two (or more) numbers have more than 1 common factor, the highest among them is called the highest common factor or H.C.F.

Consider two numbers 12 and 18.

The factors of 12 are 1, 2, 3, 6 and 12.

The factors of 18 are 1, 2, 3, 6 and 18.

1, 2, 3 and of 6 are the common factors of 12 and 18 and 6 is the highest among them.

So, H.C.F. of 12 and 18 is 6.

H.C.F. by finding common factors

Example 20, 24
Factors of 20 = 1, 2, 4, 5, 10 and 20
Factors of 24 = 1, 2, 3, 4, 6, 8, 12 and 24
Common factors = 2, 4
Highest Common Factor of 20 and 24 = 4

Exercise 1

a. Find the H.C.F. by finding factors.

   i. 14, 10

      Factors of 14 = ...

      Factors of 10 = ...

      Common factors = ...

      Highest Common Factor = ...

   ii. 18, 24

      Factors of 18 = ...

      Factors of 24 = ...

      Common factors = ...

      Highest Common Factor = ...

   iii. 16, 20   iv. 21, 18

   v. 45, 56   vi. 35, 45

   vii. 12, 16   viii. 10, 20

   ix. 15, 24   x. 18, 16

   xi. 21, 27   xii. 32, 8

b. Find the highest common factor by finding the factors by division method.

   i. 12, 15   ii. 22, 20

   iii. 14, 28   iv. 15, 20

   v. 20, 28   vi. 12, 10

   vii. 30, 36   viii. 8, 24

   ix. 54, 42   x. 24, 32

c. Find the highest common factor by multiplication method.

   i. 15, 25

   ii. 54, 36

   iii. 16, 18

   iv. 22, 20

   v. 30, 45

   vi. 24, 36

   vii. 21, 14

   viii. 63, 45

   ix. 16, 10

   x. 36, 45

d. Solve the riddles given below.

   i. I am a number between 45 and 50. Two of my factors are 2 and 6. I am a common multiple of 6 and 3. What number am I?

   ii. I am a factor of 84 and a common multiple of 3 and 7. The sum of my digits is 3. My digits are one apart. What number am I?

   iii. I am a number between 55 and 60. I have only two factors. My digits are four apart. What number am I?

   iv. I am more than 20 but less than 50. Two of my factors are 2 and 3. My first digit is double the second digit. What number am I?

   v. I am a number between 40 and 50. I am a multiple of a number between 8 and 10 and also a multiple of 15. What number am I?

Highest Common Factor (H.C.F.) using Prime Factors

You can find H.C.F. by using the Factor Tree Method.

Example: 30, 36

Step 1: Find all the prime factors of both the numbers by the factor tree method.

Step 2: Write both numbers as multiplication of prime factors.

Step 3: Find the factors which are repeating in both the numbers and multiply to get H.C.F.

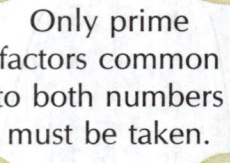

Only prime factors common to both numbers must be taken.

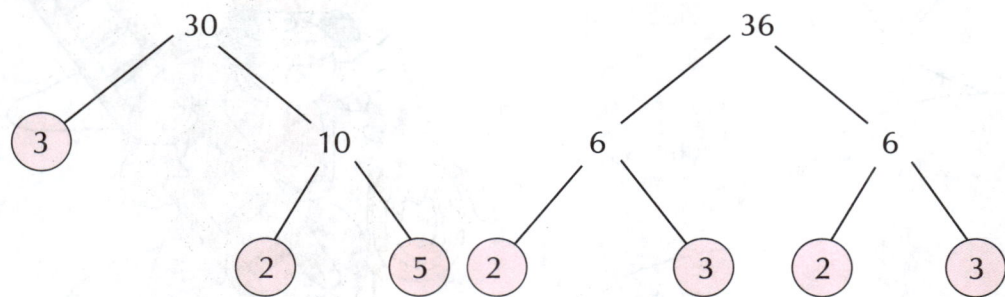

$30 = \boxed{3} \times \boxed{2} \times 5$

$36 = \boxed{3} \times \boxed{2} \times 2 \times 3$

Multiply the common factors of the 2 numbers to get the highest common factor.

$3 \times 2 = 6$

So, H.C.F. of 30 and 36 = 6

Exercise 2

Now, solve the following to find the HCF using prime factors. (You may use your notebook for this.)

a. 18, 15	b. 40, 60	c. 24, 30	d. 14, 24
e. 16, 20	f. 20, 25	g. 36, 42	h. 15, 24
i. 20, 50	j. 32, 36	k. 12, 60	l. 28, 49

Is it possible to find the highest common multiple of two numbers? Find out the answer.

Lowest Common Multiple (L.C.M.)

Since multiples are never ending, it is not possible to find the highest common multiple. So, try to find the lowest common multiple.

There are many methods of finding the L.C.M. Let us look at all of them.

Method 1

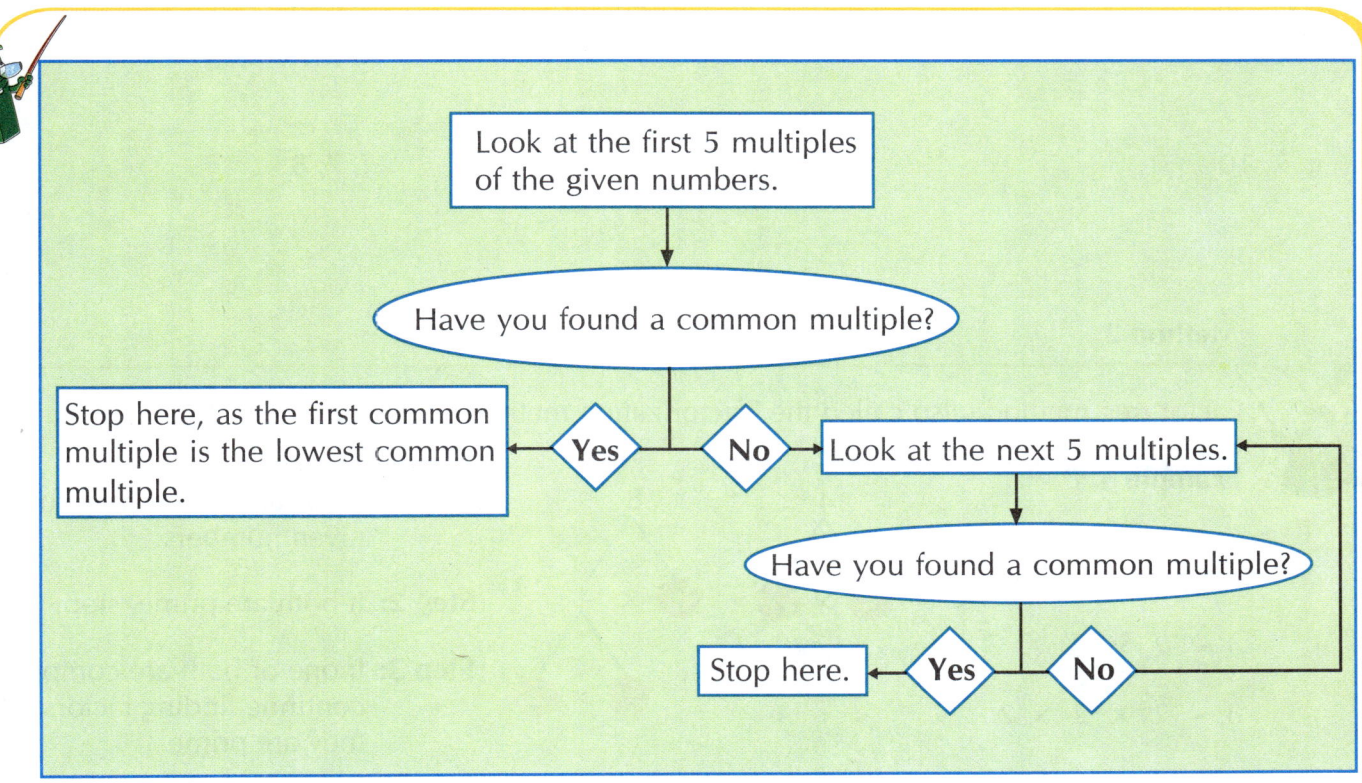

Example: Find the lowest common multiple (LCM) of 4, 6.

Step 1: Find the first 5 multiples of 4.

Step 2: Find the first 5 multiples of 6.

Step 3: Look if the 2 numbers have a common multiple. If they have, stop working further. Here, 12 is common to both 4 and 6. So, 12 is the lowest common multiple of 4 and 6.

Multiplies of 4 = 4, 8, 12 , 16, 20

Multiplies of 6 = 6, 12 , (stop)

12 is the first multiple common to 4 and 6. Hence, it is the lowest common multiple.

Note: If you do not get a common factor within the first 5 multiples do the same with the next 5 multiples of the 2 numbers.

Exercise 3

Find the lowest common multiple for the given numbers.

a. 4, 8
b. 6, 12
c. 9, 12

d. 8, 10
e. 4, 5
f. 3, 9

g. 7, 10
h. 5, 12
i. 7, 8

Method 2

Factor tree method (also called the "factorization method"), using prime factors

Example 4, 8

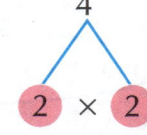

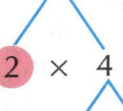
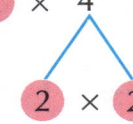

$4 = 2 \times 2$

$8 = 2 \times 2 \times 2$

Step 1: Find any 2 factors for the given numbers.

Step 2: If both are prime, stop.

Step 3: If one or both are composite continue finding factors till they are prime.

To get the L.C.M., multiply, taking the common factors once and all the other remaining factors together. Here, there is just one 2 left. So L.C.M. = 2 × 2 × 2 = 8.

Exercise 4

Find the L.C.M. using the factor tree method.

a. 7, 12
b. 5, 15
c. 8, 10

d. 6, 12
e. 3, 8
f. 4, 7

g. 5, 4
h. 3, 9
i. 12, 16

Method 3

Division method

Divide both the numbers by a common prime number, if possible. Otherwise, divide one number at a time and keep bringing down the other number till you are able to divide the other number by a prime number. Do so until you reach one.

Example 1   12, 20

2	12,	20
2	6,	10
3	3,	5
5	1,	5
	1,	1

L.C.M. = 2 × 2 × 3 × 5 = 60

Example 2   15, 55

5	15,	55
3	3,	11
11	1,	11
	1,	1

L.C.M. = 5 × 3 × 11 = 165

Exercise 5

Find the L.C.M. using the division method.

a. 8, 10

b. 6, 9

c. 10, 15

d. 9, 12

e. 14, 18

f. 20, 25

g. 13, 15

h. 16, 24

i. 6, 8

Maths Lab Activity 2

Materials required
- A worksheet, as given below, for every child
- A crayon
- A pencil

Method (Note for the Teacher)

Ask the students to circle all the letters that go with prime numbers. They should then write the letters that go with composite numbers at the bottom in order to find the hidden message.

E 13	F 24	I 67	A 45	O 59	B 11	C 56	T 35	U 89	P 7	O 10
M 5	J 23	R 74	Y 43	S 90	Z 2	K 29	A 54	E 47	R 60	H 7
E 42	R 11	T 53	F 49	T 61	U 36	N 80	G 29	B 66	L 83	U 55
A 13	T 72	F 31	D 47	X 53	M 28	O 67	V 2	P 43	U 99	J 7
L 31	S 37	L 18	R 11	U 13	S 17	T 6	B 29	I 8	Y 37	D 53
G 71	P 92	C 61	V 97	L 85	K 41	A 13	E 22	J 67	Q 19	Z 13
H 7	V 29	S 100	P 67	S 3	A 60	U 7	W 11	R 13	R 77	M 91
E 16	F 79	I 2	K 5	M 27	B 19	L 23	A 4	K 79	Z 17	D 15
H 83	D 92	F 89	A 17	J 31	E 94	M 97	V 67	N 33	Q 13	P 19
A 23	M 53	I 44	J 37	O 13	J 79	N 50	W 83	S 47	V 97	G 38

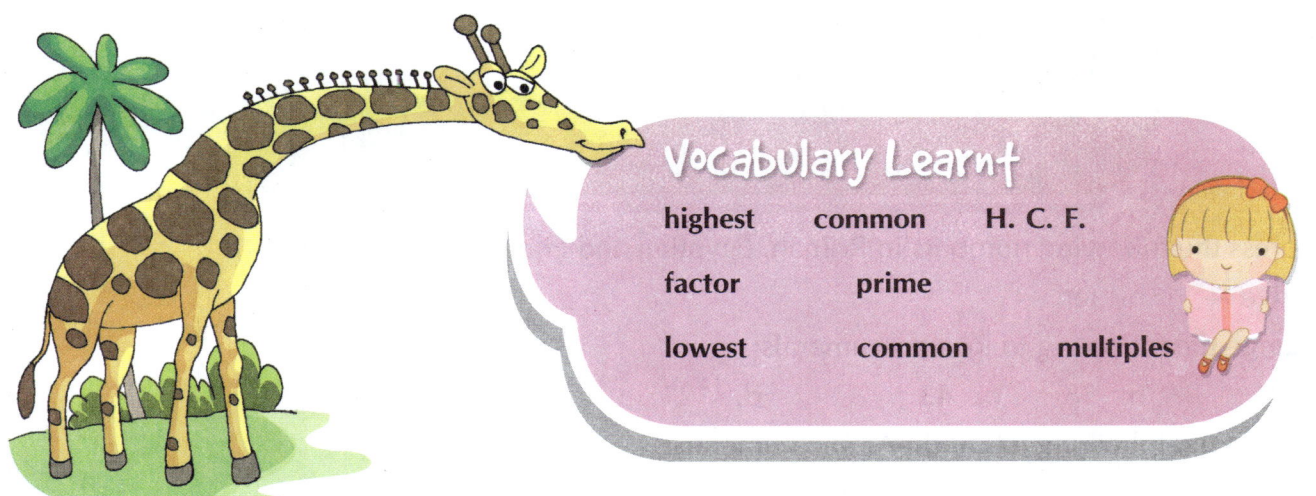

Vocabulary Learnt

highest   common   H. C. F.

factor   prime

lowest   common   multiples

Maths Lab Activity 3

FA

Materials required
- A worksheet with instructions and answer boxes as given below
- Crayons

Method (Note for the Teacher)

Ask the students to colour the c ouds according to the colour code given.

a. If it is a multiple of 2 numbers, colour in yellow.
b. If it is a multiple of 3 numbers, colour in blue.
c. If it is a multiple of 4 or more numbers, colour in green.

Do not consider 1, as every number is a multiple of 1.

Numbers in clouds: 21, 20, 18, 15, 19, 40, 14, 8, 25, 2, 6, 40, 28, 24, 22, 32, 42, 7, 12

Summative Assessment 2
(For chapters 5 to 7)

1. Express the following numbers in Roman, Egyptian and Hindu-Arabic system:
   a. five — b. ten —

2. Change the following to Roman numerals:
   a. 14   b. 58   c. 43   d. 121

3. Change the following to Hindu-Arabic numerals:
   a. XXIV   b. XIII   c. CDII   d. XC

4. Tick the boxes to say if the numbers are divisible by the given number.

Numbers	2	3	4	5	6	9	10
49851							
9344							
37507							
12580							
41386							

5. What will you add as the last digit to make the numbers divisible by the given numbers in brackets?
   a. (by 2) 8765 ____   b. (by 5) 4318 ____   c. (by 3) 6121 ____

6. Find a 3-digit number that can be divided by 2 and 3.

7. Find a 3-digit number that can be divided by 5 and 10.

8. Find a 3-digit number that can be divided by 2 and 4.

9. Find a 3-digit number that can be divided by 3 and 9.

10. Write any five prime numbers.

11. Find the common factors of   a. 32 and 36   b. 45 and 70

12. Find the H.C.F. of   a. 14 and 24   b. 21 and 18

13. Find the L.C.M. of the following using tree method.
    a. 9 and 12   b. 12 and 15

14. Find the L.C.M. of the following using division method.
    a. 12 and 20   b. 16 and 18

8 Fractions

> **You know ...**
> - what a fraction is
> - the meaning of numerator and denominator
> - how to compare, add or subtract like fractions
> - a fraction can be part of a set taken as one unit
> - how to find the fraction of a number.

You have already learnt what a fraction is. It can be a part of one whole or of a group of objects or numbers taken as one whole. A fraction is written by using two numbers, which are called the '**terms**'. A line separates the two terms. The number above the line is called the **numerator** and the number below the line is called the **denominator**. Denominator tells how many parts the whole is divided into and the numerator tells how many parts are shaded or taken out of the whole.

Maths Lab Activity 1

Fraction painting

Materials required
- Paints of different colours
- Small measuring spoons

Method (Note for the Teacher)

Ask a student to choose two colours. Let the student guess which colour would be formed if a certain amount of those two colours are mixed. Let the student actually mix the colours to check. Ask all students to try different combinations of paints.

Example

$\frac{1}{2}$ spoon of red and $\frac{1}{4}$ spoon of yellow

$\frac{1}{2}$ spoon of blue and $\frac{1}{2}$ spoon of red

$\frac{1}{2}$ spoon of red and 1 spoon of white

1 spoon of yellow and $\frac{1}{2}$ spoon of green

Ask the students to record their findings on a chart. They could write their guess in one column and the actual result of their experiment in another column.

Exercise 1

Complete the following table. One has been done for you.

Fraction	Numerator	Denominator
$\frac{1}{2}$	1	2
$\frac{1}{3}$		
$\frac{5}{6}$		
$\frac{7}{8}$		
$\frac{9}{11}$		

Like and Unlike Fractions

When two or more fractions have the same denominator, they are called **like fractions**.

Example $\frac{8}{3}, \frac{7}{3}, \frac{5}{3}, \frac{1}{3}$ and $\frac{2}{3}$ are like fractions.

When fractions have different denominators, they are called **unlike fractions**.

Example $\frac{1}{4}, \frac{2}{5}, \frac{3}{7}$ are unlike fractions.

Addition of Like Fractions

While adding like fractions, if both the required parts can be taken from one whole, it is enough if you draw one box diagram. However, shade the two parts with two different colours to show the addition of two fractions.

Example $\frac{3}{8}$ $\frac{2}{8}$ $\frac{4}{6}$ $\frac{1}{6}$

Here, both the fractions are shown in one diagram itself.

What do you think their totals are? $\frac{3}{8} + \frac{2}{8} = \frac{5}{8}$ and $\frac{4}{6} + \frac{1}{6} = \frac{5}{6}$

So you just have to add the numerators to get the answers.

Exercise 2

Add the following like fractions using the box diagram.

a. $\dfrac{1}{3} + \dfrac{2}{3}$

b. $\dfrac{4}{9} + \dfrac{2}{9}$

c. $\dfrac{7}{9} + \dfrac{1}{9}$

d. $\dfrac{2}{5} + \dfrac{1}{5}$

e. $\dfrac{1}{5} + \dfrac{3}{5}$

f. $\dfrac{1}{4} + \dfrac{1}{4}$

g. $\dfrac{2}{8} + \dfrac{5}{8}$

h. $\dfrac{3}{7} + \dfrac{2}{7}$

i. $\dfrac{1}{3} + \dfrac{1}{3}$

j. $\dfrac{2}{9} + \dfrac{5}{9}$

Remember

While adding like fractions, denominator will remain the same, just add the numerators.

Exercise 3

Add without the box diagram.

a. $\dfrac{1}{9} + \dfrac{4}{9} + \dfrac{2}{9}$

b. $\dfrac{2}{8} + \dfrac{3}{8} + \dfrac{1}{8}$

c. $\dfrac{3}{12} + \dfrac{4}{12} + \dfrac{4}{12}$

d. $\dfrac{4}{18} + \dfrac{5}{18} + \dfrac{6}{18}$

Subtraction of Like Fractions

To subtract like fractions, it is enough to draw one box diagram and cancel the required parts from the shaded parts.

$\dfrac{5}{8} - \dfrac{2}{8} = \dfrac{3}{8}$

$\dfrac{9}{11} - \dfrac{4}{11} = \dfrac{5}{11}$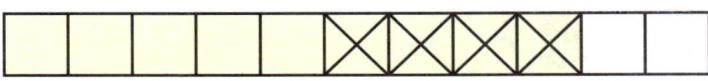

Exercise 4

Subtract the following using the box diagram.

a. $\dfrac{8}{9} - \dfrac{3}{9}$

b. $\dfrac{5}{8} - \dfrac{1}{8}$

c. $\dfrac{7}{9} - \dfrac{1}{9}$

d. $\dfrac{13}{17} - \dfrac{11}{17}$

e. $\dfrac{18}{20} - \dfrac{4}{20}$

f. $\dfrac{10}{11} - \dfrac{3}{11}$

Exercise 5

Subtract the following without using the box diagram.

a. $\dfrac{7}{14} - \dfrac{1}{14}$ b. $\dfrac{2}{8} - \dfrac{1}{8}$

c. $\dfrac{14}{17} - \dfrac{3}{17}$ d. $\dfrac{13}{19} - \dfrac{2}{19}$

e. $\dfrac{6}{8} - \dfrac{3}{8}$ f. $\dfrac{7}{10} - \dfrac{4}{10}$

g. $\dfrac{5}{6} - \dfrac{2}{6}$ h. $\dfrac{3}{7} - \dfrac{1}{7}$

i. $\dfrac{8}{9} - \dfrac{4}{9}$ j. $\dfrac{3}{4} - \dfrac{1}{4}$

Remember

While subtracting like fractions, denominator will remain the same, just subtract the numerators.

Proper and Improper Fractions

In proper fractions, the numerator is smaller than the denominator. So it is possible to take out the required number of parts from one whole cut into parts.

Example $\dfrac{1}{4}$

Here you know that the whole has been cut into four parts and you are required to take out one part. Is it possible? Yes. So it is a proper fraction.

In improper fractions, the numerator is bigger than the denominator. So it is not possible to take out the required parts from one whole.

Example $\dfrac{4}{3}$

Exercise 6

Colour all the proper fractions in red and improper fractions in green.

$\dfrac{1}{2}$ $\dfrac{8}{4}$ $\dfrac{5}{4}$ $\dfrac{3}{5}$ $\dfrac{7}{9}$ $\dfrac{8}{11}$ $\dfrac{1}{5}$ $\dfrac{5}{10}$

$\dfrac{6}{5}$ $\dfrac{2}{3}$ $\dfrac{13}{3}$ $\dfrac{9}{11}$ $\dfrac{9}{7}$ $\dfrac{8}{20}$ $\dfrac{15}{7}$ $\dfrac{2}{4}$

Changing Improper Fractions to Mixed Numbers

Look at the fraction $\frac{3}{2}$.

In this fraction, the numerator is greater than the denominator. So it is an improper fraction and you cannot take out 3 parts from 2. So, what do you do?

Think like this.

You have a bar of chocolate. You divide it into two equal parts to share it with your sister. Just then your friend comes and he wants a share equal to yours. How would you give him an equal quantity of chocolate without dividing this chocolate any further? Think of an answer.

You have to get another chocolate of the same size and give him one part.

First take one whole with 2 parts and shade both the parts to indicate that you and your sister are sharing it.

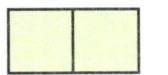

Then take another whole, which is of the same size, and cut it into 2 parts and give one part to your friend. So, you have taken 3 parts out of 2 wholes. The denominator will not change because both the chocolates have been cut into 2 parts only.

So, $\frac{3}{2}$ is an improper fraction. This can also be represented as a mixed number.

Look at this.

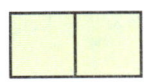 +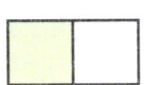

$\frac{2}{2}$ + $\frac{1}{2}$

When you take all the parts, you are taking 1 whole ($\frac{2}{2}$ or 1).

So, $\qquad 1 + \frac{1}{2} = 1\frac{1}{2}$

$1\frac{1}{2}$ has one whole number and one fractional number. So it is called a **mixed number**.

To convert an improper fraction to a mixed number, follow the steps give below:

Step 1: First look at the denominator and draw a diagram with that many parts and colour.

Step 2: Draw another diagram of the same size with the same number of parts and shade the balance parts.

Step 3: Now add them both to get the answer.

Exercise 7

Show the following improper fractions using diagrams (as shown above) and then convert them into mixed numbers.

a. $\dfrac{5}{4}$ b. $\dfrac{5}{3}$ c. $\dfrac{6}{5}$ d. $\dfrac{7}{5}$ e. $\dfrac{7}{3}$ f. $\dfrac{9}{4}$

Remember

When the numerator and the denominator are same, the value of the fraction becomes 1.

MENTAL MATH

1. How many whole units are used to represent $\dfrac{13}{4}$ pictorially?
2. Is $1\dfrac{1}{2}$ an improper fraction or $\dfrac{3}{2}$ an improper fraction?
3. What is $\dfrac{1}{4}$ of 28?
4. What are $\dfrac{1}{8}, \dfrac{3}{8}, \dfrac{5}{8}$ and $\dfrac{7}{8}$ called?
5. When $\dfrac{3}{4}, \dfrac{2}{6}$ and $\dfrac{1}{5}$ are converted to like fractions, what will be their denominator?

You cannot be always drawing to find the answers. So, let us see how to change an improper fraction numerically to a mixed number.

Exercise 8

Example $\dfrac{5}{3}$ means 5 divided by 3

$3\overline{)5}$ subtract 3, remainder 2. You get 1 set of 3 and 2 is left as remainder. So, we say 1 and $\dfrac{2}{3}$.

$= 1\dfrac{2}{3}$

Convert the following into mixed numbers by dividing.

a. $\dfrac{3}{2}$ b. $\dfrac{5}{4}$ c. $\dfrac{9}{6}$ d. $\dfrac{4}{3}$

e. $\dfrac{8}{3}$ f. $\dfrac{8}{5}$ g. $\dfrac{7}{6}$ h. $\dfrac{11}{3}$

i. $\dfrac{19}{3}$ j. $\dfrac{14}{8}$ k. $\dfrac{9}{2}$ l. $\dfrac{7}{5}$

m. $\dfrac{9}{4}$ n. $\dfrac{11}{7}$ o. $\dfrac{14}{6}$ p. $\dfrac{5}{3}$

q. $\dfrac{7}{3}$ r. $\dfrac{9}{5}$ s. $\dfrac{12}{5}$ t. $\dfrac{18}{7}$

Maths Lab Activity 2

Materials required
- Multiples of equal-sized rectangular strips of paper
- Crayons

Method (Note for the Teacher)

Divide the students into groups. Give two strips to each student in a group. Ask one group to fold the strips into 2 and 4 equal parts respectively. Ask another group to divide their two strips into 3 and 6 equal parts and so on. Next, ask the first group to colour just one part out of 2 and second group to colour one out of 3 parts of the strip and so on. Now ask the groups to take the second strip and colour parts that are equal to the one part of the first strip.

The first group would have coloured 2 out of 4, the second, 2 out of 6 and so on. Ask them to place the two strips side by side and see that though the number of parts coloured is different, the size of the coloured parts is same.

To subtract, they need to colour parts equal to the first fraction first and cancel the number of parts equal to the second fraction from the coloured parts.

Equivalent Fractions

What do we mean by equivalent? When two or more things are same, they are called equivalent. Look at these two diagrams.

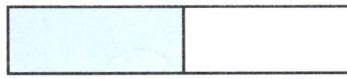 This one shows $\frac{1}{2}$ shaded

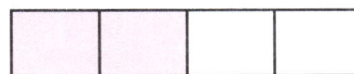 This one shows $\frac{2}{4}$ shaded

Is there any difference between the sizes of the parts? **Yes**. One shows bigger parts and the other shows smaller parts. Is there any difference in the size of the shaded parts? **No**.

In the first diagram, 1 out of 2 is shaded. In the second, 2 out of 4 are shaded. So, the same quantity is shaded in both but they are called differently, i.e., $\frac{1}{2}$ and $\frac{2}{4}$. These two fractions are called equivalent fractions. All you have to remember is that the whole unit should be of the same size in both. Now look at these.

Here, $\frac{1}{3}$ and $\frac{2}{6}$ are equivalent.

Exercise 9

Shade the two diagrams in such a way that they show equivalent fractions. Write the fractions in the circles.

◯ and ◯ are equivalent.

◯ and ◯ are equivalent.

◯ and ◯ are equivalent.

◯ and ◯ are equivalent.

◯ and ◯ are equivalent.

◯ and ◯ are equivalent.

Observe that in equivalent fractions,
- the numerator of the second fraction is multiple of the numerator of the first fraction.
- the denominator of the second fraction is multiple of the denominator of the first fraction.

Here is a fraction board. Study it carefully. It represents equivalent fractions.

Remember the two fractions must be of equal value, even if they are cut into different sizes.

Example $\dfrac{1}{2} = \dfrac{2}{4} = \dfrac{3}{6} = \dfrac{4}{8} = \dfrac{5}{10} = \dfrac{6}{12} = \dfrac{7}{14} = \dfrac{8}{16}$ are all equivalent fractions.

If we shade 1 part out of 2 in the first row of fraction board, it will represent $\dfrac{1}{2}$. If we shade two parts out of 4 in the third row, it will represent $\dfrac{2}{4}$ and so on.

Exercise 10

Write five equivalent fractions in the boxes.

a. $\dfrac{1}{4}$ =

b. $\dfrac{1}{6}$ =

c. $\dfrac{1}{3}$ =

d. $\dfrac{1}{5}$ =

We cannot always use drawings to find equivalent fractions. That is not always practical. So, to find equivalent fractions, we can look at the multiples of the numerator and the denominator.

Example

$\dfrac{1}{3} =$

2	3	4	5	6	7	8	9	10	Multiples of 1
6	9	12	15	18	21	24	27	30	Multiples of 3

Exercise 11

a. Find equivalent fractions for the following.

  i. $\dfrac{2}{3} =$ ☐☐☐☐☐☐☐☐☐ Multiples of _____ / Multiples of _____

  ii. $\dfrac{4}{8} =$ ☐☐☐☐☐☐☐☐☐ Multiples of _____ / Multiples of _____

  iii. $\dfrac{4}{9} =$ ☐☐☐☐☐☐☐☐☐ Multiples of _____ / Multiples of _____

b. Write any four equivalent fractions for the following.

  i. $\dfrac{2}{5}$ ☐☐☐☐   ii. $\dfrac{1}{4}$ ☐☐☐☐

  iii. $\dfrac{4}{9}$ ☐☐☐☐   iv. $\dfrac{4}{8}$ ☐☐☐☐

  v. $\dfrac{2}{9}$ ☐☐☐☐   vi. $\dfrac{1}{3}$ ☐☐☐☐

  vii. $\dfrac{1}{8}$ ☐☐☐☐   viii. $\dfrac{6}{8}$ ☐☐☐☐

  ix. $\dfrac{5}{6}$ ☐☐☐☐   x. $\dfrac{3}{8}$ ☐☐☐☐

c. Find the missing numerator or the denominator in the following equivalent fractions.

  i. $\dfrac{1}{10} = \dfrac{\Box}{20}$ ii. $\dfrac{4}{6} = \dfrac{8}{\Box}$ iii. $\dfrac{1}{8} = \dfrac{\Box}{40}$ iv. $\dfrac{2}{5} = \dfrac{\Box}{20}$

  v. $\dfrac{4}{9} = \dfrac{\Box}{81}$ vi. $\dfrac{4}{\Box} = \dfrac{16}{24}$ vii. $\dfrac{1}{21} = \dfrac{3}{\Box}$ iv. $\dfrac{2}{5} = \dfrac{\Box}{25}$

Reducing Fractions to their Lowest Terms

To find equivalent fractions with terms bigger than the given fraction, simply multiply the numerator and the denominator of the given fraction by a common number. To find equivalent fractions with terms smaller than the given fraction, simply divide the numerator and the denominator of the given fraction by a common factor.

Example

To increase $\frac{3}{4}$ to an equivalent fraction with bigger terms, multiply 3 by 5 and 4 by 5 and you will get $\frac{15}{20}$.

To reduce $\frac{15}{20}$ to an equivalent fraction with smaller terms, divide 15 by 5 and 20 by 5 and you will get $\frac{3}{4}$.

While reducing fractions to their lowest terms, it is important to first find out the highest common factor for both the terms. Otherwise more than one step will be involved.

Example

$\frac{15}{30}$

We know that 3 is a factor of 15 and 30. So let us divide both 15 and 30 by 3.

$15 \div 3 = 5$
$30 \div 3 = 10$

So, $\frac{5}{10}$ is an equivalent fraction of $\frac{15}{30}$ with lower terms. But you are asked to find the equivalent fraction with the lowest term.

$\frac{5}{10}$ is not a fraction with the lowest terms. So you need to again reduce $\frac{5}{10}$ to a lower term by dividing by a common factor, (5) and you will get $\frac{1}{2}$. To avoid this long process, you can divide by the highest common factor the first time itself. Here 15 is the highest common factor of 15 and 30. So, $15 \div 15 = 1$ and $30 \div 15 = 2$. So, $\frac{15}{30} = \frac{1}{2}$.

Exercise 12

Reduce the following to the lowest terms.

a. $\frac{3}{6}$ b. $\frac{9}{36}$ c. $\frac{5}{15}$ d. $\frac{4}{12}$ e. $\frac{8}{32}$

f. $\frac{10}{16}$ g. $\frac{20}{35}$ h. $\frac{9}{12}$ i. $\frac{9}{27}$ j. $\frac{12}{15}$

k. $\frac{5}{15}$ l. $\frac{4}{16}$ m. $\frac{9}{15}$ n. $\frac{11}{22}$ o. $\frac{8}{16}$

Comparison of Fractions

You have already learnt how to compare whole numbers and find out which is greater or smaller. In the same way, fractions can also be compared.

When you compare things, be it numbers, objects or people, you must remember that they should be of the same quality, value or strength. You cannot compare a mouse with an elephant. It is neither correct nor fair.

In the same way, while comparing fractions, make sure the wholes are of the same size and only the parts are divided differently.

Example $\frac{1}{2}$ and $\frac{1}{3}$

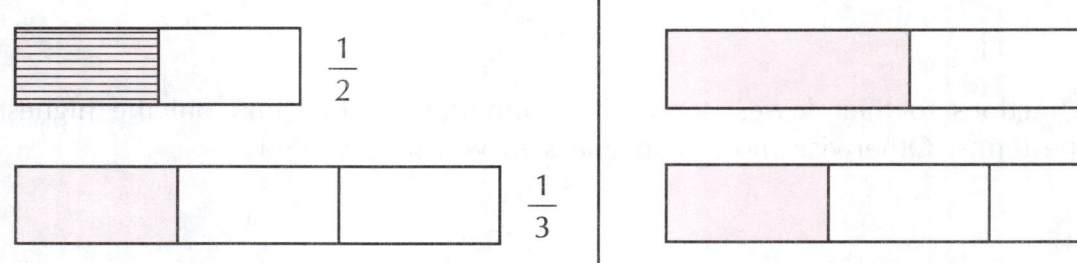

The first set of diagrams shows $\frac{1}{2}$ and $\frac{1}{3}$. Here it is not possible to compare and say which is bigger, though $\frac{1}{3}$ seems bigger, because the **diagrams** are not of the same size.

In the second set of diagrams, both are of the same size, you can see that actually $\frac{1}{2}$ is bigger than $\frac{1}{3}$.

So you must remember that if you compare parts of 2 things that are not the same in size, you may end up giving the wrong answer.

From this you can also understand that while comparing one part of two diagrams that have been divided into different number of parts, like $\frac{1}{2}$ and $\frac{1}{3}$, the one that has less number of parts (the fraction with a smaller denominator) will always be bigger. Here, $\frac{1}{2}$ is bigger than $\frac{1}{3}$.

Exercise 13

Now, use diagrams to find which is greater and use the < or > sign. One has been done for you.

a. $\frac{1}{3}$ > $\frac{1}{5}$

b. $\frac{1}{6}$ ☐ $\frac{1}{2}$

c. $\frac{1}{7}$ ☐ $\frac{1}{3}$

d. $\frac{1}{9}$ ☐ $\frac{1}{10}$

e. $\frac{1}{5}$ ☐ $\frac{1}{8}$

f. $\frac{1}{6}$ ☐ $\frac{1}{4}$

Remember
The wholes should be of the same size when you compare fractions.

Exercise 14

Now, find out which is greater without using diagrams.

a. $\frac{1}{4}$ ☐ $\frac{1}{2}$ b. $\frac{1}{3}$ ☐ $\frac{1}{9}$

c. $\frac{1}{6}$ ☐ $\frac{1}{8}$ d. $\frac{1}{7}$ ☐ $\frac{1}{3}$

e. $\frac{1}{8}$ ☐ $\frac{1}{10}$ f. $\frac{1}{9}$ ☐ $\frac{1}{6}$

Maths Lab Activity 3

Materials required
- Same-sized long strips of paper
- Crayons

Method (Note for the Teacher)

Give each student three strips of paper. Ask them to show $\frac{1}{2}$, $\frac{1}{4}$ and $\frac{1}{3}$ using the three strips by colouring 1 part in each. Now, ask them to place the strips besides one another and observe them carefully. You may then ask questions like

a. Which one of these do you think is more or greater, half or quarter? (half)

b. Which one of these do you think is more or greater, half or one third? (half)

c. Which one of these do you think is more or greater, quarter or one third? (one third)

d. What do you notice from this?

(They should be able to say that with more divisions the parts get smaller in size. They should also be able to conclude that while comparing fractions with the same numerator, the fraction with the smaller denominator is bigger).

Exercise 15

Look at the following diagrams. Colour the required number of parts and say which is bigger.

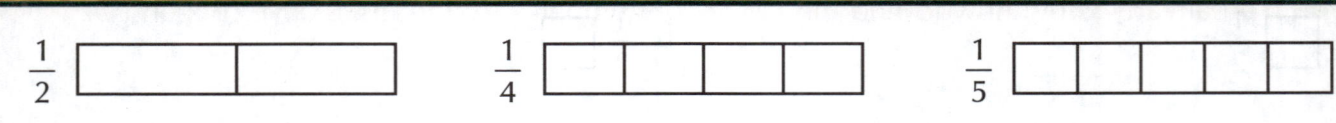

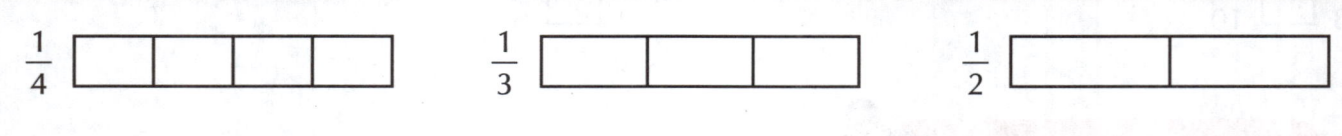

While what you have done is an easy way of finding out which is bigger or smaller while comparing 2 fractions, there is a method to be used for this purpose.

You must first convert the 2 fractions to like fractions by finding the L.C.M. of the 2 denominators.

Example $\frac{1}{2}$ and $\frac{1}{5}$

The first fraction shows $\frac{1}{2}$, which means the whole has been divided into 2 parts. The second fraction shows $\frac{1}{5}$, which means the whole has been divided into 5 parts. First, we should change both the fractions into like fractions.

Which means we need to change their denominators to the same number. How do you do it?

Method 1

Find equivalent fractions for them till both have the same denominator.

$$\frac{1}{2} = \frac{2}{4} = \frac{3}{6} = \frac{4}{8} = \frac{5}{10}$$

$$\frac{1}{5} = \frac{2}{10}$$

So $\frac{1}{2}$ can be written as $\frac{5}{10}$ and $\frac{1}{5}$ can be written as $\frac{2}{10}$.

Now, compare $\frac{5}{10}$ and $\frac{2}{10}$.

It is obvious that 5 parts out of 10 are more than 2 parts out of 10. So, $\frac{1}{2}$ is greater than $\frac{1}{5}$.

Method 2

$\dfrac{1}{2}$ and $\dfrac{1}{5}$

You already know how to find the L.C.M. of numbers. So find the L.C.M. of 2 and 5.

$$\begin{array}{c|cc} 2 & 2 & 5 \\ \hline 5 & 1 & 5 \\ \hline & 1 & 1 \end{array} \qquad 2 \times 5 = 10$$

The L.C.M. is 10.

Now change both the denominators to the L.C.M found above, that is 10 by multiplying by a suitable number. Remember to multiply the numerator also by the same number to keep the value of the fraction same.

$\dfrac{1}{2} \times \dfrac{5}{5} = \dfrac{5}{10} \qquad \dfrac{1}{5} \times \dfrac{2}{2} = \dfrac{2}{10}$.

Now, compare $\dfrac{5}{10}$ and $\dfrac{2}{10}$.

$\dfrac{5}{10}$ is greater than $\dfrac{2}{10}$. So $\dfrac{1}{2} > \dfrac{1}{5}$.

Exercise 16

a. Find and circle the greater of the fractions by using **Method 1** in each case.

 i. $\dfrac{1}{3}, \dfrac{1}{5}$ 　　　　 ii. $\dfrac{1}{5}, \dfrac{1}{6}$ 　　　　 iii. $\dfrac{1}{3}, \dfrac{4}{5}$

 iv. $\dfrac{1}{2}, \dfrac{4}{5}$ 　　　　 v. $\dfrac{9}{10}, \dfrac{5}{6}$ 　　　　 vi. $\dfrac{2}{4}, \dfrac{1}{3}$

 vii. $\dfrac{7}{8}, \dfrac{3}{4}$ 　　　　 viii. $\dfrac{2}{3}, \dfrac{3}{9}$ 　　　　 ix. $\dfrac{2}{3}, \dfrac{4}{7}$

 x. $\dfrac{1}{6}, \dfrac{3}{8}$ 　　　　 xi. $\dfrac{7}{9}, \dfrac{3}{4}$ 　　　　 xii. $\dfrac{1}{4}, \dfrac{3}{5}$

 xiii. $\dfrac{2}{8}, \dfrac{3}{7}$ 　　　　 xiv. $\dfrac{3}{9}, \dfrac{10}{12}$ 　　　　 xv. $\dfrac{1}{2}, \dfrac{5}{6}$

b. Find and circle the greater of the fractions by using **Method 2** in each case.

 i. $\dfrac{2}{5}, \dfrac{3}{4}$ 　　　　 ii. $\dfrac{3}{9}, \dfrac{1}{4}$ 　　　　 iii. $\dfrac{1}{6}, \dfrac{2}{9}$

iv. $\dfrac{3}{5}, \dfrac{7}{8}$ v. $\dfrac{9}{10}, \dfrac{5}{9}$ vi. $\dfrac{1}{8}, \dfrac{1}{3}$

vii. $\dfrac{2}{4}, \dfrac{1}{6}$ viii. $\dfrac{1}{3}, \dfrac{5}{6}$ ix. $\dfrac{2}{4}, \dfrac{6}{7}$

x. $\dfrac{6}{9}, \dfrac{2}{8}$ xi. $\dfrac{3}{5}, \dfrac{8}{10}$ xii. $\dfrac{7}{9}, \dfrac{5}{6}$

xiii. $\dfrac{2}{5}, \dfrac{6}{8}$ xiv. $\dfrac{1}{4}, \dfrac{3}{5}$ xv. $\dfrac{1}{5}, \dfrac{6}{10}$

Addition of Like Fractions

Maths Lab Activity 4

Materials required

- Multiples of same-sized square or rectangular papers
- Crayons

Method (Note for the Teacher)

Ask the students to take one paper and fold it into four equal parts. Give them a problem like $\dfrac{1}{4}$ plus $\dfrac{2}{4}$. Make them colour $\dfrac{1}{4}$ of that paper. Ask them if they can colour $\dfrac{2}{4}$ on the same paper. (Yes). Now ask how many parts are coloured altogether. ($\dfrac{3}{4}$)

Since both fractions can be got out of the same paper, you should just add the numerators and keep the same denominator. So, $\dfrac{1}{4} + \dfrac{2}{4} = \dfrac{3}{4}$

Give similar examples using other papers. Finally, tell them if two like fractions are added, the numerators get added. The denominators remain the same, as we are taking parts out of the same whole.

Exercise 17

Add the following.

a. $\dfrac{1}{3} + \dfrac{1}{3}$ b. $\dfrac{2}{7} + \dfrac{4}{7}$ c. $\dfrac{6}{9} + \dfrac{1}{9}$

d. $\dfrac{2}{8} + \dfrac{5}{8}$ e. $\dfrac{3}{5} + \dfrac{1}{5}$ f. $\dfrac{2}{7} + \dfrac{2}{7}$

g. $\frac{1}{9} + \frac{5}{9}$ h. $\frac{1}{4} + \frac{1}{4}$ i. $\frac{3}{10} + \frac{4}{10}$

j. $\frac{4}{11} + \frac{2}{11}$ k. $\frac{1}{6} + \frac{3}{6}$ l. $\frac{3}{11} + \frac{5}{11}$

Subtraction of Like Fractions

Like fractions can also be subtracted.

Example $\frac{3}{4} - \frac{1}{4} = \frac{2}{4}$

Here you subtract the numerators and keep denominators same.

Exercise 18

Subtract the following.

a. $\frac{5}{8} - \frac{4}{8}$ b. $\frac{8}{11} - \frac{5}{11}$ c. $\frac{5}{9} - \frac{2}{9}$

d. $\frac{3}{6} - \frac{2}{6}$ e. $\frac{9}{10} - \frac{4}{10}$ f. $\frac{6}{8} - \frac{5}{8}$

g. $\frac{7}{9} - \frac{4}{9}$ h. $\frac{5}{10} - \frac{2}{10}$ i. $\frac{8}{12} - \frac{3}{12}$

j. $\frac{10}{15} - \frac{6}{15}$ j. $\frac{7}{11} - \frac{4}{11}$ j. $\frac{7}{14} - \frac{5}{14}$

Addition of Unlike Fractions

You have already learnt how to add like fractions.

Example $\frac{1}{5} + \frac{2}{5} = \frac{3}{5}$

All you have to do is add the numerators and write the answer with the same denominator.

Now, when you want to add un ike fractions, first you need to change them to like fractions. Then, you can add easily.

Example $\dfrac{1}{3} + \dfrac{3}{6}$

Step 1: Find the L.C.M. of the denominators.
Multiples of 3 = 3, $\boxed{6}$
Multiples of 6 = $\boxed{6}$. Least common multiple = 6.

Step 2: Change both the denominators to the L.C.M.
So, change both denominators to 6.

$\dfrac{1}{3} \times \dfrac{2}{2} = \dfrac{2}{6}$ and $\dfrac{3}{6} \times \dfrac{1}{1} = \dfrac{3}{6}$

Step 3: Now add the numerators and keep the denominator same.

So, $\dfrac{1}{3} + \dfrac{3}{6} = \dfrac{2}{6} + \dfrac{3}{6} = \dfrac{5}{6}$

Exercise 19

Add the following unlike fractions.

a. $\dfrac{6}{12} + \dfrac{4}{8}$ b. $\dfrac{3}{5} + \dfrac{4}{10}$ c. $\dfrac{5}{7} + \dfrac{1}{3}$

d. $\dfrac{2}{9} + \dfrac{1}{10}$ e. $\dfrac{1}{7} + \dfrac{2}{24}$ f. $\dfrac{7}{9} + \dfrac{3}{6}$

g. $\dfrac{4}{9} + \dfrac{1}{3}$ h. $\dfrac{5}{8} + \dfrac{1}{4}$ i. $\dfrac{2}{3} + \dfrac{5}{6}$

j. $\dfrac{4}{7} + \dfrac{2}{4}$ k. $\dfrac{2}{9} + \dfrac{4}{6}$ l. $\dfrac{3}{5} + \dfrac{1}{4}$

m. $\dfrac{5}{7} + \dfrac{1}{8}$ n. $\dfrac{2}{3} + \dfrac{4}{6}$ o. $\dfrac{2}{8} + \dfrac{3}{4}$

Mixed Numbers or Mixed Fractions

A mixed number is a whole number and a fraction combined together.

Example

$4\dfrac{1}{3}$ is a mixed number. Here 4 is a whole number and $\dfrac{1}{3}$ is a fraction.

Converting mixed numbers to improper fractions

We can convert a mixed number to an improper fraction.

Example $2\frac{3}{4}$

To convert this mixed number to improper fraction, follow the steps
- Multiply the whole number part by the denominator ($2 \times 4 = 8$)
- Add that to the numerator. ($8 + 3 = 11$)
- Write the number above the denominator ($\frac{11}{4}$)

Exercise 20

Convert the following mixed numbers to improper fractions.

a. $3\frac{1}{5}$ b. $2\frac{1}{6}$ c. $7\frac{2}{5}$ d. $4\frac{1}{9}$

e. $6\frac{2}{7}$ f. $5\frac{3}{8}$ g. $3\frac{1}{7}$ h. $4\frac{6}{7}$

Addition of Mixed Numbers

A mixed number is made up of a whole number and a fraction.

Example $4\frac{1}{2}$. Here 4 is a whole number and $\frac{1}{2}$ is a fraction.

Method 1

$$4\frac{1}{2} + 1\frac{1}{4}$$

Step 1: Add the whole numbers first $(4 + 1) = \boxed{5}$. This is the first answer.

Step 2: Add the fractions after finding the L.C.M. of denominators and changing them to like fractions.

$$\frac{1}{2} + \frac{1}{4} \qquad \begin{array}{c|c} 2 & 2,\ 4 \\ \hline 2 & 1,\ 2 \\ \hline & 1,\ 1 \end{array} \qquad \frac{1}{2} \times \frac{2}{2} = \frac{2}{4} \qquad \frac{1}{4} \times \frac{1}{1} = \frac{1}{4}$$

$$\text{L.C.M.} = 2 \times 2 \times 1 = 4$$

So, $\frac{1}{2} + \frac{1}{4} = \frac{2}{4} + \frac{1}{4} = \frac{3}{4}$

$\frac{3}{4}$ is the second answer.

Step 3: Add the first and the second answers together.

$$5 + \frac{3}{4} = 5\frac{3}{4}$$

$5\frac{3}{4}$ is the final answer.

Method 2

Step 1: Change both mixed numbers to improper fractions.

$$4\frac{1}{2} = \frac{4 \times 2 + 1}{2} = \frac{9}{2}$$

$$1\frac{1}{4} = \frac{1 \times 4 + 1}{4} = \frac{5}{4}$$

Step 2: Add the fractions after finding the L.C.M. of the denominators and changing them to like fractions.

$$\frac{9}{2} \times \frac{2}{2} = \frac{18}{4} \qquad \frac{5}{4} \times \frac{1}{1} = \frac{5}{4}$$

$$\frac{18}{4} + \frac{5}{4} = \frac{23}{4}$$

Step 3: If the final answer is an improper fraction, change it to a mixed number, by dividing the numerator by the denominator to find the number of wholes and parts in the improper fraction.

$$\frac{23}{4} = 5\frac{3}{4} \qquad \text{Hence, } 5\frac{3}{4} \text{ is the final answer.}$$

Exercise 21

Use **Method 1** to add the following.

a. $2\frac{1}{3} + 3\frac{1}{6}$　　b. $5\frac{1}{9} + 2\frac{1}{8}$　　c. $5\frac{1}{6} + 3\frac{2}{8}$　　d. $2\frac{4}{5} + 2\frac{1}{2}$

e. $3\frac{1}{3} + 4\frac{1}{4}$　　f. $7\frac{1}{2} + 9\frac{1}{4}$　　g. $6\frac{1}{3} + 5\frac{2}{3}$　　h. $4\frac{1}{4} + 8\frac{4}{9}$

Exercise 22

Use **Method 2** to add the following.

a. $1\frac{2}{3} + 6\frac{1}{2}$　　b. $3\frac{1}{3} + 1\frac{4}{5}$　　c. $9\frac{1}{3} + 3\frac{2}{4}$　　d. $1\frac{1}{4} + 2\frac{2}{3}$

e. $2\frac{1}{7} + 1\frac{1}{6}$　　f. $2\frac{1}{7} + 7\frac{1}{2}$　　g. $4\frac{1}{5} + 4\frac{1}{3}$　　h. $4\frac{1}{6} + 2\frac{1}{4}$

i. $2\frac{1}{5} + 5\frac{1}{4}$　　j. $4\frac{1}{6} + 3\frac{1}{2}$　　k. $3\frac{1}{4} + 2\frac{2}{3}$　　l. $1\frac{1}{7} + 4\frac{2}{3}$

Subtraction of Unlike Fractions

Unlike fractions can also be subtracted. You have to remember to change them to like fractions, i.e., make the denominators same, before subtracting.

Example $\dfrac{8}{10} - \dfrac{3}{5}$

Step 1: Here, the two denominators are different. So, you should first find the L.C.M. of 5 and 10 by using the division method.

$$\begin{array}{c|cc} 5 & 10, & 5 \\ 2 & 2, & 1 \\ \hline & 1, & 1 \end{array}$$

L.C.M. = 5 × 2 = 10

Step 2: Now convert both the fractions to like fractions with the L.C.M. as the denominator.

$$\dfrac{8 \times 1}{10 \times 1} = \dfrac{8}{10} \qquad \dfrac{3 \times 2}{5 \times 2} = \dfrac{6}{10}$$

Step 3: Subtract $\dfrac{6}{10}$ from $\dfrac{8}{10}$. $\dfrac{8}{10} - \dfrac{6}{10} = \dfrac{2}{10}$

Exercise 23

Subtract the following.

a. $\dfrac{1}{2} - \dfrac{1}{6}$
b. $\dfrac{1}{3} - \dfrac{2}{7}$
c. $\dfrac{2}{3} - \dfrac{4}{8}$
d. $\dfrac{1}{2} - \dfrac{1}{5}$

e. $\dfrac{9}{12} - \dfrac{2}{4}$
f. $\dfrac{3}{7} - \dfrac{1}{4}$
g. $\dfrac{2}{3} - \dfrac{3}{7}$
h. $\dfrac{5}{7} - \dfrac{1}{4}$

i. $\dfrac{8}{9} - \dfrac{1}{6}$
j. $\dfrac{3}{4} - \dfrac{3}{5}$
k. $\dfrac{4}{7} - \dfrac{3}{6}$
l. $\dfrac{3}{6} - \dfrac{2}{7}$

m. $\dfrac{1}{2} - \dfrac{1}{3}$
n. $\dfrac{7}{8} - \dfrac{3}{5}$
o. $\dfrac{6}{7} - \dfrac{2}{5}$
p. $\dfrac{2}{5} - \dfrac{3}{8}$

Subtraction of Mixed Numbers

Mixed numbers, as you know, are numbers with a whole number and a fraction. For example, $3\dfrac{1}{2}$ is a mixed number.

While adding 2 or more mixed numbers, the whole numbers can be added separately and the fractions can be added separately. Then the 2 answers can be added together to get the final answer.

While it is possible to subtract the same way, it will not give the right answer always. Sometimes the fraction of the first number may be smaller than that of the second number.

Example $3\dfrac{1}{4} - 1\dfrac{1}{2}$

Now, 3 − 1 = 2. But you cannot subtract $\dfrac{1}{2}$ from $\dfrac{1}{4}$ as $\dfrac{1}{2}$ is bigger.

So what do we do?
Change the mixed numbers to improper fractions and then find the L.C.M. and proceed as in addition.

Look at this.

$$3\frac{1}{4} - 1\frac{1}{2}$$

$$\frac{13}{4} - \frac{3}{2}$$

L.C.M. of 4 and 2 = 4. Hence, $\frac{13}{4} \times \frac{3}{3} = \frac{13}{4}$ $\frac{3}{2} \times \frac{2}{2} = \frac{6}{4}$ $\frac{13}{4} - \frac{6}{4} = \frac{7}{4} = 1\frac{3}{4}$

Exercise 24

Now solve the following.

a. $3\frac{1}{2} - 1\frac{3}{4}$ b. $9\frac{2}{6} - 3\frac{1}{4}$ c. $5\frac{1}{8} - 2\frac{3}{7}$

d. $6\frac{1}{2} - 4\frac{3}{4}$ e. $10\frac{1}{3} - 7\frac{4}{6}$ f. $7\frac{2}{8} - 5\frac{1}{2}$

g. $8\frac{1}{4} - 1\frac{3}{12}$ h. $5\frac{6}{9} - 2\frac{1}{3}$ i. $9\frac{1}{2} - 8\frac{3}{5}$

j. $5\frac{2}{7} - 3\frac{3}{6}$ k. $9\frac{2}{9} - 3\frac{7}{8}$ l. $6\frac{5}{8} - 5\frac{2}{4}$

m. $7\frac{3}{7} - 4\frac{3}{5}$ n. $7\frac{3}{9} - 5\frac{2}{3}$ o. $6\frac{1}{2} - 3\frac{2}{5}$

Multiplication of Fractions

Multiplication, as you know, is rows multiplied by columns. The product is derived from the meeting place of rows and columns. The first number shows the rows and the second number shows the columns. Look at this.

Here, there are 4 rows and 3 columns. They are meeting at 12 places. So the product of 3 × 4 = 12.

In the same way, multiplication of fractions can also be done.

Example $\frac{1}{3} \times \frac{1}{4}$

Step 1: Draw 3 lines for rows and shade 1 row with lines slanted to the left.
Step 2: Draw 4 columns and shade 1 column with lines slanted to the right.
Step 3: Rows and columns meet at one box, which gives the numerator. There are 12 boxes, which give the denominator.

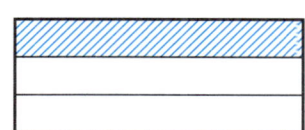 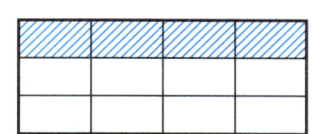 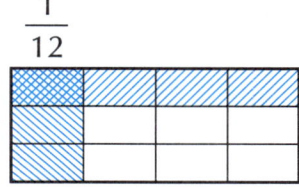

The answer is $\frac{1}{12}$.

Exercise 25

a. Find answers for the following using the above method. (Use two different colours for the rows and columns.

i. $\frac{1}{3} \times \frac{1}{2}$
ii. $\frac{1}{5} \times \frac{1}{2}$
iii. $\frac{1}{4} \times \frac{1}{6}$

iv. $\frac{1}{3} \times \frac{1}{3}$
v. $\frac{1}{5} \times \frac{1}{4}$
vi. $\frac{1}{4} \times \frac{1}{7}$

Do you notice any pattern in the answers?

_____

_____

If you multiply the two numerators together and the two denominators together, then also you get the answer.

Example

$\frac{1}{5} \times \frac{1}{4} = \frac{1 \times 1}{5 \times 4} = \frac{1}{20}$

Exercise 26

a. Find the product.

i. $\frac{2}{3} \times \frac{1}{4}$
ii. $\frac{5}{6} \times \frac{2}{4}$
iii. $\frac{3}{4} \times \frac{1}{3}$

iv. $\frac{2}{5} \times \frac{2}{7}$
v. $\frac{4}{5} \times \frac{2}{3}$
vi. $\frac{4}{6} \times \frac{2}{4}$

vii. $\frac{3}{6} \times \frac{1}{7}$
viii. $\frac{2}{9} \times \frac{3}{5}$
ix. $\frac{3}{4} \times \frac{5}{8}$

x. $\frac{3}{8} \times \frac{1}{8}$
xi. $\frac{6}{7} \times \frac{3}{8}$
xii. $\frac{1}{9} \times \frac{2}{7}$

xiii. $\frac{4}{7} \times \frac{2}{4}$
xiv. $\frac{2}{6} \times \frac{3}{6}$
xv. $\frac{6}{8} \times \frac{1}{9}$

xvi. $\frac{5}{8} \times \frac{6}{9}$
xvii. $\frac{3}{5} \times \frac{2}{5}$
xviii. $\frac{3}{7} \times \frac{2}{8}$

xix. $\dfrac{6}{7} \times \dfrac{2}{8}$ xx. $\dfrac{1}{5} \times \dfrac{2}{9}$ xxi. $\dfrac{2}{3} \times \dfrac{3}{4}$

Division of Fractions

Division is the opposite of multiplication. It is not easy to divide a number by a fraction as it has two numbers, one below the other ($\dfrac{1}{2}$).

You can divide a number only by whole numbers. So, if you are asked to divide by a fraction, you should first convert it into a whole number. The only whole number which you can convert into a fraction, without changing its value, is 1. To do this, you have to multiply the fraction by its reciprocal.

Here, the reciprocal of $\dfrac{1}{2}$ is $\dfrac{2}{1}$.

So, $\dfrac{1}{2} \times \dfrac{2}{1} = \dfrac{2}{2}$

Reciprocal
The inverse of the given fraction, e.g. reciprocal of $\dfrac{1}{2} = \dfrac{2}{1}$.

When the product of two numbers is 1, one is the **multiplicative inverse** of the other.

Exercise 27

Write the reciprocals of the following fractions in the boxes provided.

a. $\dfrac{2}{3} = \Box$ b. $\dfrac{6}{7} = \Box$ c. $\dfrac{3}{5} = \Box$ d. $\dfrac{9}{12} = \Box$ e. $\dfrac{4}{7} = \Box$

One can come across division in three forms.
a. A whole number divided by a fraction
b. A fraction divided by a whole number
c. A fraction divided by a fraction

Remember
Reciprocal means the multiplicative inverse.

Dividing a Whole Number by a Fraction
Example 1

$3 \div \dfrac{1}{2}$

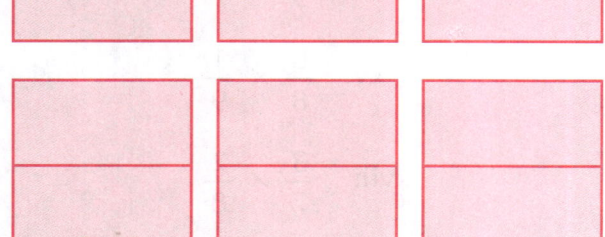

This is 3.

This is 3 divided into 2 parts. Now it has 6 parts.

That is, $3 \div \dfrac{1}{2} = \dfrac{3}{1} \times \dfrac{2}{1} = \dfrac{6}{1} = 6$.

Whole numbers take 1 as the denominator.

We have multiplied the numerators together and the denominators together, like you would do for multiplication.

Example 2

$4 \div \dfrac{1}{5}$

This is 4.

This is 4 divided into 5 parts.
So there are 20 parts in all.
$4 \div \dfrac{1}{5} = 4 \times \dfrac{5}{1} = 20$

Exercise 28

a. Solve the following by using diagrams.

   i. $3 \div \dfrac{1}{2}$ ii. $4 \div \dfrac{1}{3}$ iii. $5 \div \dfrac{1}{2}$ iv. $2 \div \dfrac{1}{4}$

b. Divide the following. (Multiply by the reciprocal of the divisor.) One has been done for you.

   i. $4 \div \dfrac{1}{4} = \dfrac{4}{1} \times \dfrac{4}{1} = 16$ ii. $5 \div \dfrac{1}{7}$ iii. $9 \div \dfrac{1}{3}$ iv. $4 \div \dfrac{2}{5}$

   v. $6 \div \dfrac{3}{6}$ vi. $7 \div \dfrac{3}{4}$ vii. $5 \div \dfrac{2}{5}$ viii. $6 \div \dfrac{2}{3}$

   ix. $5 \div \dfrac{2}{3}$ x. $6 \div \dfrac{3}{4}$ xi. $9 \div \dfrac{5}{8}$ xii. $7 \div \dfrac{2}{9}$

Dividing a Fraction by a Whole Number

Example $\dfrac{1}{3} \div 4$

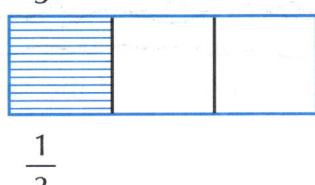

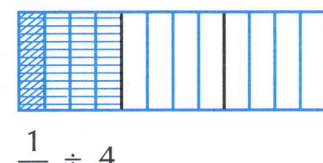

Step 1: Divide the whole into 3 equal parts.

Step 2: Divide $\dfrac{1}{3}$ of the 3 parts into 4 equal parts.

Step 3: Shade 1 part out of the 4 parts. If there can be 4 parts in the chosen $\dfrac{1}{3}$, there should be 4 parts in each of the other 2 parts also. So the answer is $\dfrac{1}{12}$.

Exercise 29

a. Draw and find the answers for the following.

   i. $\dfrac{1}{3} \div 5$ ii. $\dfrac{1}{5} \div 4$ iii. $\dfrac{1}{7} \div 2$ iv. $\dfrac{1}{4} \div 3$

   v. $\dfrac{1}{6} \div 3$ vi. $\dfrac{1}{9} \div 5$ vii. $\dfrac{1}{8} \div 4$ viii. $\dfrac{1}{2} \div 6$

b. Now, divide without the diagram, by finding the reciprocal. One has been done for you.

Remember
Denominator of whole numbers is 1.

i. $\dfrac{1}{2} \div 6$ ii. $\dfrac{1}{3} \div 5$ iii. $\dfrac{2}{5} \div 3$ iv. $\dfrac{3}{4} \div 2$ v. $\dfrac{3}{6} \div 2$

$= \dfrac{1}{2} \times \dfrac{1}{6} = \dfrac{1}{12}$

vi. $\dfrac{2}{4} \div 5$ vii. $\dfrac{4}{5} \div 3$ viii. $\dfrac{5}{7} \div 4$ ix. $\dfrac{2}{7} \div 8$ x. $\dfrac{1}{9} \div 4$

xi. $\dfrac{2}{3} \div 5$ xii. $\dfrac{4}{6} \div 3$ xiii. $\dfrac{3}{7} \div 4$ xiv. $\dfrac{2}{8} \div 2$

Dividing a Fraction by a Fraction

Look at this.

$\dfrac{1}{3} \div \dfrac{1}{4}$

Here, the first fraction shows rows.

This shows $\dfrac{1}{3}$.

$\dfrac{1}{3}$ taken 4 times =

Since you can take only three $\dfrac{1}{3}$s from one box, you take the help of another box of the same size to take the fourth $\dfrac{1}{3}$.

Hence, the answer is $\dfrac{3}{3} + \dfrac{1}{3} = \dfrac{4}{3}$ or $1\dfrac{1}{3}$.

Exercise 30

a. Now solve the following by using diagrams.

   i. $\dfrac{1}{4} \div \dfrac{1}{5}$ ii. $\dfrac{1}{5} \div \dfrac{1}{6}$ iii. $\dfrac{1}{4} \div \dfrac{1}{2}$ iv. $\dfrac{3}{5} \div \dfrac{1}{4}$

b. Divide without using the diagrams. Remember to find the reciprocal of the divisor and multiply. One has been done for you.

i. $\dfrac{1}{3} \div \dfrac{2}{5}$ ii. $\dfrac{1}{5} \div \dfrac{3}{4}$ iii. $\dfrac{2}{3} \div \dfrac{4}{6}$ iv. $\dfrac{2}{8} \div \dfrac{1}{3}$ v. $\dfrac{1}{2} \div \dfrac{4}{5}$

$= \dfrac{1}{3} \times \dfrac{5}{2} = \dfrac{5}{6}$

vi. $\dfrac{3}{5} \div \dfrac{2}{7}$ vii. $\dfrac{2}{6} \div \dfrac{2}{3}$ viii. $\dfrac{5}{8} \div \dfrac{4}{6}$ ix. $\dfrac{3}{4} \div \dfrac{2}{9}$ x. $\dfrac{2}{4} \div \dfrac{1}{4}$

xi. $\dfrac{1}{5} \div \dfrac{1}{2}$ xii. $\dfrac{1}{7} \div \dfrac{1}{5}$ xiii. $\dfrac{1}{3} \div \dfrac{1}{5}$ xiv. $\dfrac{2}{7} \div \dfrac{1}{5}$

c. Solve the riddles given below. One has been done for you.

i. A day is what fraction of a week? $\dfrac{1}{7}$

ii. A day is what fraction of September?

iii. A month is what fraction of a normal year?

iv. One year is what fraction of a century?

v. One year is what fraction of a decade?

vi. One week is what fraction of February in a leap year?

vii. Hundred years is what fraction of a millennium?

viii. What fraction is one hour of the hours in a day?

ix. What fraction is one minute of an hour?

x. What fraction is one of a dozen?

Exercise 31

1. Rita and Julie had ribbons of same length. Rita cut her ribbon into halves and used one piece. Julie cut her ribbon into thirds and used one piece. Who used more ribbon?

2. Rahim said, $\frac{3}{3}$ is more than $\frac{4}{4}$. Shyam said, No, $\frac{3}{3}$ and $\frac{4}{4}$ are the same. Payal who was listening to this said, "You both are wrong, $\frac{3}{3}$ is smaller than $\frac{4}{4}$. Who is correct? Give reasons for your answer.

3. John had 100 stones with him. He gave $\frac{1}{4}$ of them to his sister and took the rest with him to play. Priyam his friend, asked for some stones. So John gave him $\frac{1}{3}$ of the remaining stones and kept the rest with him. Just then Vijay, another friend came there and asked for some. So John gave him half of what he had and took the rest home.
   a. How many stones did his sister get?
   b. How many stones did Priyam get?
   c. How many stones did Vijay get?
   d. How many stones did John keep?

4. Salman gave $2\frac{3}{4}$ of his chocolates to his friends. The number of chocolates he gave is between,
   a. 3 and 4
   b. 2 and 3
   c. 5 and 6
   d. 1 and 2

5. How much liquid is there in the glasses below?

   a. 3 glasses
   b. $3\frac{1}{2}$ glasses
   c. $3\frac{3}{4}$ glasses
   d. $3\frac{1}{4}$ glasses

6. One of the pieces below is $\frac{1}{5}$ of a cake, and the other is $\frac{1}{10}$ of the same cake. Circle the piece that is showing one-fifth of the cake.

7. Tina spends $\frac{1}{2}$ hrs studying Chemistry and $\frac{3}{4}$ hrs studying Biology. How many hours does she study in all?

8. There are 35 students in a class. If $\frac{3}{5}$ of the students prefer basketball over cricket, how many students like cricket?

9. The local shoe store sells sports shoes for ₹ 3000. The shop owner says that I can buy them for $\frac{2}{5}$ th the actual price. How much money would I need to pay?

10. Anurag is 176 cm tall and his brother, Shyam is $\frac{7}{8}$ as tall as him. How tall is Shyam?

Vocabulary Learnt
reciprocal like unlike proper
term improper inverse equivalent
mixed reduce

Fraction Crossword

Solve this crossword puzzle with the help of the clues given below.

Across
1. In $\frac{5}{7}$, 7 is called the _____
7. In $\frac{1}{4}$, 1 is called the _____
9. $\frac{2}{3}$, $\frac{4}{3}$, and $\frac{1}{3}$ are called _____ fractions.
10. $\frac{5}{3}$ is _____ of $\frac{3}{5}$.

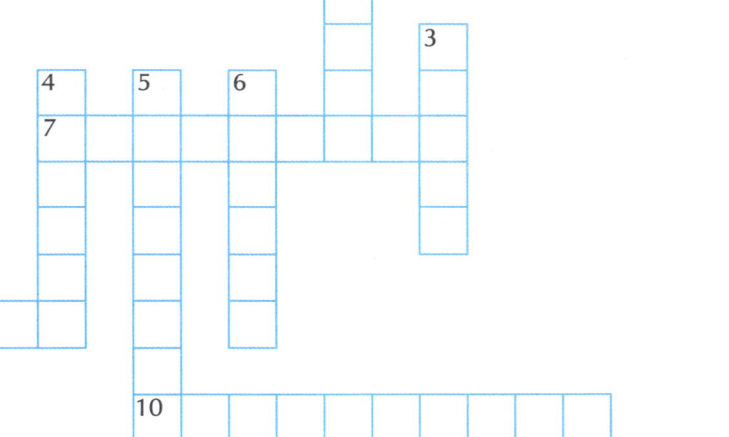

Down
2. $\frac{1}{2}$ and $\frac{2}{4}$ are _____ fractions.
3. The two number of a fraction are called the _____ of a fraction.
4. $\frac{1}{7}$, $\frac{2}{5}$, $\frac{3}{8}$ are _____ fractions.
5. $\frac{7}{3}$ is a _____ fraction.
6. $\frac{1}{3}$ is a _____ fraction.
8. $2\frac{3}{5}$ is a _____ number.

9 Decimals

> **You know ...**
> - fractions are parts of a whole
> - a fraction has 2 terms — numerator and denominator.
> - there are 2 types of fractions — proper and improper.

Like fractions, decimals are also a part of a whole. Let us compare the two.

Fractions	Decimals
a. A fraction is a part of a whole unit, divided into equal-sized pieces.	a. A decimal is a part of a whole unit, divided into equal-sized pieces.
b. A proper fraction is always less than 1.	b. Any number written after the decimal point is less than 1.
c. A fraction has two terms, the numerator and the denominator. They are written one below the other with a line in-between.	c. A decimal has two terms, the numerator and the denominator, though the denominator is never written. A decimal is written with a point.
d. A fraction can have any number as the denominator.	d. A decimal can have only 10, 100, 1000, ... as denominators.

Exercise 1

Rohit drew 24 faces that show different moods. $\frac{2}{6}$ of what he drew had happy faces and $\frac{1}{6}$ had sad faces. $\frac{1}{2}$ of the remaining had angry faces and $\frac{1}{4}$ of them had crying faces. Fill in the boxes.

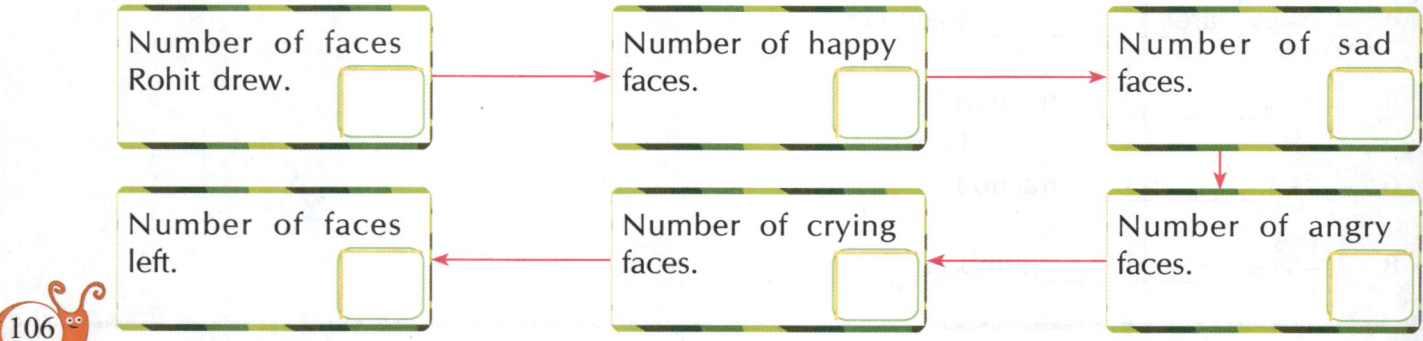

Remember

Any number written after the point, no matter how big, is always less than one..

Maths Lab Activity 1

Given below is a grid with several decimal numbers. Since none of them has a whole number, they are all less than one. Find pairs of numbers next to one another which when added give 1.

Example

a. 0.8 + 0.2 = 1.0   b. 0.84 + 0.16 = 1.00   c. 0.0.006 + 0.094 = 1.000

Method (Note for the Teacher)

Remind the students that all decimal numbers without a whole number are less than 1 no matter how many digits are there after the point, for example, 0.09807. Next, ask them to find and colour alike as many pairs that add up to 1 as they can. The pairs may be placed vertically or horizontally.

0.99	0.36	0.1	0.85	0.004	0.11	0.74	0.081
0.01	0.389	0.61	0.74	0.996	0.3	0.12	0.919
0.714	0.14	0.85	0.2	0.118	0.75	0.41	0.583
0.61	0.740	0.15	0.3	0.14	0.412	0.17	0.71
0.002	0.141	0.99	0.1	0.51	0.586	0.66	0.29
0.998	0.78	0.33	0.75	0.25	0.2	0.81	0.494
0.6	0.8	0.361	0.99	0.418	0.582	0.98	0.1
0.2	0.415	0.639	0.3	0.200	0.71	0.65	0.9
0.5	0.4	0.99	0.121	0.006	0.82	0.29	0.456
0.22	0.6	0.7	0.666	0.094	0.007	0.41	0.31
0.70	0.8	0.84	0.16	0.001	0.80	0.202	0.69

When we talk about whole numbers, we refer to each place as ones or units, tens, hundreds, thousands, etc. (right to left). However, when there is a number written with a point, we call it a decimal number and the digits after the point also have place value. They are tenths, hundredths, thousandth and so on (left to right). There are no units here, because it is the unit that is being called tenths when cut in to 10 parts, hundredths when cut in to 100 parts and thousandths when cut in to 1000 parts and so on.

Every digit before the point shows a whole number and every digit after the point refers to a part of 1.
Look at this number: 2 3 . 4 5
Do you see a point between the digits?
This point which separates the whole numbers from fractional numbers is called the decimal point. Every digit before the point refers to a whole number, while every digit after the point refers to a part of 1. The decimal point is placed between ones and one tenths.

Thousands	Hundreds	Tens	Ones	•	One tenths	One hundredth	One thousandths	One ten thousandths

No matter how many digits are there after the point, we read each one of them independently as their value is less than 1. In whole numbers, the place values are read from right to left, while in decimal numbers the place values are read from left to right. The first place before the point is taken by units, but the first place after the point is taken by tenths, because a whole unit is cut into 10 parts in this place and every number that occupies this place is that many tenths of a unit. When the whole number is cut into 100 parts, each one becomes one hundredth and the second place represents that. When the whole number is cut into 1000 parts, each part becomes one thousandth and the third place represents that, and this goes on.

You should also remember that every place to the left of ones or units is ten times more than the previous value. Similarly, every place to the right of the decimal point is ten times less than the previous value.

Now look at this number:

a. 124.2. This number indicates 124 whole numbers and 2 parts out of the next whole number which is cut into 10 parts.

b. 341.76. This number indicates 341 whole numbers and 76 parts out of the next whole number which is cut into 100 parts.

c. 605.381. This number indicates 605 whole numbers and 381 parts out of the next whole number which is cut into 1000 parts.

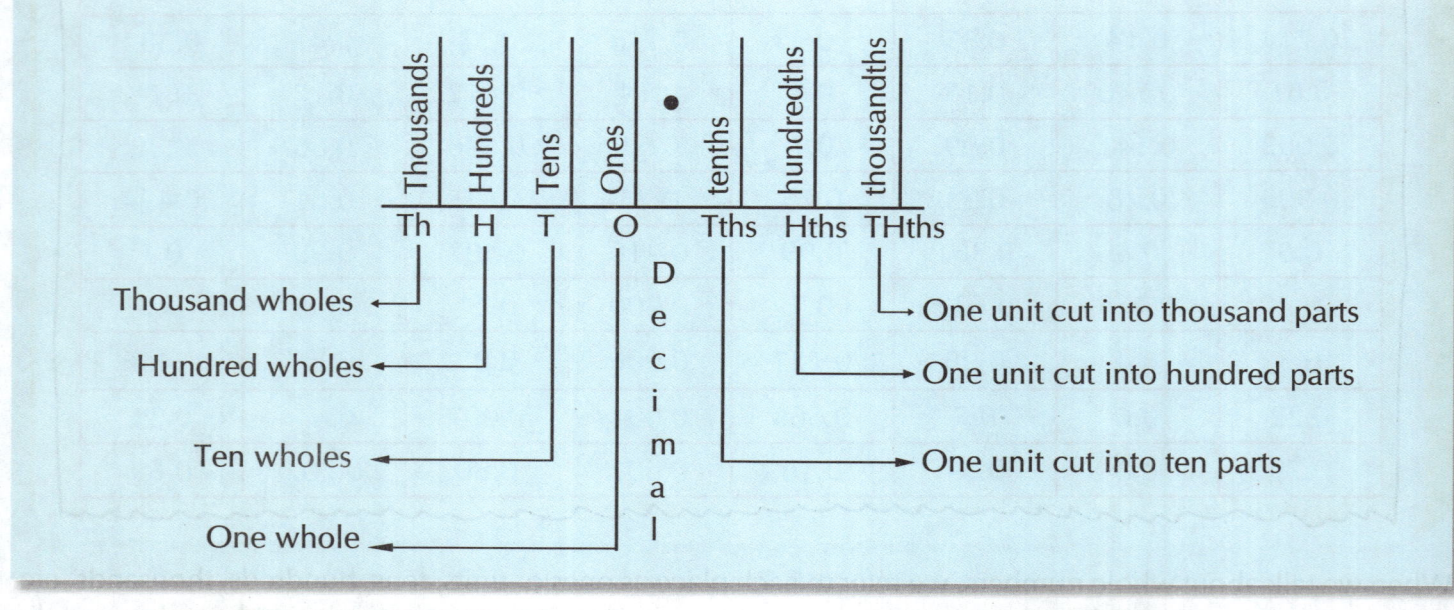

This is one whole, cut into 10 parts. Since all the parts are shaded, we are taking the whole unit. So we write 1.0.

This is also one whole cut into 10 parts but only 6 out of the 10 parts are shaded. So we write 0.6, which means six out of ten.

Remember
Put a zero before the decimal to indicate that there are no whole numbers.

This is also one whole, divided into 100 parts. Since all the parts are shaded, we are taking the whole unit. So we write 1.0.

This is one whole divided into 100 parts, but only 25 parts out of 100 parts are shaded. So we write 0.25, which means 25 out of 100 parts are taken.

This is also one whole cut into 100 parts, but only 3 parts out of 100 are shaded. So we write 0.03, as the first place belongs to tenths and 3 is out of hundred, which is the second place.

Exercise 2

Write the numbers represented by these in the blanks given below.

a. 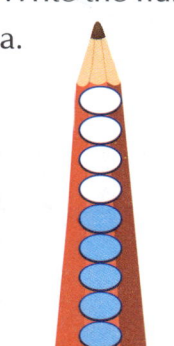   b. 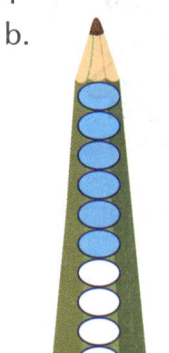   c. 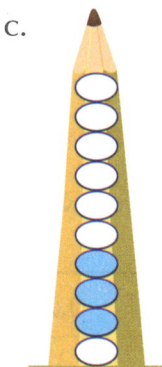   d. 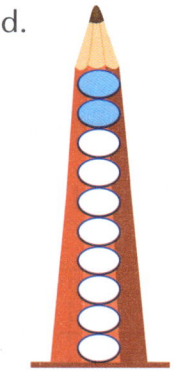   e.

f.　　　　g.　　　　　h.　　　　　　i.　　　　　　j.

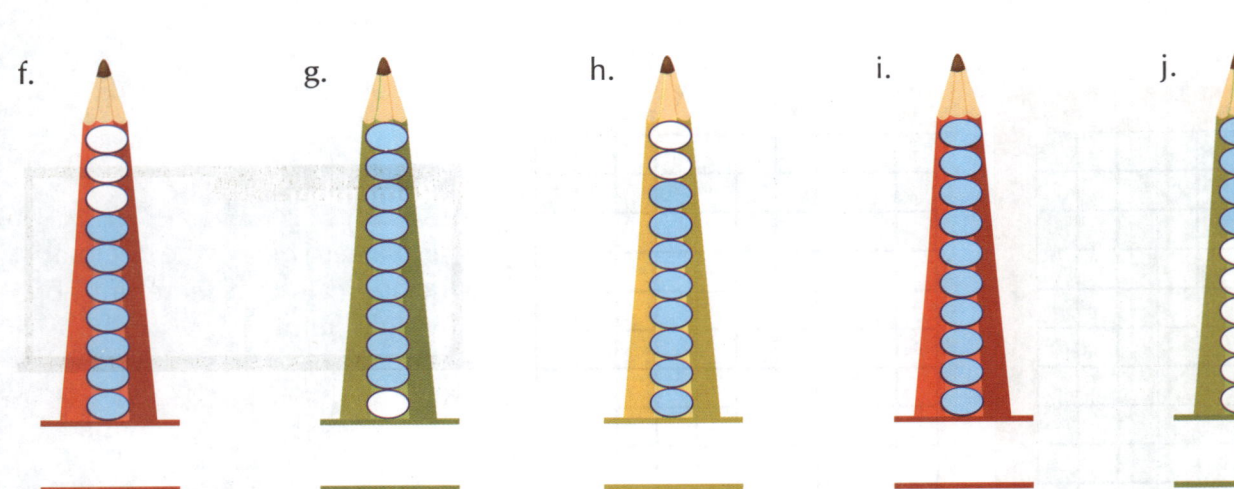

Exercise 3

Shade to represent the numbers given.

0.5
0.8
0.1
0.4
0.9
0.2
0.6
0.3
0.7
1.0

MENTAL MATH

Match the fraction and the decimal by colouring alike. Remember some of the fractions are in their lowest terms.

0.06	0.50	0.25	0.33	0.10	0.40	0.75	0.66	0.08	0.03
$\frac{2}{25}$	$\frac{3}{100}$	$\frac{1}{10}$	$\frac{3}{4}$	$\frac{6}{100}$	$\frac{1}{2}$	$\frac{33}{100}$	$\frac{33}{50}$	$\frac{1}{4}$	$\frac{2}{5}$

Exercise 4

Write the decimal fraction for the following in the oval given below each figure.

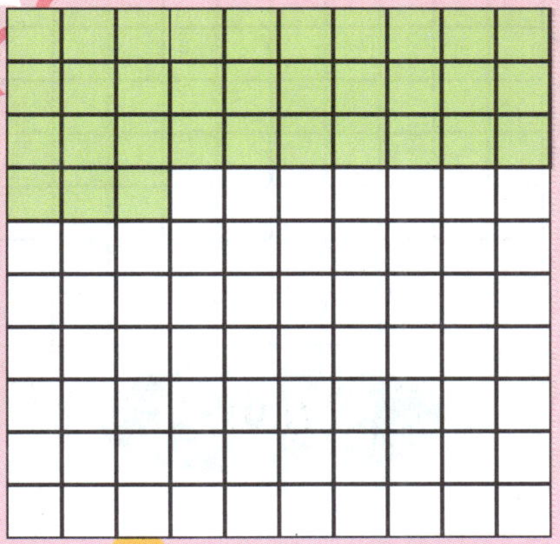

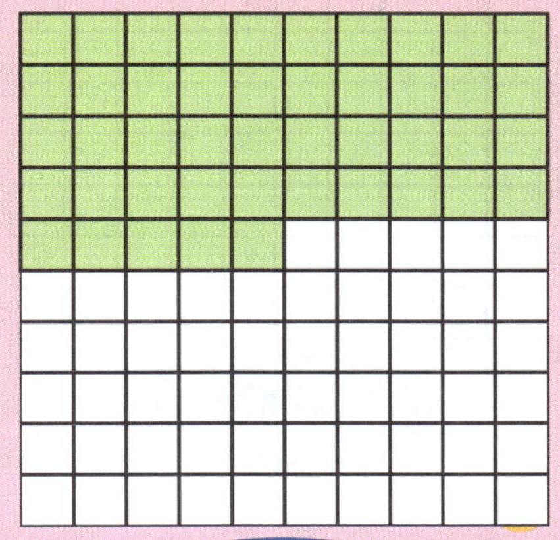

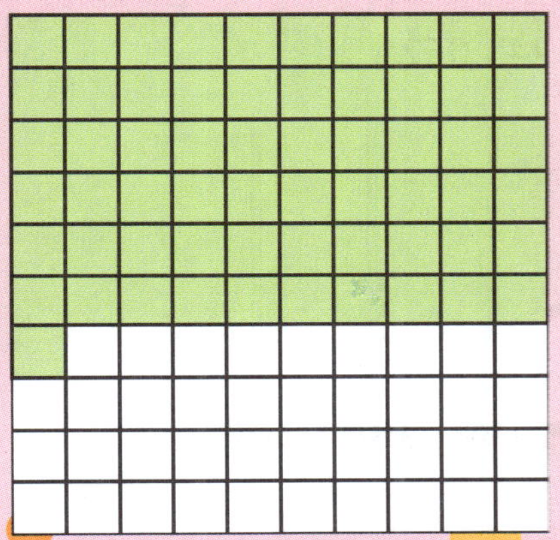

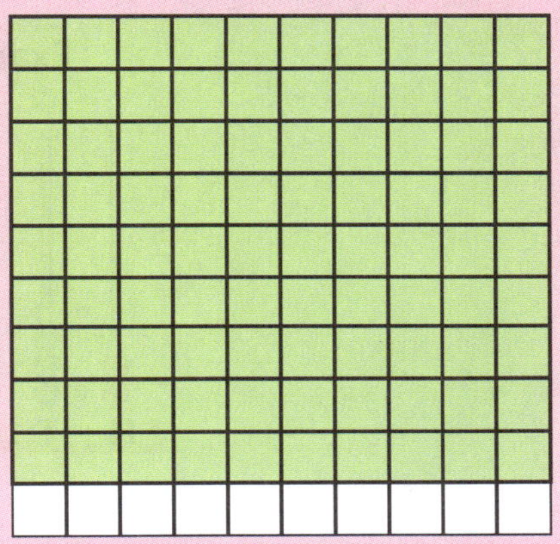

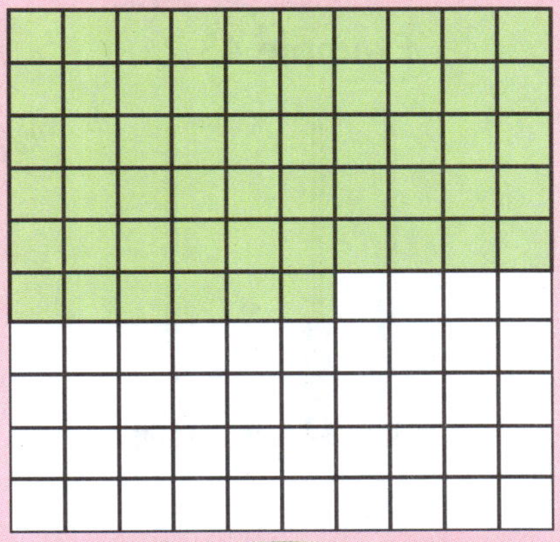

Exercise 5

Shade the squares to represent the decimal fractions given below.

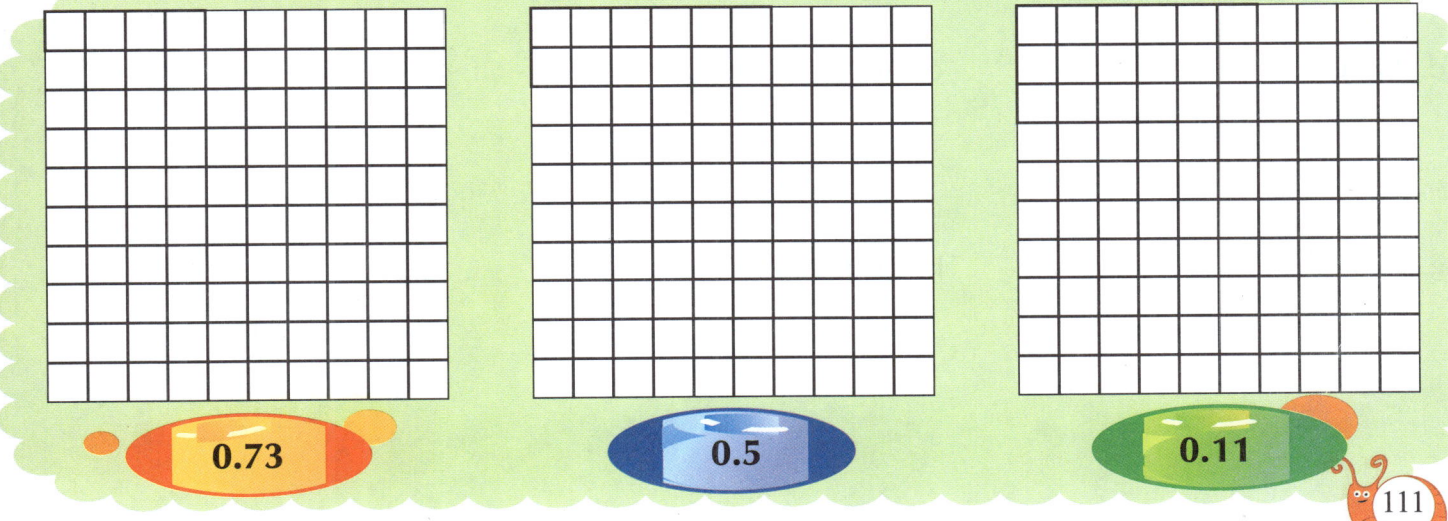

0.73   0.5   0.11

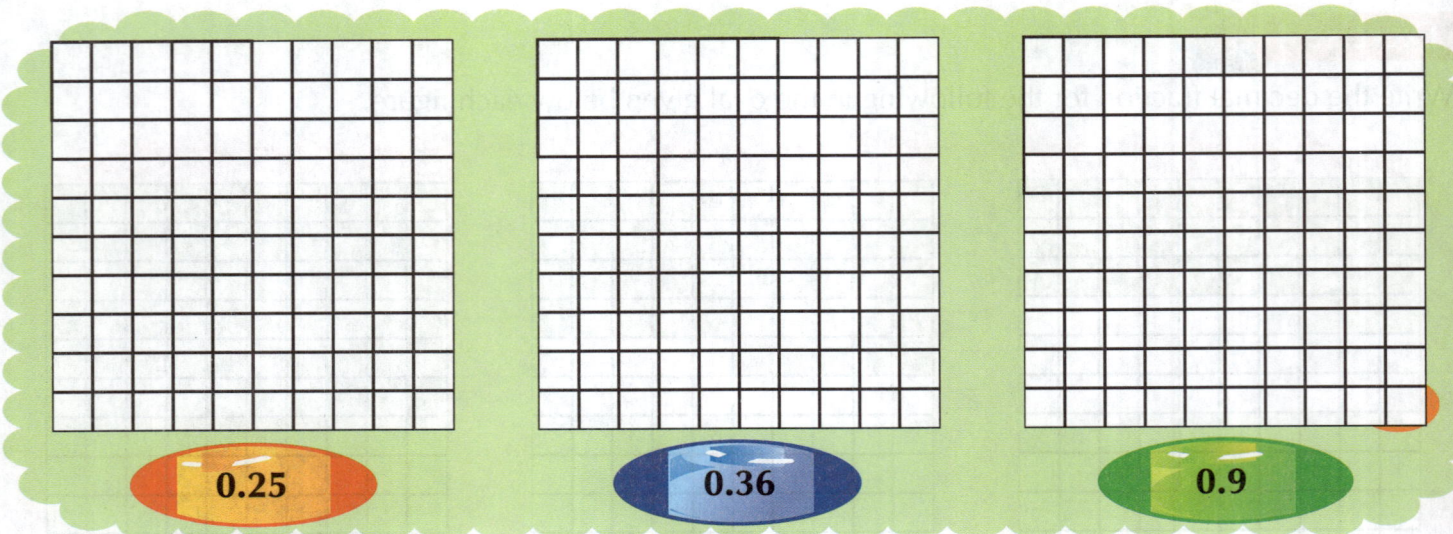

Decimal Number on the Abacus

A decimal number can also be shown on an abacus.

Example 43.2

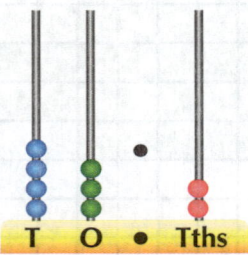

Example 243.052

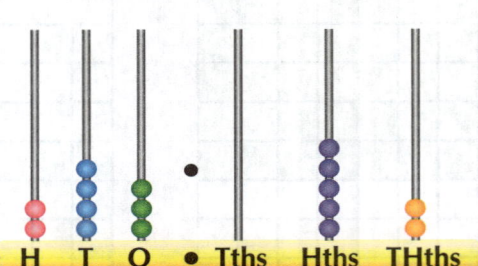

Exercise 6

Show the following numbers on the abacus.

a. 8.009   b. 620.21   c. 53.07

d. 449.081   e. 4.003   f. 486.312

g. 15.310   h. 11.009   i. 12.23

Reading and Writing Decimals

When you have a whole number and a decimal number like 36.41, you should read it as thirty-six point four one and not as thirty-six point forty one, because any number after the point is less than one and cannot be read like a whole number.

Exercise 7

a. Write as you would read.

  i.   9.64   _____
  ii. 1.58   _____
  iii. 76.1   _____
  iv. 6.439   _____
  v.   19.123   _____
  vi. 0.004   _____
  vii. 0.9   _____
  viii. 0.11   _____
  ix. 381.189 _____
  x.   6.444   _____
  xi. 1.5896   _____
  xii. 748.009 _____
  xiii. 24.1080 _____
  xiv. 513.02   _____
  xv. 9168.1234 _____

b. Fill in the blanks.

  i.   0.58   = _____ ones, _____ tenths and _____ hundredths.
  ii.   0.671 = _____ ones _____ tenths _____, hundredths and _____ thousandths.
  iii. 0.3   = _____ ones and _____ tenths.
  iv.   31.8   = _____ tens, _____ ones and _____ tenths.
  v.   36.280 = _____ tens, _____ ones, _____ tenths, _____ hundredths and _____ thousandths.
  vi.   45.893 = _____ tens, _____ ones, _____ tenths _____ hundredths and _____ thousandths.
  vii. 51.02 = _____ tens, _____ ones, _____ tenths and _____ hundredths.
  viii. 5.007 = _____ ones _____ tenths, _____ hundredths and _____ thousandths.
  ix.   7.58   = _____ ones _____ tenths and _____ hundredths.
  x.   1.682 = _____ one _____ tenths, _____ hundredths and _____ thousandths.

Decimals as Fractions

Example

What is the meaning of 0.5? It means 5 parts out of 10, as tenths is the value of the first place after the point. So, 0.5 = 5/10.

Now look at this.

0.05. Here, the number 5 means 5 parts out of 100. There is a 0 in the tenths place to tell you that we are not talking about tenths at all.

So, $0.05 = \dfrac{5}{100}$.

What do you think 0.005 will be? It will be $\dfrac{5}{1000}$.

Look at these to understand the relationship between decimals and fractions.

Remember
While in fractions you can cut the whole into as many parts as you wish, in decimals you cannot. In decimals, the whole can be cut into parts only according to the place value after the point, i.e., 10, 100, 1000 and so on. Denominators can be 10 or powers of 10.

Look at these to understand the relationship between **decimals** and **fractions**.

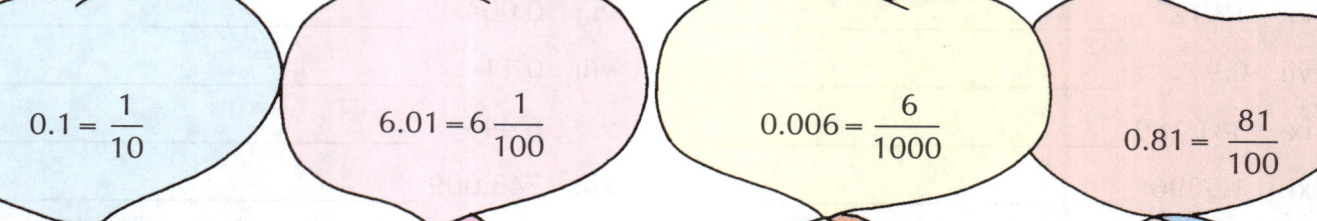

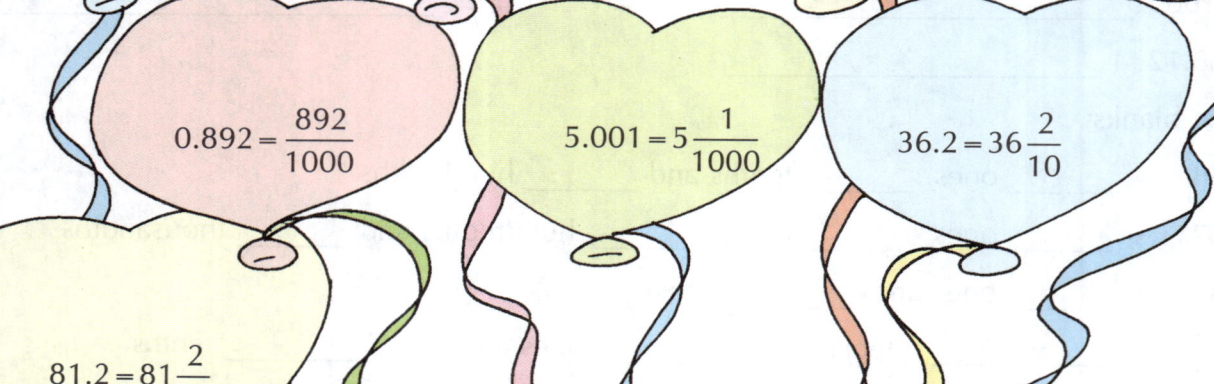

Remember
In whole numbers, a zero to the right of a number increases its value 10 times, while a zero after the point and to the left of a number reduces its value 10 times.

Exercise 7

a. Change to a fraction.

Example $0.89 = \dfrac{89}{100}$

i. 0.87 =   ii. 0.776 =   iii. 0.005 =   iv. 0.09 =

v. 1.09 =   vi. 2.89 =   vii. 34.007 =   viii. 99.001 =

ix. 567.807 =   x. 21.005 =   xi. 2.601 =   xii. 80.007 =

b. Change to decimals.

i. $\frac{6}{10}$ =   ii. $\frac{9}{10}$ =   iii. $\frac{83}{100}$ =   iv. $\frac{6}{100}$ =

v. $\frac{50}{1000}$ =   vi. $\frac{8}{100}$ =   vii. $\frac{779}{1000}$ =   viii. $\frac{3}{1000}$ =

ix. $\frac{5}{10}$ =   x. $\frac{53}{100}$ =   xi. $3\frac{2}{10}$ =   xii. $6\frac{3}{10}$ =

xiii. $7\frac{40}{100}$ =   xiv. $7\frac{804}{1000}$ =   xv. $3\frac{4}{100}$ =   xvi. $2\frac{9}{10}$ =

c. Write in expanded form.

Example $16.39 = 10 + 6 + \frac{3}{10} + \frac{9}{100}$

i. 17.39

ii. 49.096

iii. 592.015

iv. 49.1345

v. 9.001

vi. 62.43

vii. 12.106

viii. 64.981

ix. 5.09

x. 6.35

xi. 16.351

xii. 6434.39

xiii. 540.521

xiv. 144.44

xv. 764.003

xvi. 206.101

xvii. 344.24

xviii. 508.209

xix. 11.001

xx. 5.003

d. Write as a decimal number.

Example 1 $3 + \frac{1}{10} + \frac{2}{100} = 3.12$

Example 2 $100 + 60 + 7 + \frac{8}{1000} = 167.008$

i. $4 + \frac{7}{10}$ =

ii. $5 + \frac{3}{100}$ =

iii. $6 + \dfrac{5}{1000}$ = 　　　　iv. $10 + 6 + \dfrac{1}{10}$ =

v. $40 + 2 + \dfrac{4}{100}$ = 　　　　vi. $50 + 6 + \dfrac{7}{100}$ =

vii. $70 + 7 + \dfrac{7}{100}$ = 　　　　viii. $50 + 3 + \dfrac{6}{10}$ =

ix. $40 + 8 + \dfrac{2}{10} + \dfrac{4}{100}$ = 　　　　x. $900 + 10 + 3 + \dfrac{7}{10}$ =

xi. $600 + 70 + 6 + \dfrac{9}{100} + \dfrac{3}{1000}$ = 　　　　xii. $20 + 7 + \dfrac{9}{1000}$ =

xiii. $6000 + 60 + 6 + \dfrac{5}{10} + \dfrac{2}{100}$ = 　　　　xiv. $700 + 60 + 6 + \dfrac{3}{100} + \dfrac{8}{1000}$ =

xv. $500 + 6 + \dfrac{4}{10} + \dfrac{3}{100} + \dfrac{8}{1000}$ = 　　　　xvi. $7000 + 70 + \dfrac{6}{10} + \dfrac{9}{100}$ =

e. Write in expanded form.

i. 0.876 = 　　　　　　ii. 89.07 =

iii. 8.097 = 　　　　　　iv. 8.93 =

v. 450.807 = 　　　　　　vi. 0.451 =

vii. 128.002 = 　　　　　　viii. 345.876 =

ix. 701.003 = 　　　　　　x. 333.999 =

Ordering Decimal Numbers

Like fractions, decimal numbers must also have like denominators if you want to compare two or more decimal fractions.

Example

1/3 and 1/5 can be compared only if they have the same denominators. So you find the L.C.M. of 3 and 5, which is 15, and convert both the fractions to like fractions.

$$\dfrac{1 \times 5}{3 \times 5} = \dfrac{5}{15} \qquad\qquad \dfrac{1 \times 3}{5 \times 3} = \dfrac{3}{15}$$

The ascending order of 5/15 and 3/15 is 3/15, 5/15. Hence, the ascending order of the two fractions is $\dfrac{1}{5}, \dfrac{1}{3}$.

In the same way, to find the ascending order of 0.8 and 0.31, we should find a like denominator for them.

0.8 means $\dfrac{8}{10}$ and 0.31 means $\dfrac{31}{100}$

Since their denominators are not the same, you have to find the L.C.M. of 10 and 100, which is 100, and convert them both into like fractions.

$$\frac{8 \times 10}{10 \times 10} = \frac{80}{100} \qquad \frac{31 \times 1}{100 \times 1} = \frac{31}{100}$$

The ascending order of $\frac{8}{10}$ and $\frac{31}{100}$ is $\frac{31}{100}, \frac{80}{100}$ or 0.31, 0.8.

Exercise 9

a. Tick (✓) the greater number.

i. 0.5, 0.90   ii. 0.5, 0.78   iii. 0.543, 0.11

iv. 0.78, 0.3   v. 0.34, 0.231   vi. 0.99, 0.5

vii. 0.980, 0.563   viii. 0.98, 0.111   ix. 0.6, 0.34

x. 0.321, 0.8   xi. 0.594, 0.549   xii. 0.89, 0.369

b. Cross (✗) the smaller number.

i. 0.089, 0.5   ii. 0.78, 0.987   iii. 0.777, 0.7

iv. 0.909, 0.99   v. 0.545, 0.55   vi. 0.111, 0.1

vii. 0.888, 0.65   viii. 0.1, 0.101   ix. 0.4, 0.2

x. 0.532, 0.53   xi. 0.79, 0.97   xii. 0.436, 0.5

Addition of Decimal Numbers

Adding numbers with a decimal point is very similar to adding whole numbers. Just remember to align the points exactly one below the other, both in the numbers to be added and the answer, and you will not go wrong.

Example

Exercise 10

Add the following.

a. 6.21
  + 2.10

b. 2.66
  + 1.59

c. 1.33
  + 2.45

d. 7.348
  + 1.210

e. 8.41
  + 1.18

f. 4.89
  + 3.21

g. 7.14
  + 0.25

h. 9.628
  + 2.570

i. 3.10
  + 5.21

j. 213.28
  + 197.67

Addition of a Whole Number with a Decimal Number

To add a whole number with no decimal place to a whole number with decimal place, you should make sure there are as many places after the point in the whole number as in the decimal number. This does not change the value of the whole number.

Look at this.

23 + 1.789

The whole number 23 should be written as 23.000. (Add 3 zeroes after 23 with a decimal point as there are 3 places after the decimal point in the second number.)

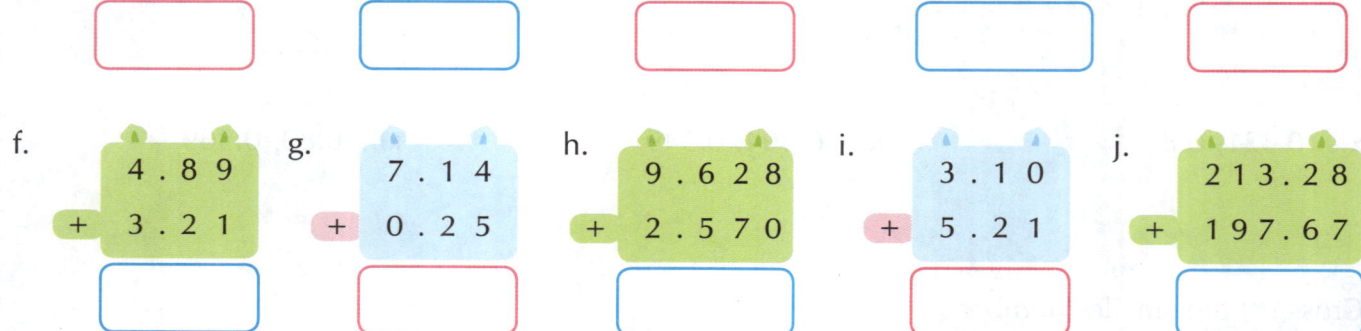

   23.000
 + 1.789
   24.789

Here are some more examples.

a. 5 + 2.1
```
   5.0
+  2.1
-----
   7.1
```

b. 7 + 2.25
```
   7.00
+  2.25
-----
   9.25
```

c. 7 + 1.250
```
   7.000
+  1.250
-----
   8.250
```

d. 2.456 + 8
```
   2.456
+  8.000
-----
  10.456
```

Remember
The number of zeroes that we add to the decimal place of the whole number will depend on how many places there are after the point in the second number.

Exercise 11

Add the following.

a. 6 + 5.1   b. 5 + 2.20   c. 9 + 2.235   d. 6 + 1.01   e. 6 + 4.08

f. 5.2 + 3   g. 7 + 1.009   h. 8 + 2.31   i. 12 + 14.3   j. 15 + 6.001

k. 23.09 + 5.008   l. 154.9 + 9.08   m. 6 + 3.002   n. 12.054 + 324.7530   o. 67.9 + 4

Subtraction of Decimal Numbers

Subtracting numbers with a decimal point is very similar to subtracting whole numbers. Just remember to align the points exactly one below the other, both in the numbers to be subtracted and the answer, and you will not go wrong.

Look at this.

```
   38.58
 - 21.37
-------
   17.21
```

Exercise 12

Solve the following.

a. 24.67 – 5.78

b. 46.123 – 43.789

c. 56.890 – 12.752

d. 67.900 – 2.892

e. 408.74 – 43.11

f. 89.764 – 1.808

g. 789.999 – 34.231

h. 76.9 – 33.8

i. 453.121 – 76.232

j. 574.09 – 23.005

k. 300.451 – 12.09

l. 67.0007 – 34.5921

Subtraction of Whole Numbers and Decimal Numbers

To subtract whole numbers from decimal numbers or decimal numbers from the whole numbers, it is important to convert both of them to like decimals so that there are equal number of places after the point in both the numbers.

How do you do this?

Add zeroes to the number that has no digits after the point, before doing the operation.

Look at these examples.

Example 1

23 – 12.56

```
  23.00   ←(Borrow and do the subtraction)
- 12.56
  -----
  10.44
```

Example 2

56.781 – 41

```
  56.781
- 41.000
  ------
  15.781
```

Exercise 13

Solve the following in the space provided.

a. 34.986 − 21　　　b. 456.87 − 410　　　c. 78.806 − 4　　　d. 67.210 − 56

e. 67.957 − 44　　　f. 960.064 − 73　　　g. 375.8 − 23　　　h. 998.674 − 765

i. 641.308 − 31　　　j. 4962.009 − 231　　k. 379.21 − 21　　　h. 59.28 − 51

Problem Solving

a. The weights of 4 boys in a class are 25.05 kg, 12.25 kg, 16.23 kg and 20.1 kg, respectively. Find their total weight.

b. Sam bought 56.3 kg of wheat in January, 49.66 kg of wheat in February and 12.156 kg of wheat in March. How much wheat did he buy in all?

c. From a rope that was 234.70 m long, 128.9 m was cut. How much rope was left?

d. Pamela went to the market to buy fruits. The cost of one basket of fruits was ₹ 167.50. She had only ₹ 89.05 with her. How much more money did she need to buy the fruits?

e. What should be subtracted from 356.9 to get 12.796?

f. A shopkeeper had 102.567 kg of sugar in the morning when he opened the shop. At the end of the day, he was left with only 45.9 kg of sugar. How much sugar did he sell during the day?

g. During a race, a cyclist travelled 128.5 km in the first stage, 126.78 km in the second stage and 125.23 km in the third. How many kilometres did he cover in all?

h. If 69 out of 100 students in a school are boys, how would you write a decimal for the part of the school that consists of boys? Also, write the decimal expression for the number of girls in the school.

i. Radhika purchased fruits worth ₹ 140.67 at the grocery. She paid the cashier ₹ 200. How much amount should be returned to her by the cashier?

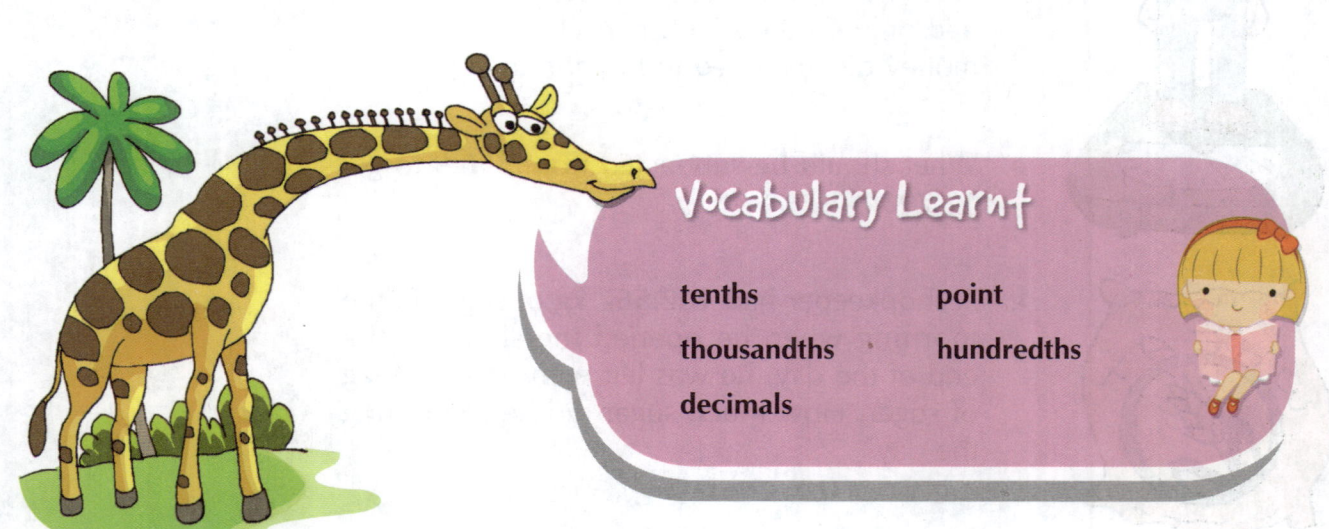

Vocabulary Learnt

tenths   point

thousandths   hundredths

decimals

Maths Lab Activity 2

Materials required
- Worksheet, as given below
- Pencil

Method (Note for the Teacher)
Ask the students to complete the table by adding the numbers in vertical boxes with those in the horizontal boxes.

	0.069	1.523	0.659	0.009	0.62
0.931					
0.112					
0.341					
3.555					
0.38					

10 Profit and Loss

> **You know ...**
> - buying and selling involve exchange of money.

Profit and loss are the two terms that arise when you are buying and selling things.

The price at which an article is bought is called its **cost price**.

The price at which an article is sold is known as its **selling price**.

When you buy something for ₹ 20.00 and sell it for ₹ 30.00, you make a **profit** because you are getting ₹ 10.00 more than the cost price.

So,
Profit = Selling price – Cost price

When you buy something for ₹ 20.00 and sell it for ₹ 15.00, you make a **loss** because you are getting ₹ 5.00 less than the price at which it was bought.

So,
Loss = Cost price – Selling price

When something is bought for ₹ 45.00 and sold for a profit of ₹ 15.00, will the selling price be more or less than the cost price?

It will be more because you make a profit only when you sell at a higher price than the cost price.

So,
Selling price = Cost price + Profit

When something is bought at ₹ 80.00 and sold at a loss of ₹ 25.00, will the selling price be more or less than the cost price?

It will be less because you make a loss only when the selling price is less than the cost price.

So,
Selling price = Cost price – Loss

Look at these.

Example 1

Tom bought a cycle for ₹ 1850.00. After some time, he sold it for ₹ 1250.00. Is there a profit or a loss?

There is a loss because the selling price is less than the buying price.

	₹ p	
Cost price	1850 . 00	
Selling price	1250 . 00	(Loss = Cost price – Selling price)
Loss =	600 . 00	

Example 2

Vani bought a chain for ₹ 540.00 and sold it for ₹ 610.00. Did she have a loss or a profit?

She made a profit because the selling price is more than the cost price.

	₹ p	
Selling price	610 . 00	
Cost price	– 540 . 00	(Profit = Selling price – Cost price)
Profit =	70 . 00	

Example 3

Mansi bought a book for ₹ 15.00 and, after reading it several times, sold it at a loss of ₹ 4.50. What do you think was the selling price of the book?

When you sell at a loss, it means your selling price is less than your cost price. So you should subtract the loss from the cost price to find the selling price.

	₹ p	
Cost price	15 . 00	
Loss	– 4 . 50	(Selling price = Cost price – Loss)
Selling price	10 . 50	

Example 4

Rashid bought a bicycle for ₹ 475.00 and sold it at a profit of ₹ 100.50. What was the price at which Rashid sold the bicycle?

When there is a profit at the time of selling, it means your selling price is more than your cost price. So you should add the profit to the cost price to find the selling price.

	₹ p	
Cost price	475 . 00	
Profit	+ 100 . 50	(Selling price = Cost price + Profit)
Selling Price =	575 . 50	

Exercise 1

Find the profit.

Cost price	Selling price	Profit
a. ₹ 659.00	₹ 734.50	
b. ₹ 325.50	₹ 567.50	
c. ₹ 412.00	₹ 552.50	
d. ₹ 123.50	₹ 432.50	
e. ₹ 45.50	₹ 56.50	
f. ₹ 1134.00	₹ 1314.00	
g. ₹ 2654.00	₹ 2673.50	

Exercise 2

Find the loss.

Cost price	Selling price	Loss
a. ₹ 56.50	₹ 45.50	
b. ₹ 342.50	₹ 234.50	
c. ₹ 432.00	₹ 420.50	
d. ₹ 1200.00	₹ 1050.00	
e. ₹ 3500.00	₹ 2850.00	
f. ₹ 1350.00	₹ 1289.00	
g. ₹ 2450.00	₹ 2319.00	

Exercise 3

Find the cost price.

Selling price	Profit	Cost price
a. ₹ 762.00	₹ 80.00	
b. ₹ 679.00	₹ 69.00	

Selling price	Loss	Cost price
a. ₹ 489.00	₹ 78.00	
b. ₹ 365.00	₹ 29.00	

Exercise 4

Find the selling price.

Cost price	Profit	Selling price
a. ₹ 582.00	₹ 83.00	
b. ₹ 4756.00	₹ 78.00	

Cost price	Loss	Selling price
a. ₹ 148.00	₹ 98.00	
b. ₹ 765.00	₹ 79.00	

Problem Solving

a. Raj bought pens for ₹ 130 a dozen. He sold it for ₹ 20 each. What was his profit?

b. Mr. Rao bought a television for ₹ 18,850 and sold it at a loss of ₹ 5780. Find the selling price.

c. A second hand truck was sold for ₹ 1,80,000, at a loss of ₹ 1800. Find the cost price of the truck.

d. James sold his piano for ₹ 40,000. He had bought the piano for ₹ 67,500. Find out the loss incurred.

e. By selling a videogame for ₹ 88, a storeowner gains ₹ 25.75. What is the cost price of the videogame?

f. Ajay purchased a computer for ₹ 25,725 and after using it for a year, he sold it for ₹ 21,570. Find out the loss.

Vocabulary Learnt

selling price   cost price

profit   loss

Maths Lab Activity 1

Materials required
- Notebook
- Pencil

Method (Note for the Teacher)

Ask the students to make a list of things they would like to buy from the market. Make them find the cost of those things. Assuming less selling rates, ask them to calculate loss in each case. Again, assuming more selling rates, ask them to calculate profit in each case.

11 Metric Measures

You know ...
- metric system evolved because non-standard units of measure were not accurate
- there are different units of measurement for length, weight and capacity
- how to convert one unit into another within the system
- how to add or subtract by using the metric measures.

Maths Lab Activity 1

Materials required
- Cards with pictures of measuring jars showing certain quantities of liquids that are not marked
- Cards with pictures of weighing scales with certain quantities of goods on them with no measurements marked
- Cards with different line segments showing a distance that is not marked
- Cards with the pictures of objects which can be measured by units shown in the picture cards mentioned above

Method (Note for the Teacher)

Divide the students into two groups. Give to one group the picture cards and to the other group the cards that show the measurements.

Ask one student from the first group to show a picture card and one student from the other group to show the card that shows the weight, length or capacity of the first card. If the two match, the group gets a point.

The game can be played again, with the groups exchanging the cards. This game will help the students estimate and find the correct answers. The skills acquired can help them in problem-solving situations in real life.

Remember, the answers for the cards must be written at the back of the cards.

Do you know the different ways of measuring lengths and heights?

But they cannot give accurate measurements. So, please use the metric system.

We can use our

So, we use

> metre – to measure length and height
> gram – to measure weight
> litre – to measure capacity

Look at the following. Here, the units are divided according to the decimal system.

Units Used to Measure Lengths and Heights

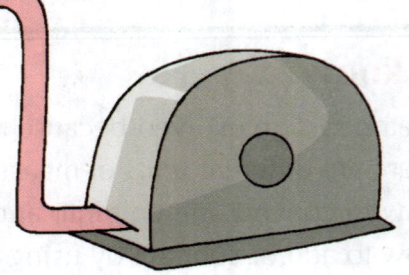

10 millimetres (mm)	=	1 centimetre (cm)
10 centimetres	=	1 decimetre (dm)
10 decimetres	=	1 metre (m)
10 metres	=	1 decametre (dam)
10 decametres	=	1 hectometre (hm)
10 hectometres	=	1 kilometre (km)

Units Used to Measure Weight

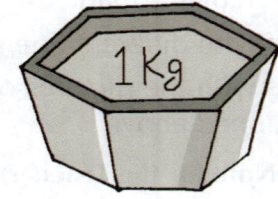

10 milligrams (mg)	=	1 centigram (cg)
10 centigrams	=	1 decigram (dg)
10 decigrams	=	1 gram (g)
10 grams	=	1 decagram (dag)
10 decagrams	=	1 hectogram (hg)
10 hectograms	=	1 kilogram (kg)

Units Used to Measure Capacity

10 millilitres (ml)	=	1 centilitre (cl)
10 centilitres	=	1 decilitre (dl)
10 decilitres	=	1 litre (l)
10 litres	=	1 decalitre (dal)
10 decalitres	=	1 hectolitre (hl)
10 hectolitres	=	1 kilolitre (kl)

You will see that the basic unit of length is metre, the basic unit of weight is gram, and the basic unit of capacity is litre. In this system, we represent thousands by kilo, hundreds by hecto, tens by deca, tenths by deci, hundredths by centi, and thousandths by milli.

The metric system is a decimal system as each unit is 10 times the next smaller unit. However, all the units that are crossed out in the chart given below are units not much used in general. So it is enough if you know how to use the rest of the units.

Main unit

Th	H	T	O	T. Ths	H. Ths	Th. Ths
km	~~hm~~	~~dam~~	m	~~dm~~	cm	mm
kg	~~hg~~	~~dag~~	g	~~dg~~	~~cg~~	mg
kl	~~hl~~	~~dal~~	l	~~dl~~	~~cl~~	ml

It is important to learn to convert one unit into the other as metric measurements are used by us daily in problem-solving situations.

Length

Length is the measurement of something from one end to the other. The unit used to measure length is metre. It is a small unit of measure. We use kilometre to measure long distances. Very short lengths are measured in centimetres and millimeters. We take measurement of lengths with the help of measuring tapes, ruler, etc.

Exercise 1

Convert into centimetre.

Remember
1 m = 100 cm

Example 1 m 47 cm = 100 cm + 47 cm = 147 cm

a. 2 m 16 cm	b. 1 m 91 cm	c. 5 m	d. 4 m 22 cm
e. 3 m 7 cm	f. 6 m 12 cm	g. 5 m 82 cm	h. 3 m 19 cm
i. 2 m 66 cm	j. 7 m	k. 1 m 19 cm	l. 2 m 15 cm

Exercise 2

Convert into metre and centimetre.

Remember
100 cm = 1 m

Example 152 cm = 100 cm + 5 cm = 1 m 52 cm

a. 623 cm	b. 801 cm	c. 219 cm	d. 618 cm
e. 506 cm	f. 316 cm	g. 501 cm	h. 222 cm
i. 420 cm	j. 412 cm	k. 321 cm	l. 146 cm

Exercise 3

Convert into millimetre.

Remember
1 m = 1000 mm

Example 6 m 36 mm = 6000 mm + 36 mm = 6036 mm

a. 6 m 24 mm	b. 7 m 218 mm	c. 5 m 318 mm	d. 3 m 532 mm
e. 6 m 9 mm	f. 2 m 86 mm	g. 1 m 127 mm	h. 9 m 128 mm
i. 8 m 298 mm	j. 3 m 146 mm	k. 7 m 7 mm	l. 5 m 165 mm

Exercise 4

Remember
1 m = 1000 mm

Convert into metre and millimetre.

Example 1265 mm = 1000 mm + 265 mm 1 m 265 mm

a. 7065 mm
b. 9601 mm
c. 1008 mm
d. 9601 mm
e. 3031 mm
f. 20200 mm
g. 6117 mm
h. 9807 mm
i. 7666 mm
j. 4312 mm
k. 1336 mm
l. 5006 mm

Exercise 5

Remember
1 cm = 10 mm

Convert into millimetre.

Example 1 cm 4 mm = 10 mm + 4 mm = 14 mm

a. 6 cm 4 mm
b. 2 cm 8 mm
c. 1 cm 9 mm
d. 8 cm
e. 1 cm 8 mm
f. 5 cm 6 mm
g. 1 cm 5 mm
h. 9 cm
i. 7 cm 2 mm
j. 6 cm 5 mm
k. 4 cm 7 mm
l. 3 cm

Exercise 6

Remember
10 mm = 1 cm

Convert into centimetre and millimetre.

Example 35 mm = 30 mm + 5 mm = 3 cm + 5 mm

a. 66 mm
b. 23 mm
c. 61 mm
d. 43 mm
e. 64 mm
f. 11 mm
g. 54 mm
h. 65 mm
i. 83 mm
j. 46 mm
k. 39 mm
l. 71 mm

Exercise 7

Remember
1 km = 1000 m

Convert into metre.

Example 1 km 861 m = 1000 m + 861 m = 1861 m

a. 5 km 218 m
b. 6 km 323 m
c. 1 km 65 m
d. 2 km 212 m
e. 6 km 31 m
f. 9 km 45 m
g. 2 km 698 m
h. 8 km 612 m
i. 9 km 245 m
j. 6 km 124 m
k. 4 km 4 m
l. 7 km 12 m

Exercise 8

Remember
1000 m = 1 km

Convert into kilometre and metre.

Example 1869 m = 1000 m + 869 m = 1 km 869 m

a. 2089 m
b. 4365 m
c. 7193 m
d. 8625 m
e. 7323 m
f. 6215 m
g. 9191 m
h. 5005 m
i. 6151 m
j. 1001 m
k. 5346 m
l. 5961 m

Addition and Subtraction using the Metric System

Addition or subtraction using the metric measures is the same as addition or subtraction using whole numbers. However, you should remember to leave space between the two different units that are taken and write the name of the unit on top.

Addition

Example 1

m	cm
4	86
5	12
9	98

9 m 98 cm

Example 2

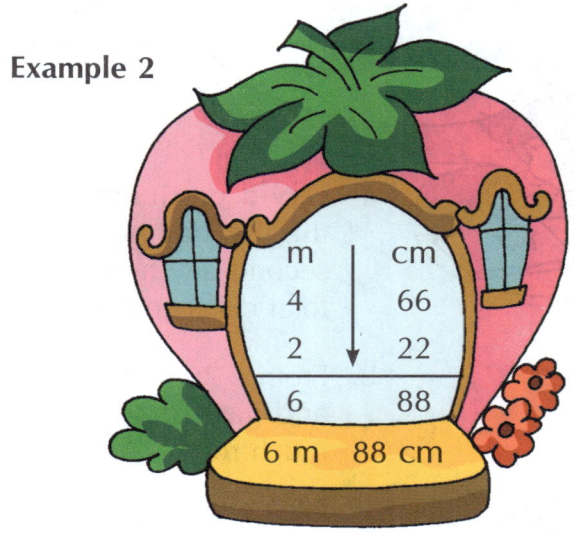

m	cm
4	66
2	22
6	88

6 m 88 cm

Exercise 9

a. Add the following.

i.
m	cm
2	24
+ 3	21

ii.
m	cm
6	14
+ 5	20

iii.
m	cm
6	41
+ 9	35

iv.
m	cm
3	24
+ 3	08

v.
m	mm
4	226
+ 3	128

vi.
m	mm
6	201
+ 2	222

vii.
m	mm
2	016
+ 2	189

viii.
km	m
8	869
+ 1	218

xi.
km	m
7	369
+ 6	789

x.
km	m
1	147
+ 6	953

b. Subtract the following.

i.
m	cm
8	85
− 2	25

ii.
m	cm
7	38
− 2	86

iii.
m	cm
5	25
− 3	89

iv.
m	cm
5	95
− 3	20

v.
m	mm
9	38
− 1	12

> **Remember**
> Before solving word problems, look at the facts, the question, the operation and the reason.

Problem Solving

a. David participated in a marathon race. On the first day he ran 23 km 345 m and on the second day he ran 19 km 378 m. What is the total distance that he ran?

b. From a 20-m-long rope, Babu cut 12 m 34 cm and gave it to his friend to tie a box. How much rope is left with him?

c. Shyam wanted to climb a 2180 m high peak. After he climbed up 1 km, how much distance was left for him to reach the top?

d. The total distance from Chennai to Bengaluru is 320 km, from Bengalure to Mysore is 128 km and from Mysore to Ooty is 89 km. What is the total distance to be covered to go from Chennai to Ooty?

e. Joel travelled 453 km by bus, 256 km by train and 10 km by scooter to reach his town from Delhi city. What is the total distance that he travelled?

Weight

Weight is the measurement relating to the heaviness of an object. The unit used to measure weight is called **gram**. It is a small unit. To measure heavier objects, **kilogram** is used and to measure very light objects, **milligram** is used.

Exercise 10

Convert into gram.

Example 3 kg 600 g = 3000 g + 600 g = 3600 g

a. 4 kg 652 g
b. 5 kg 30 g
c. 2 kg 6 g
d. 3 kg 825 g
e. 2 kg 968 g
f. 8 kg 156 g

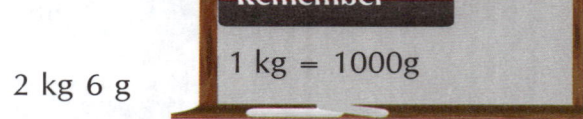
> **Remember**
> 1 kg = 1000g

Exercise 11

Convert into kilogram and gram.

Example 3234 g = 3000 g + 234 g = 3 kg + 234 g

a. 6821 g
b. 6211 g
c. 4166 g
d. 1201 g
e. 1166 g
f. 6313 g
g. 7843 g
h. 2095 g
i. 5900 g
j. 6655 g
k. 8888 g
l. 5006 g

Remember
1000 g = 1 kg

Exercise 12

Convert into gram and milligram.

Example 5128 mg = 5000 mg + 128 mg = 5 g 128 mg

a. 6128 mg
b. 2323 mg
c. 1506 mg
d. 9899 mg
e. 9016 mg
f. 9111 mg
g. 7869 mg
h. 6256 mg
i. 6253 mg
j. 3002 mg
k. 2007 mg
l. 5585 mg

Remember
1000 mg = 1 g

Exercise 13

Convert into milligram.

Example 1 g 375 mg = 1375 mg

a. 6 g 215 mg
b. 5 g 143 mg
c. 8 g 103 mg
d. 2 g 320 mg
e. 7 g 140 mg
f. 9 g 182 mg
g. 6 g 213 mg
h. 9 g 5 mg
i. 11 g 4 mg
j. 4 g 143 mg
k. 6 g 30 mg
l. 3 g 442 mg

Remember
1 g = 1000 mg

Exercise 14

a. Add the following.

	g	mg
i.	5	429
+	2	140

	g	mg
ii.	2	43
+	3	156

	g	mg
iii.	6	30
+	9	198

	g	mg
iv.	6	208
+	3	25

	g	mg
v.	8	227
+	1	496

	g	mg
vi.	5	223
+	1	611

	g	mg
vii.	4	43
+	9	876

	g	mg
viii.	6	50
+	1	111

	g	mg
xi.	5	943
+	2	258

	g	mg
x.	7	460
+	6	62

b. Subtract the following.

i.	g	mg		ii.	g	mg		iii.	g	mg		iv.	g	mg		v.	g	mg
	7	408			8	349			5	402			5	231			7	246
−	2	256		−	6	429		−	2	326		−	1	220		−	1	240

vi.	g	mg		vii.	g	mg		viii.	g	mg		xi.	g	mg		x.	g	mg
	5	742			7	214			6	692			7	502			7	841
−	1	816		−	4	19		−	2	463		−	1	416		−	6	55

Capacity

Capacity means the maximum quantity of liquid that a container can hold. The unit used to measure capacity is called *litre*. It is a small unit of measure. We use *kilolitre* to measure large quantities of liquids. Very small quantities of capacity are measured in *millilitres*. There are measuring cups available with different units of measures marked on them for finding capacity.

Here are the units of measure you need to remember.

$$1 \text{ litre} = 1000 \text{ ml}$$
$$1 \text{ kl} = 1000 \text{ } l$$

Exercise 15

Convert into millilitre.

Example 7 *l* 462 ml = 7000 ml + 462 ml = 7462 ml

a. 6 *l* 75 ml
b. 3 *l* 105 ml
c. 9 *l* 23 ml
d. 2 *l* 120 ml
e. 6 *l* 532 ml
f. 4 *l* 50 ml

Remember
1000 ml = 1 *l*

Exercise 16

Convert into litre and millilitre.

Example 5268 ml = 5000 ml + 268 ml = 5 *l* 268 ml

a. 2133 ml
b. 6215 ml
c. 8811 ml
d. 9112 ml
e. 6655 ml
f. 8338 ml

Remember
1 *l* = 1000 ml

Exercise 17

Convert into litre.

Example 4 kl 128 l = 4000 l + 128 l = 4128 l

a. 12 kl 14 l
b. 1 kl 289 l
c. 2 kl 159 l
d. 6 kl 5 l
e. 2 kl 75 l
f. 3 kl 2 l

Remember
1 kl = 1000 l

Exercise 18

Convert into kilolitre and litre.

Example 6835 l = 6000 l + 835 l = 6 kl 835 l

a. 2029 l
b. 5652 l
c. 3500 l
d. 6213 l
e. 9009 l
f. 8982 l

Remember
1000 l = 1 kl

Exercise 19

a. Add the following.

i.
l	ml
1	614
+ 2	210

ii.
l	mg
5	38
+ 4	219

iii.
l	ml
3	152
+ 1	596

iv.
l	ml
2	142
+ 3	596

v.
l	ml
7	691
+ 1	249

vi.
l	ml
3	45
+ 4	182

vii.
l	ml
4	792
+ 1	79

viii.
l	ml
6	348
+ 12	143

xi.
l	ml
2	61
+ 13	229

x.
l	ml
5	289
+ 1	385

b. Subtract the following.

i.
l	ml
6	591
− 2	289

ii.
l	ml
6	490
− 1	259

iii.
l	ml
5	282
− 1	811

iv.
l	ml
8	459
− 2	53

v.
l	ml
16	491
− 3	341

vi.
l	ml
13	790
− 3	36

vii.
l	mg
13	889
− 2	111

viii.
l	ml
12	880
− 1	100

xi.
l	ml
6	162
− 1	825

x.
l	ml
5	129
− 2	314

Problem Solving

a. Priya and her friends bought four 1 litre bottles of water on a hot day. If 650 ml of water was left after they drank, how much had been used up?

b. The petrol pump owner started his business with 5650 litres of petrol in the morning and was left with 2109 litres of petrol at the end of the day. How much petrol was sold during the day?

c. Rishi added 150 ml of water to 120 ml of curd to mix well and make butter milk. How much of butter milk did he get?

d. Sujatha mixed 250 ml of orange juice, 350 ml of grape juice, 20 ml of ginger juice and 200 ml of pineapple juice to make a mocktail. What was the total quantity of the mocktail that she made?

e. A milkman took 5 litres of milk for distribution to the houses in the village. He gave 1 l and 300 ml in the first house, 1 l and 250 ml in the second house and 750 ml in the third house. How much did he carry back home?

f. The tank lorry carrying 13000 litres of milk loaded 3350 litres in the first vending machine and 4200 litres in the second vending machine. The balance was loaded into the third vending machine. How much was loaded in the third vending machine?

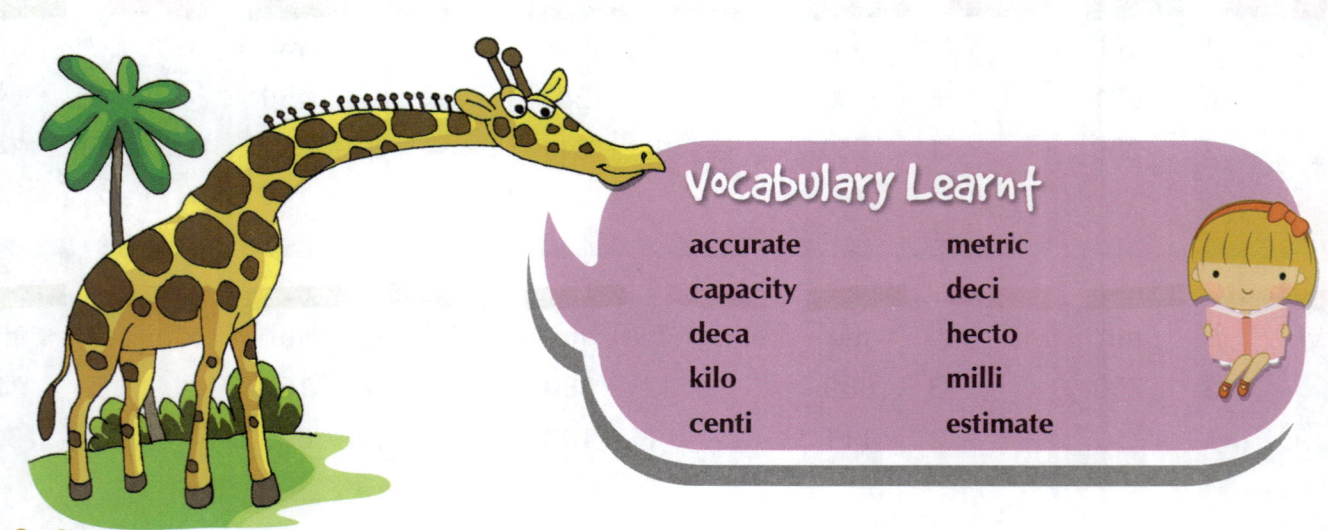

Vocabulary Learnt

accurate	metric
capacity	deci
deca	hecto
kilo	milli
centi	estimate

Maths Lab Activity 2

Materials required
- A sheet with pictures of different sized jars, each denoting a different weight, (1000 g, 500 g, 200 g, 100 g, 50 g, 20 g, 10 g and 5 g) for each student
- A pair of scissors

Method (Note for the Teacher)

Divide the students into groups. Ask each student to cut out all the jars separately and keep with him/her. You call out a certain weight, say 2 kg and 670 g. Each group must pool in their jars and try to give you jars equivalent to the weight you asked.

Repeat different combinations of weights and each time the group must see how they can give you the weights for the sum presented by you. Discuss the differences between the groups so that the children understand that the same total can be achieved with different combinations. For example, 2 kg can be given as four 500 g or as one 1 kg and two 500 g, or as two 1 kg and so on.

12 Angles, Circles and Nets

> **You know ...**
> - what are plane and solid shapes
> - what is a point, a line segment and a ray.

Angle

An angle is formed when two rays meet at a point. The rays are called the **arms** of the angle. The meeting point of the two rays is called the **vertex**. An angle is always named with a capital letter. For example, angle A, angle B, etc.

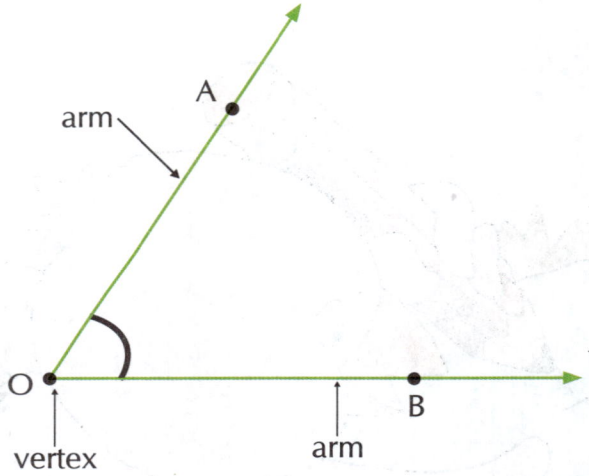

Angles are usually measured in units called **degrees**. The symbol for degrees is °. There are 360° in a circle and 180° (half of 360°) form a straight angle. An instrument called a protractor is used to measure angles.

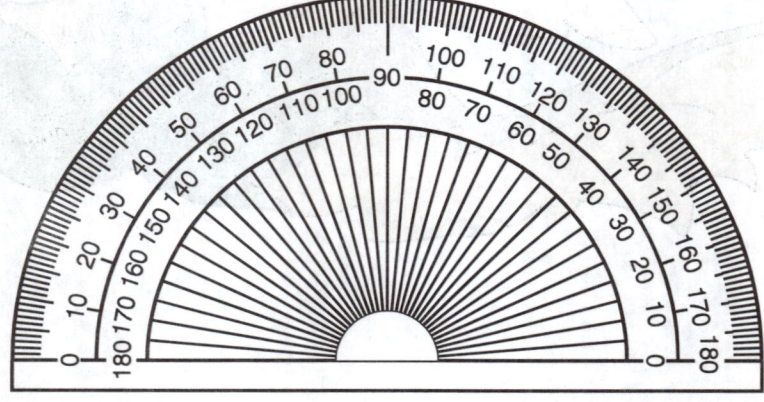

A protractor has numbers 0 to 180 marked on it from both sides. This helps to measure angles from both sides. The centre of the protractor shows 90°.

Measuring Angles

A protractor is used to measure angles. In this section, we will consider the use of a protractor that has the shape of a semi-circle and two scales marked from 0° to 180°.

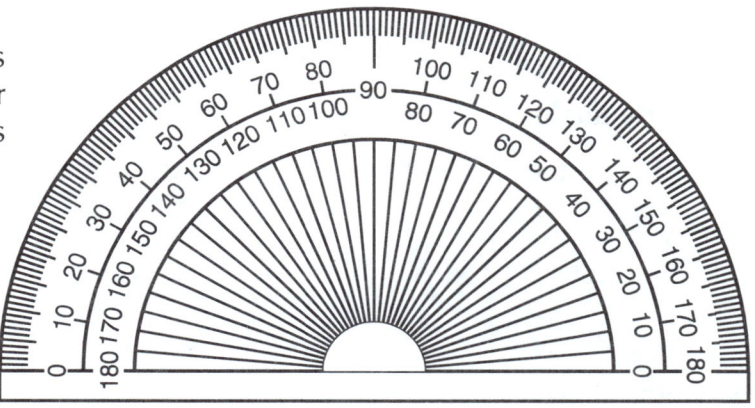

The two scales make it easy for us to measure angles facing different ways.

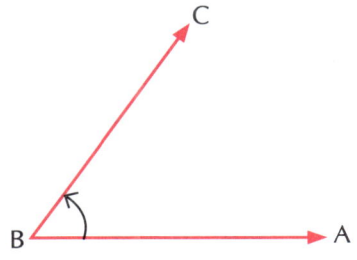

To measure the size of angle ABC, place the protractor over the angle so that centre of the protractor is directly over the angle's vertex, B; and the base line of the protractor is along the arm BA, of the angle.

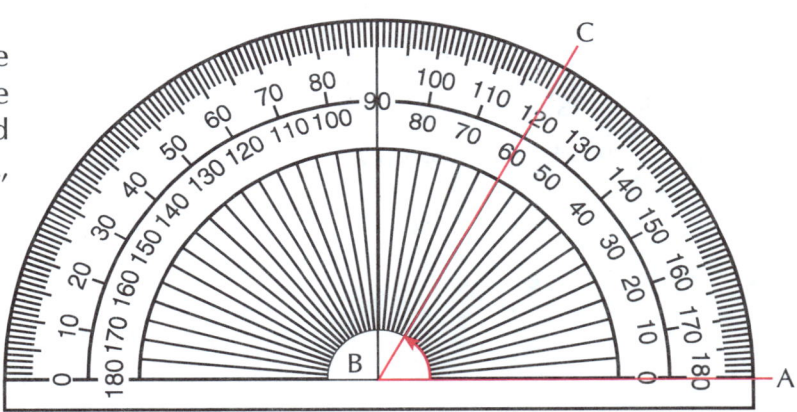

We use the inner scale to measure the angle ABC, as the arm AB passes through the **zero** of the **inner scale**. Following the inner scale around the protractor, we find that the other arm, BC, passes through the inner scale at 60°. So, the size of angle ABC is 60 degrees. We write this as follows:

∠ABC = 60°

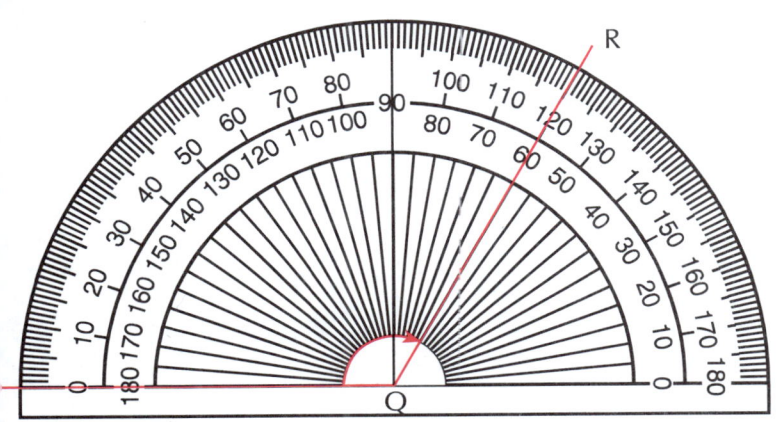

To measure the size of angle PQR, place the protractor over the angle so that the centre of the protractor is directly over the angle's vertex, Q; and the base line of the protractor is along the arm, PQ, of the angle.

We use the outer scale to measure the angle PQR, as the arm PQ passes through the zero of the **outer scale**. Following the outer scale around the protractor, we find that the other arm, QR, passes through the outer scale at 120. So, the size of angle PQR is 120 degrees. We write this as follows:

∠PQR = 120°

Types of Angles

There are different types of angles.

a. Acute angle

An angle that is less than 90° is called an acute angle.

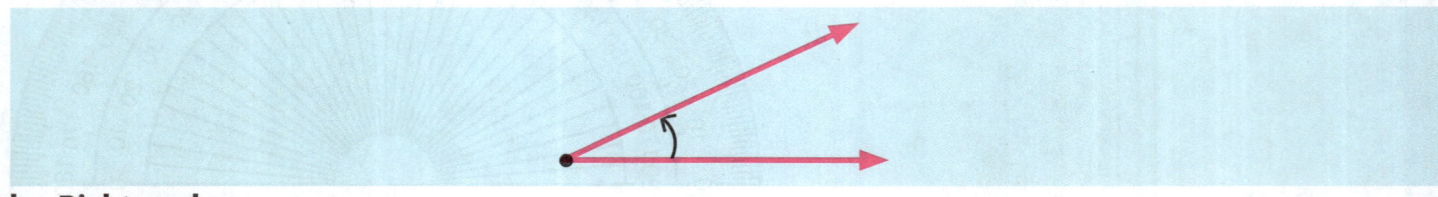

b. Right angle

An angle that is exactly 90° is called a right angle.

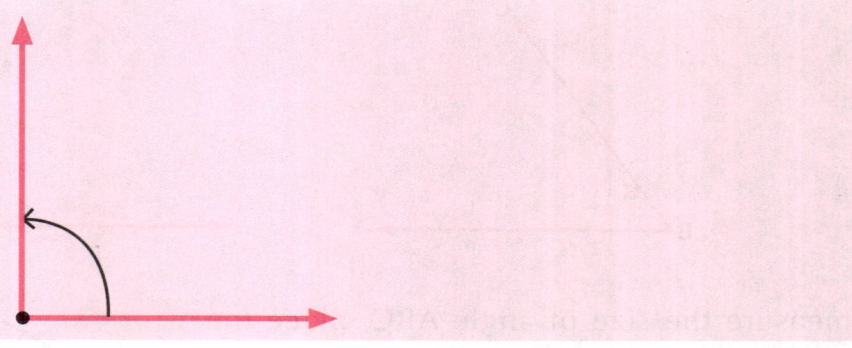

c. Obtuse angle

An angle that is more than 90° but less than 180° is called an obtuse angle.

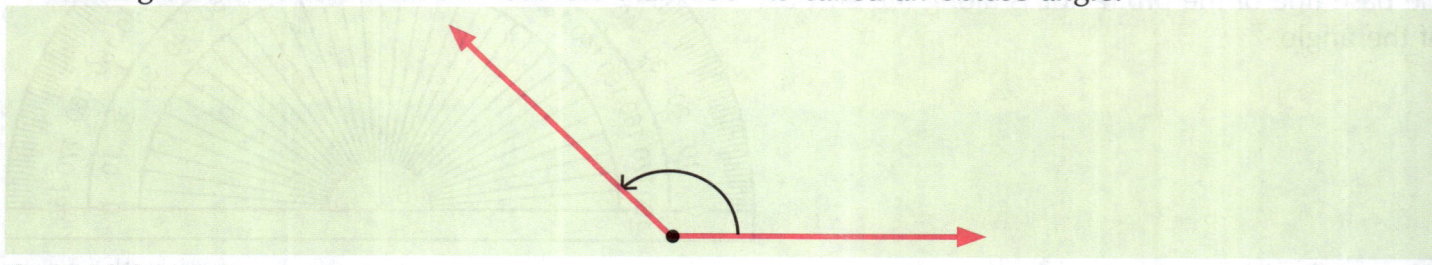

d. Straight angle

An angle that is exactly 180° is called a straight angle.

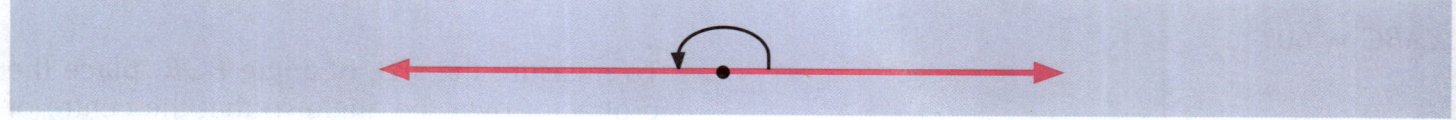

e. Reflex angle

An angle that is more than 180° but less than 360° is called a reflex angle.

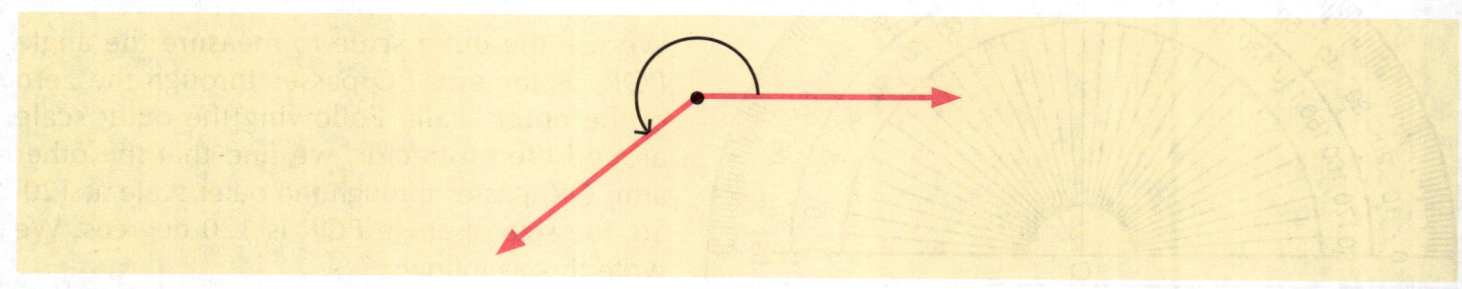

Measuring Reflex Angles

Recall that:

A protractor can be used to measure the size of an acute angle (between 0 and 90) and an obtuse angle (between 90° and 180°).

Now, we will use a protractor to measure the reflex angle **PQR**.

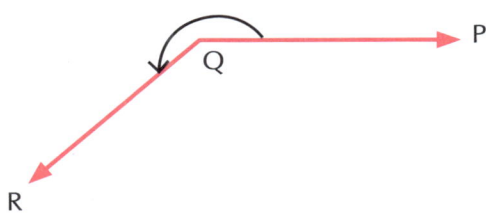

To measure the reflex angle *PQR*, extend the arm *PQ* to A to form *PQA* which is a straight angle. Then measure the size of the angle *AQR* and add 180°.

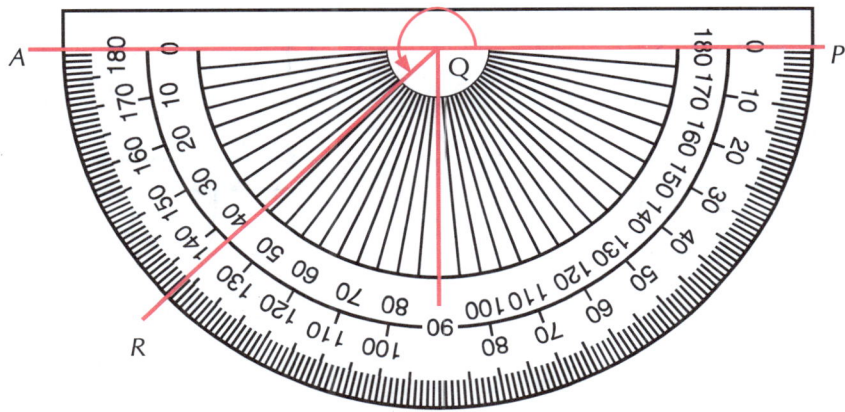

Reflex ∠PQR = Straight angle + ∠AQR
= 180° + 45°
= 225°

Exercise 1

Match the two boxes that mean the same by colouring them alike.

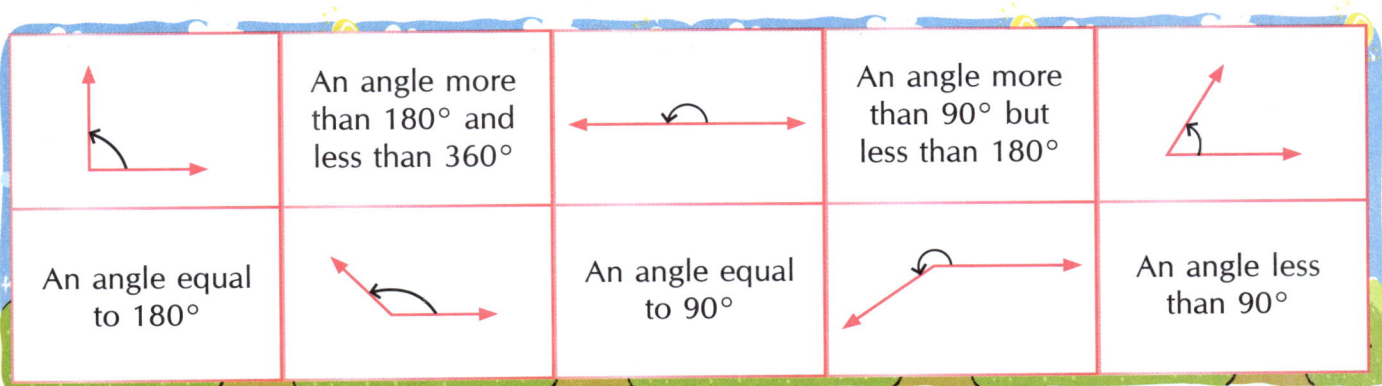

Exercise 2

Here are three angles showing three different measurements. Keeping them as your guidelines, can you estimate the measures of the following angles? Write the estimated measure in the boxes given below. Then measure them actually using a protractor and write their exact measure in the angle.

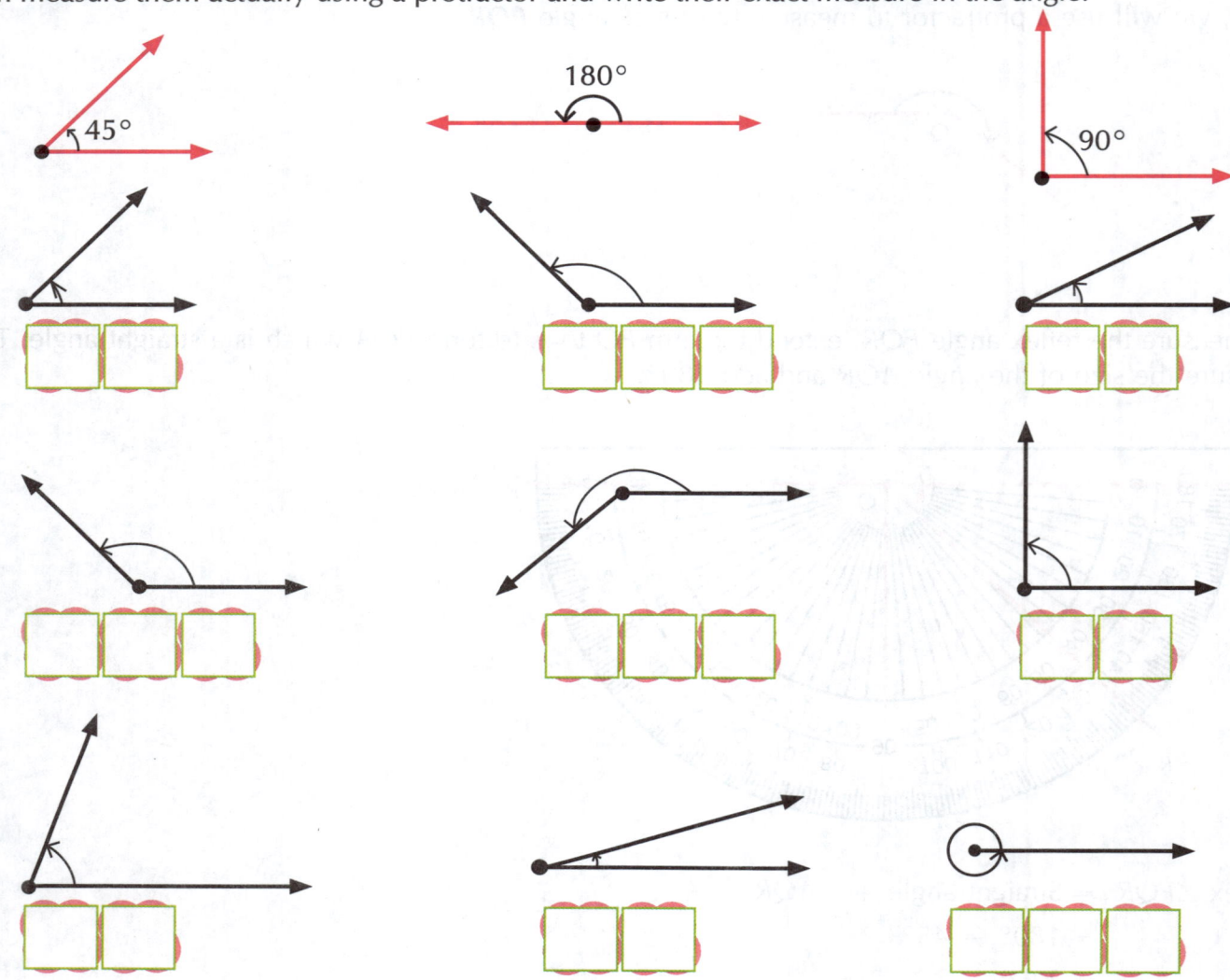

Exercise 3

Estimate the measures of the angles A, B, and C for both the triangles, then measure using a protractor and give yourself a rating as per the colour code. excellent: red   good: blue   fail: yellow

a.

b.

Shape	Angle	Estimate	Actual	Rating
a	A			
	B			
	C			
b	A			
	B			
	C			

Exercise 4

Measure the following angles and write in the boxes given below.

a.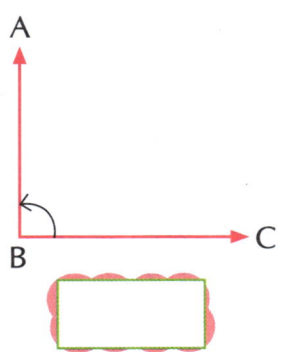

b.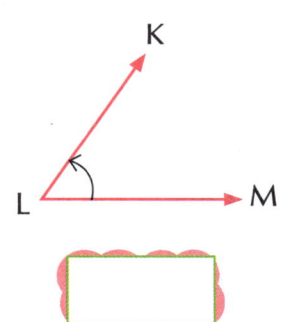

c.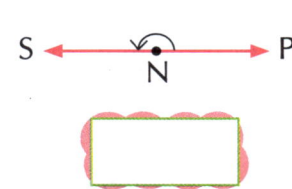

d.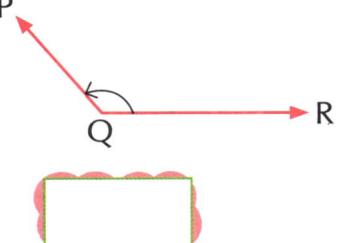

e.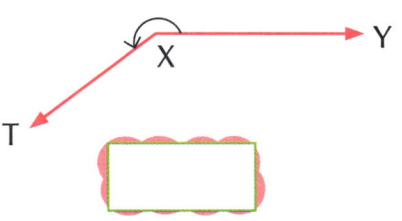

f.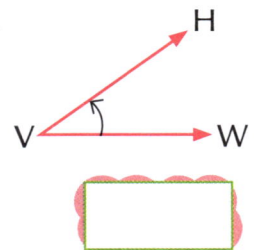

g.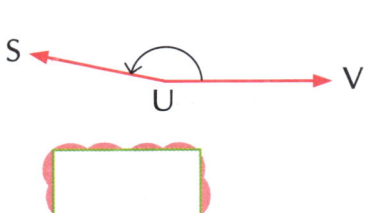

h.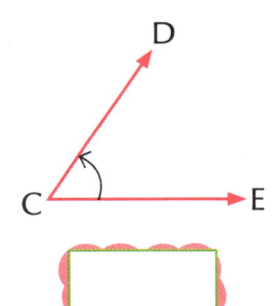

i.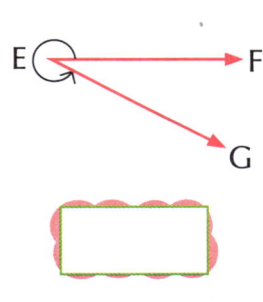

Drawing Angles less than 180° with a Protractor

To draw an **angle** with **protractor**, proceed as follows:
- Draw a straight line (i.e. an arm of the angle).
- Place a dot at one end of the arm. This dot represents the **vertex** of the angle.
- Place the centre of the protractor at the vertex dot and the baseline of the protractor along the arm of the angle.
- Find the required angle on the scale and then mark a small dot at the edge of the protractor.
- Join the small dot with the vertex with a ruler to form the second arm of the angle.
- Label the angle with capital letters.

Example 1

Draw = ∠ABC = 60° with a ruler and protractor.

Solution:

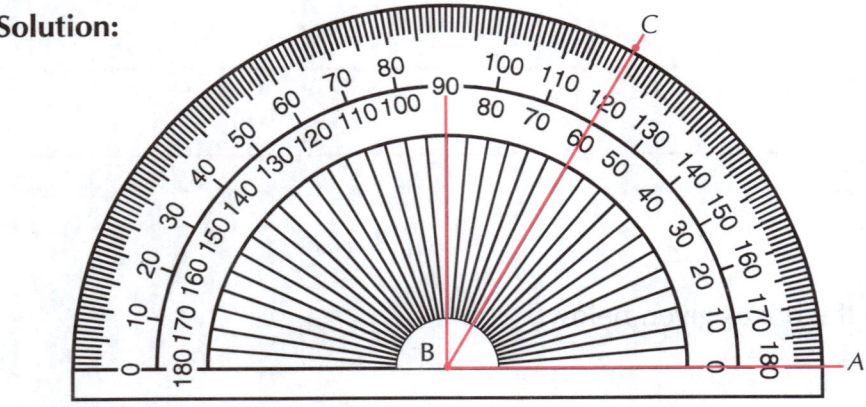

- Draw a straight line AB.
- Place a dot at B. This dot represents the vertex of the angles.
- Place the centre of the protractor at B and the baseline of the protractor along the arm BA.
- Find 60 on the scale and mark a small dot at the edge of the protractor and mark it as C.
- Join the vertex B to the small dot with a ruler to form the second arm, BC, of the angle.
- Mark the angle with a small arc as shown below.

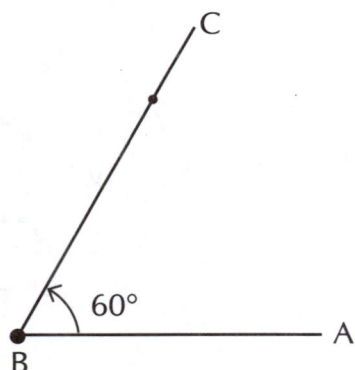

Drawing Reflex Angles

To draw a reflex angle (i.e. angle greater than 180° and less than 360°), proceed as follows:
- Subtract the reflex angle from 360°. Then draw the resulting angle as described earlier.
- The required angle is outside the one that has been drawn.
- Mark the angle with a small arc.
- Label the angle.

Example 2

Draw ∠PQR = 240° with a ruler and protractor.

Solution:

To construct the reflex angle PQR = 240°, draw ∠PQR = 360° − 240°
= 120°

- Draw a straight line PQ.
- Place a dot at Q. This dot represents the vertex of the angle.
- Turn the protractor upside down and place the centre of the protractor at Q and the baseline of the protractor along the arm PQ.
- Use the outer scale to find 120° and mark a small dot at the edge of the protractor

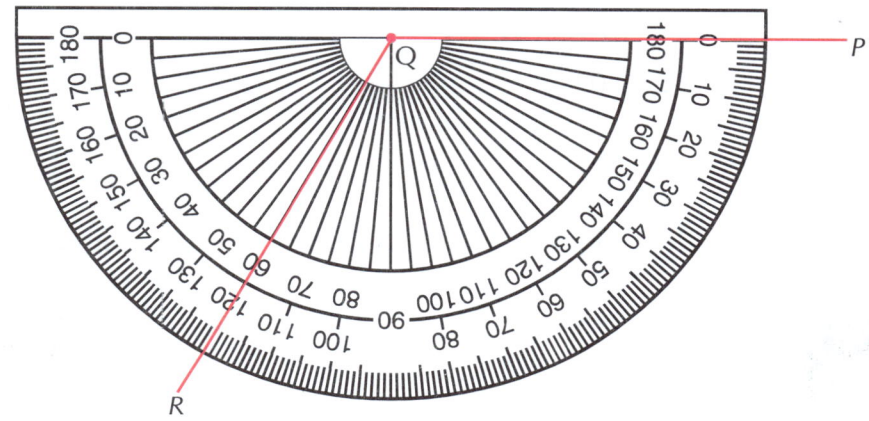

- Then remove the protractor and join the vertex, Q, to the small dot with a ruler to form the second arm, QR, of the angle.
- Mark the angle with a small arc as shown below.

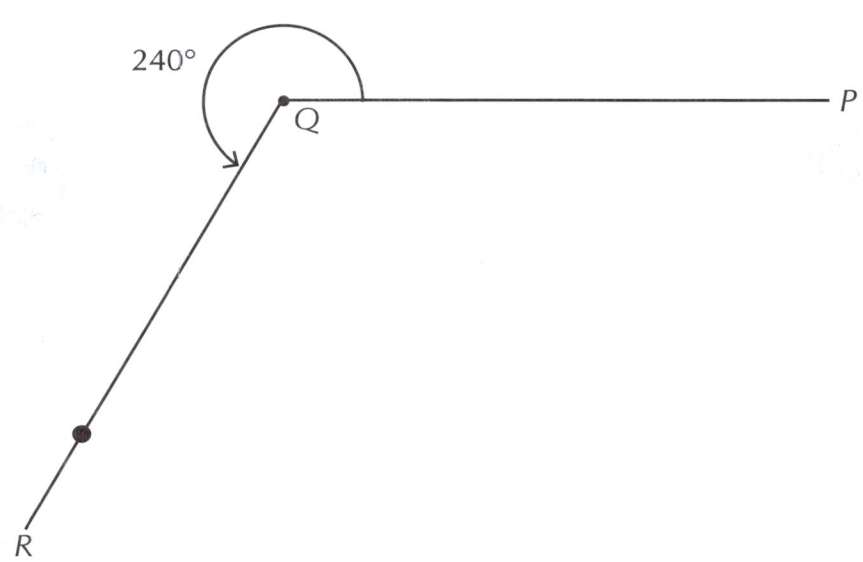

Exercise 4

Construct the following angles.

a. 40°   b. 85°   c. 90°

d. 120°   e. 220°   f. 105°

g. 25°   h. 152°   i. 320°

j. 300°   k. 100°   l. 270°

Exercise 5

Name 2 angles in each picture using capital letters and say what angles are formed in them.

_____   _____
_____   _____
_____   _____

_____   _____
_____   _____
_____   _____

Maths Lab Activity 2

Materials required
- A sheet of paper
- Pencil

Method (Note for the Teacher)
Let the students choose two angles of any measurement, for example, an obtuse angle and an acute angle or an angle of 60° and 90°. Ask them to write a conversation between them on one page.

1.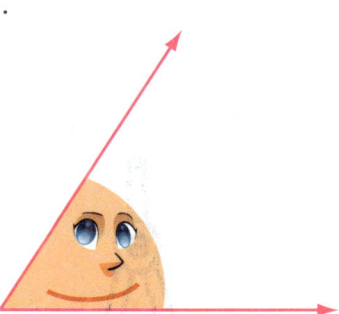

2.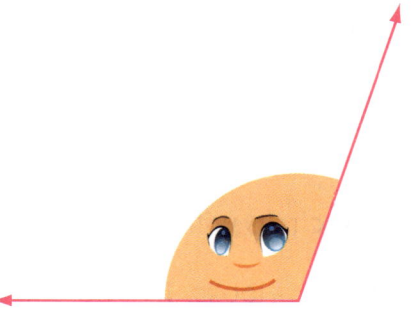

Circles

A circle is a plane shape like the square, triangle or rectangle. It is a closed figure with a curved boundary called the circumference. It is unlike the other shapes that have boundaries with line segments.

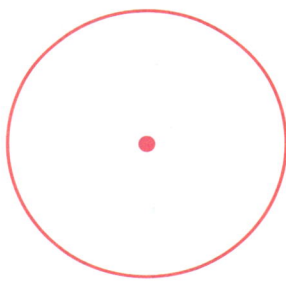

Centre, Radius and Diameter

You need a fixed point to be able to draw a perfect circle around it. This point is called the **centre**. Every point on the boundary of a circle is at the same distance from the centre. For example, points A, B, C and D are all at the same distance from O.

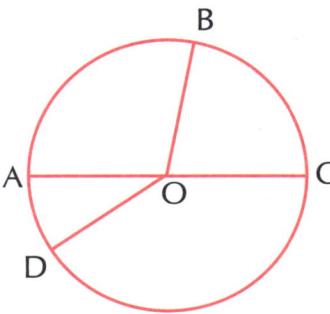

So, we can say that AO = BO = CO = DO.

This fixed distance from centre O to any point on the boundary is called the **radius**. There can be any number of radii (the plural of radius) for a circle.

Do you see the line segment AH passing through O? The points A and H are on the boundary of the circle. A line segment that starts from one point (A) on the circle, goes through the centre (O) and ends at another point (H) on the circle, is called the **diameter**. There can be infinite number of diameters for a circle but all of them must pass through the centre.

Here, CG, AH, DE, FB are all diameters as they all pass through the centre.

Look carefully at the radius and the diameter. You will notice that the diameter is actually twice (two times) the radius.

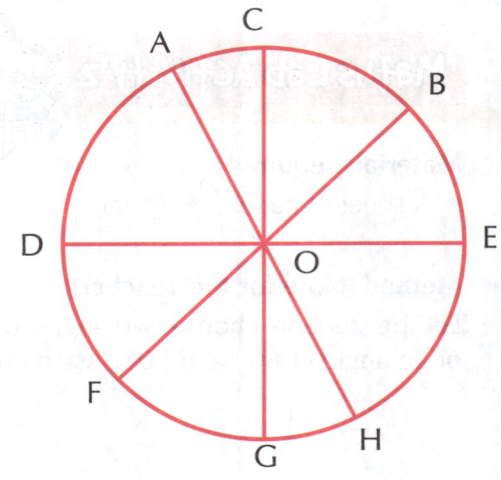

Drawing a Circle

You can draw a circle with the help of a compass and ruler.

See how a **compass** looks. Its one end holds the pencil while the other sharp end helps to draw the circle. To draw a circle, you must place the sharp end of the compass on the paper. This point will be the centre O. Fix this sharp end on the paper and move the other end holding the pencil around the centre to complete the circle.

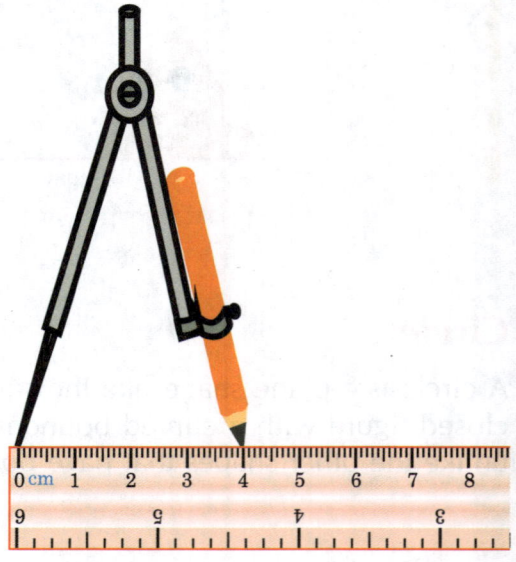

It is not just enough to have the instrument. You should also know how big your circle should be. For that, you need the measurement of the radius. Suppose, the length of the radius is 4 cm. Measure that distance by opening the compass. The sharp metal tip should rest at O and the pencil tip should be stretched up to 4 cm on the ruler.

Mark a point O on a paper or your notebook. Fix the sharp metal tip of the compass at point O. With O as the centre and radius equal to 4 cm, rotate the compass with the pencil touching the paper until you have gone one full round. Remove your compass and you will see your circle. As you already know the diameter is equal to two radii, measure and see if the diameter of the circle is 8 cm. If it is, you have done a good job.

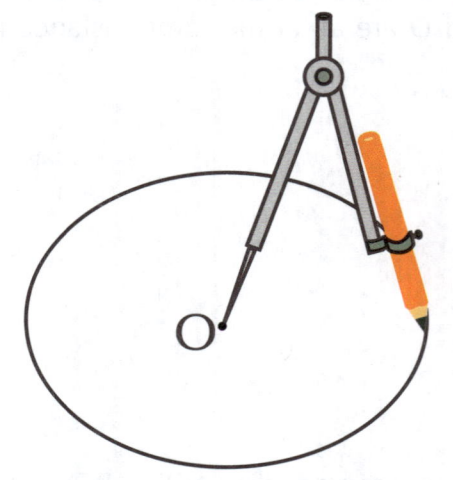

Exercise 6

Complete the following.

a. A circle is a _____ shape.

b. Circles have _____ diameters.

c. A diameter divides the circle into two _____ parts.

d. A circle can be drawn with a _____ .

e. The word semi refers to _____ .

f. A circle has no _____ or breadth.

g. The radius is _____ of the diameter.

h. Many _____ can be drawn from the centre.

Exercise 7

Draw circles of the following radii on your notebook.

a. 3.5 cm

b. 3 cm

c. 2.5 cm

d. 1.4 cm

e. 3.6 cm

f. 5.5 cm

Exercise 8

Measure the radius of the circles and calculate the diameters.

a.

Radius = _____
Diameter = _____

b.

Radius = _____
Diameter = _____

c.

Radius = _____
Diameter = _____

d.

Radius = _____
Diameter = _____

e.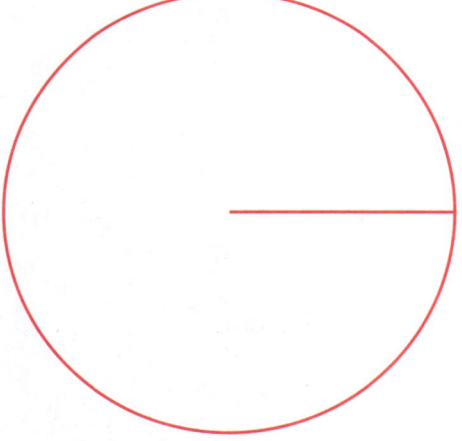

Radius = _____
Diameter = _____

f.

Radius = _____
Diameter = _____

Maths Lab Activity 2

Materials required

- Different objects with a circular base (lids, caps, CDs, bangles, etc.)
- A rectangular piece of cardboard
- Glue

Method (Note for the Teacher)

Ask the students to find pictures that can be created only by using circular objects. Let them stick what they have collected at suitable places on the picture and make a collage. They can hang the best collage in the classroom.

Cubes

A solid figure having six square faces is called a cube. You must have played with a pair of dice. A die (singular of dice) is a cube. It has six square faces.

Nets

Take a cubical box and unfold it as shown. You get a net. Try to make the box again by folding the faces.

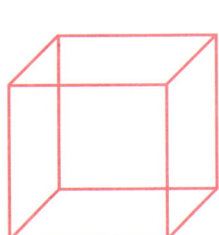
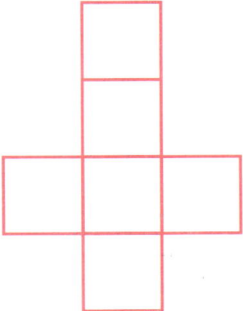

Exercise 9

Which of the following nets do you think will make a cube with no lid and no base? (Use ✓ or ✗)

a.
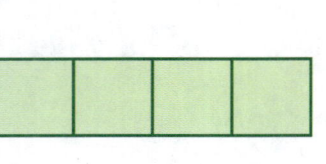

b.

c.
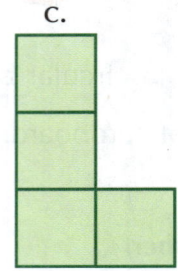

d.
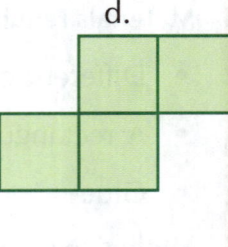

Exercise 10

Which nets do you think will make a cube with no lid? (Use ✓ or ✗)

a.

b.
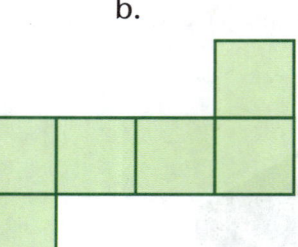

c.

d.
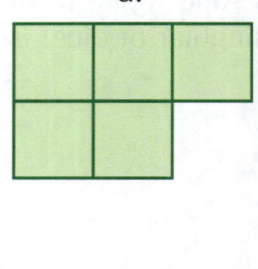

Exercise 11

Which nets do you think will make a complete cube? (Use ✓ or ✗)

a.

b.
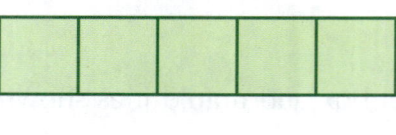

c.
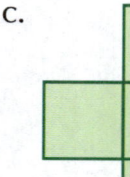

d.
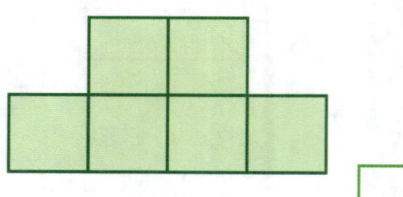

Summative Assessment 3
(For chapters 7 to 12)

1. What is the difference between a prime number and a composite number?
2. Find the factors of the following and say whether they are prime or composite.
   a. 17   b. 24   c. 29   d. 36
3. Find prime factors for the following using tree method.
   a. 20   b. 42
4. Which of the following fractions has the highest numerator?
   a. $\frac{3}{4}$ b. $\frac{5}{6}$ c. $\frac{7}{8}$ d. $\frac{2}{4}$
5. Add the following:
   a. $\frac{1}{3} + \frac{1}{3} =$ b. $\frac{2}{5} + \frac{1}{5} =$ c. $\frac{4}{9} + \frac{2}{9} =$
6. Subtract the following:
   a. $\frac{10}{11} - \frac{5}{11}$ b. $\frac{7}{8} - \frac{4}{8}$ c. $\frac{6}{9} - \frac{4}{9}$
7. Tick the proper fractions and circle the improper fractions:
   a. $\frac{5}{9}$ b. $\frac{11}{10}$ c. $\frac{7}{9}$ d. $\frac{13}{11}$
8. Multiply the following:
   a. $\frac{2}{3} \times \frac{3}{4}$ b. $\frac{4}{5} \times \frac{2}{3}$
9. Find the profit for the following:
   a. Cost price = ₹ 530.00   Selling price = ₹ 920.00
   b. Cost price = ₹ 7652.00   Selling price = ₹ 10,485.00
10. Find the cost price of the following:
    a. Selling price = ₹ 1085.0   Profit = ₹ 263.00
    b. Selling price = ₹ 3486.00   Loss = ₹ 699.00
11. Change the following to m and mm:
    a. 8049 mm   b. 5967 mm
12. Change the following to gram.
    a. 4 kg 501 g =   b. 12 kg 16 g =
13. Say true or false.
    a. An angle is measured using a pair of compasses.
    b. A 90° angle is a right angle.
    c. An obtuse angle is more than 180° but less than 360°.

d. An angle has two arms and a vertex.

e. An angle that shows more than 90° but less than 180° is a straight line.

14. Name the following angles:

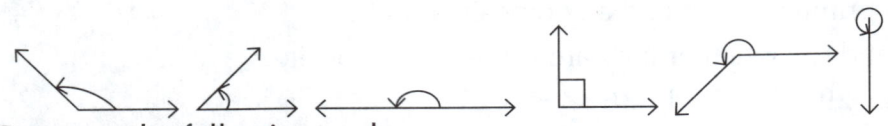

15. Construct the following angles:
    a. 45°   b. 20°   c. 140°   d. 250°
    e. 180°   f. 140°

16. Change the following to cm:
    a. 4 m 36 cm =   b. 8 m 71 cm =

17. Divide the following:
    a. $7 \div \frac{3}{4}$ b. $\frac{2}{6} \div \frac{2}{3}$

18. Change to a fractional number.
    a. 0.1   b. 0.26   c. 0.75

19. Circle the smaller number.
    a. 0.818, 0.812   b. 0.188, 0.818

20. Change the following to improper fractions:
    a. $2\frac{1}{3}$ b. $1\frac{3}{8}$

21. Reduce to the lowest term:
    a. $\frac{12}{16}$ b. $\frac{15}{20}$ c. $\frac{20}{50}$

# 13

Time

> **You know ...**
> - time is measured with the help of clocks and calendars
> - to distinguish between day and night and plan activities accordingly
> - time is very precious and it should not be wasted
> - time, once lost, cannot be recovered.

Maths Lab Activity 1

Materials required
- 4 cm × 4 cm square cards (as many as the number of students in the class)
- Crayons
- Pencils
- Erasers

Method (Note for the Teacher)

Divide the cards into two sets. On one set, draw clock faces showing different times. On the other set, write down the time, corresponding to the time in the cards of set one, in words.

Divide the class into two groups. Ask one student from the first group to show his/her clock to the students in the other group. The student in the second group, who has the card with the corresponding time, should get up and read the time on his card. Those with the correct responses score points for their teams.

We all know that time is very precious and it should not be wasted. If we do not recognise the passage of time, we cannot be organised and do things on time. So, it is important to know how to read a clock to recognise hours, minutes and seconds and also to recognise the calendar, weeks and days as units for measuring time.

Do you sometimes feel that time is passing very quickly and at other times feel it is passing very slowly? What do you think is the reason?

Time is always passing at the same speed, but we feel that it has passed very quickly when we are engaged in an activity that we enjoy. We do not want it to end. However, if the activity is something that we do not enjoy, even five minutes may seem like an hour.

Exercise 1

List three activities which make you feel that time is passing very quickly.

_____

List three activities which make you feel that time is moving very slowly.

_____

Exercise 2

Look at the calendar given below.

Sun	Mon	Tue	Wed	Thur	Fri	Sat
	1	2	3	4	5	6
7	8	9	10	11	12	13
14	15	16	17	18	19	20
21	22	23	24	25	26	27
28	29	30	31			

Now, mark your answers in the calendar as instructed.

a. The Republic Day of India is on the fourth Friday. Draw a star in the box.
b. Your school Sports Day is on the 28th. What day is it? Draw a star in this box.
c. Colour all holidays in orange.
d. You are going on a picnic on the third Thursday. What is the date on that day? Draw a star in that box.
e. The English New Year is on the first of this month. Draw a star in that box.
f. Draw a star in the box which has the date of your birthday.
g. Can you guess the name of this month?

Seasons

You know that there are 12 months in a year. These 12 months are divided into different seasons depending on the weather conditions. These seasons may vary in different countries.

In India, there are four main seasons. There are: summer, rainy season, winter and the spring.

People wear clothes according to the seasons. Also different fruits are found in different seasons.

Look at the table to learn more about seasons.

Seasons	Calender months	Fruits available
Summer	April to June	
Rainy season	July to September	
Winter	October to January	
Spring	February to March	

158

We also wear clothes according to the season. People wear light clothes in summer and warm clothes or woollens in winter. Similarly, we wear a raincoat when it rains.

Exercise 3

Write the name of the season by looking at the clothes that people are wearing.

_____   _____   _____   _____

Exercise 4

You know that the same tree will look different in different seasons. Can you complete the trees given below to show your understanding of the four seasons in sequence? Also, write the names of the seasons.

159

Conversion of Time into Lower Units

All along you have been learning how to read the time on a clock. Now you can learn how to convert from one unit of time to another.

Converting Hours into Minutes

Example

3 hours

1 hr = 60 min

3 × 60 = 180 min

> To convert hours into minutes, you should multiply the given hours by 60.

Exercise 5

1 hour = 60 min

Convert hours into minutes.

a. 2 hr
b. 4 hr
c. 5 hr
d. 9 hr
e. 3 hr
f. 6 hr

Converting Hours and Minutes into Minutes

Example

1 hr 30 min

1 hr = 60 min

60 min + 30 min = 90 min

> To convert hours and minutes into minutes, you should multiply the given hour by 60 and add the given minutes to the answer.

Exercise 6

Convert hours and minutes into minutes.

a. 2 hr 10 min
b. 4 hr 35 min
c. 1 hr 50 min
d. 3 hr 15 min
e. 5 hr 10 min
f. 6 hr 30 min

Converting Minutes into Seconds

Example

2 min

2 × 60 = 120 sec

1 min = 60 sec

> To convert minutes into seconds, multiply the given minutes by 60.

Exercise 7

1 min = 60 sec

Convert the minutes into seconds.

a. 5 min
b. 4 min
c. 7 min
d. 12 min
e. 15 min
f. 20 min

Converting Minutes and Seconds into Seconds

Example

1 min 45 sec

1 min = 60 sec

60 sec + 45 sec = 105 sec

> To convert minutes into seconds, multiply the number of minutes by 60 and add the given seconds to the answer.

Exercise 8

Convert minutes and seconds into seconds.

a. 4 min 20 sec
b. 3 min 18 sec
c. 8 min 49 sec
d. 9 min 25 sec
e. 2 min 54 min
f. 1 min 39 sec

Converting Hours and Minutes into Seconds

Example

1 hr 20 min

1 hr = 60 min

60 min + 20 min = 80 min

1 min = 60 sec

80 min = 80 × 60 = 4800 sec

> To convert hours and minutes into minutes, multiply the number of hours by 60 and add the given minutes. To convert minutes into seconds, again multiply by 60.

Exercise 9

Convert hours and minutes into seconds.

a. 2 hr 16 min
b. 3 hr 35 min
c. 8 hr 12 min
d. 4 hr 22 min
e. 9 hr 54 min
f. 5 hr 23 min

Converting Years into Months

Example

2 years

1 year = 12 months

2 × 12 = 24 months

> To convert years into months, you should multiply the given years by 12.

Exercise 10

1 year = 12 months

Convert years into months.

a. 34 years
b. 67 years
c. 89 years
d. 90 years
e. 63 years
f. 100 years

Converting Months into Weeks

Example

1 month = 4 weeks (approximately)

2 months = 2 × 4 = 8 weeks

> 1 month = 4 weeks

To convert months into weeks, multiply the given month by 4.

Exercise 11

Convert months into weeks.

a. 3 months
b. 5 months
c. 7 months
d. 9 months
e. 11 months
f. 6 months

Converting Months and Weeks into Weeks

Example

1 month 2 weeks

4 weeks + 2 weeks = 6 weeks

To convert months into weeks, multiply the given months by 4 and add the given weeks.

Exercise 12

Convert months and weeks into weeks.

a. 2 months 7 weeks
b. 7 months 9 weeks
c. 5 months 8 weeks
d. 6 months 5 weeks
e. 4 months 6 weeks
f. 3 months 10 weeks

Converting Weeks into Days

Example

1 week = 1 × 7 days = 7 days

To convert weeks into days, multiply the given weeks by 7.

Exercise 13

Convert weeks into days.

a. 4 weeks
b. 8 weeks
c. 12 weeks
d. 16 weeks
e. 23 weeks
f. 6 weeks

Converting Weeks and Days into Days

Example

2 weeks 9 days

To convert weeks and days into days, multiply the given weeks by 7 and add the given days.

Exercise 14

Convert weeks and days into days.

a. 1 week 9 days
b. 35 weeks 8 days
c. 67 weeks 6 days
d. 56 weeks 3 days
e. 29 weeks 5 days
f. 14 weeks 14 days

Conversion of Time into Upper Units

You multiply to change into lower units and divide to change into upper units.

Converting Days into Weeks

Example

21 days

7 days = 1 week

So 21 ÷ 7 = 3 weeks.

> To convert days into weeks, you should divide the given days by 7.

Exercise 15

Convert days into weeks.

a. 49 days   b. 119 days   c. 154 days
d. 105 days   e. 70 days   f. 630 days

Converting Days into Weeks and Days

Example

32 days

32 ÷ 7 = 4, with remainder 4.

You know that 7 days make 1 week. If you divide 32 by 7, you get 4 as quotient and 4 as remainder. The quotient shows the number of weeks and the remainder shows the number of days.

So, 32 days = 4 weeks and 4 days

MENTAL MATH

Complete the time table

Time				
10.25 p.m.	25 minutes later		1 hour, 10 minutes later	
7.55 a.m.	40 minutes later		1 hour 50 minutes later	
11.55 a.m.	15 minutes later		2 hours, 5 minutes later	
10.05 p.m.	10 minutes before		1 hour 20 minutes before	
2.15 a.m.	35 minutes before		1 hour 5 minutes before	

Exercise 16

Convert days into weeks and days.

a. 123 days   b. 58 days   c. 169 days
d. 43 days   e. 60 days   f. 100 days

> To convert days into weeks and days, divide the given days by 7. The quotient shows the number of weeks and remainder shows the number of days.

Converting Months into Years

Example

24 months

12 months = 1 year

24 ÷ 12 = 2 years

To change months into years, you should divide the given months by 12.

Exercise 17

1 year = 12 months

Convert months into years.

a. 96 months
b. 108 months
c. 144 months
d. 72 months
e. 48 months
f. 24 months

Problem Solving

a. A train left Chennai railway station at 4.30 p.m. on Sunday to go to Delhi. It reached Delhi after 28 hours. At what time did it reach Delhi?

b. Raju woke up at 5.00 a.m. and went jogging for an hour, did yoga for 45 minutes, homework for 1 hour and 10 minutes and then left for school. At what time did he leave for school?

c. Shyama went to her native village. She travelled by bus for 11 hours 15 minutes, by bullock cart for 4 hours and 20 minutes and walked a distance of 3 kilometres in 1 hour and 15 minutes. When do you think she reached the village if she left home at 7.00 a.m. on Monday?

d. A man left his house at 7.30 a.m. for work. He travelled for 1 hour to work and stayed at the office for 8 hours 30 minutes. He took half an hour extra to return home due to heavy traffic. What time did he reach home?

e. A lady's wristwatch stopped at 8.30 a.m. on Monday and she reset it at 5.00 p.m. on Tuesday after changing the battery cell. How long was the watch not functioning?

Vocabulary Learnt

passing   convert   seasons

measure   precious

Materials required
- A story to work on
- Clocks to mark on

Method (Note for the Teacher)

Ask the students to read the story carefully and mark the time on the clocks accordingly.

Leela started her morning walk at 6:00. She walked for 1 hour and 15 minutes. At what time did Leela finish walking?	Her father started jogging at the same time as Leela. He took 25 minutes less than Leela to complete his jogging. At what time did he finish?	10 minutes after her walk, Leela started watering the plants in the garden. It took her 1 hour and 30 minutes to finish. At what time did she finish watering?
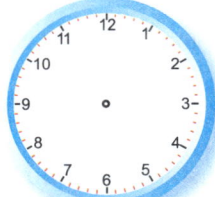		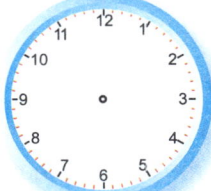

While Leela started watering the garden, her mother started clearing the weeds. She was tired after 30 minutes of work.

When did she stop working? (Mark on the given clock)

How much extra time did Leela spend in the garden than her mother? (Use the blank to write your answer.)

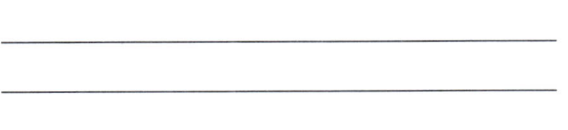

Their gardener came to work at 9:00 a.m. He worked there for 2 hours and 15 minutes. When did he finish the work?

14 Perimeter and Area

You know ...
- Geometry is a branch of Mathematics
- Geometry is all about points, lines and shapes
- how to recognise and name the basic plane shapes and solid shapes
- how to identify shapes based on their properties.

Maths Lab Activity 1

Materials required
- Cards with closed shapes
- Scale to measure

Method (Note for the Teacher)

Give several cards with closed shapes drawn on them to the students. Use quadrilaterals such as rectangles, squares and a few irregular shapes. Ask them to measure the distance around each shape in cm. Here are some questions that can be asked.

a. What is the total distance around the shape given to you?

b. How did you find the answer? (when a student gets a regular shape like a square or a rectangle)

c. Is there any quick way of finding the distance around your shape?

d. Can you do the same thing for an irregular shape? If not, why? Give reasons.

Once all the students have had an opportunity to talk about how they found the distance around their shapes, they could be told that 'perimeter' is the special name for the distance around any closed shape. It is usually measured in cm, m or km, depending on the dimensions of the shape.

You have learnt about different plane and solid shapes in the previous class. While plane shapes have only length and breadth, solid shapes also have height.

Now you can learn how to find out the measurement around the boundary of shapes and inside the boundary. The distance around a closed shape is called its perimeter. The space inside a closed shape is called its area.

Exercise 1

Measure the distance around the following by using a ruler or a metre tape.

a. Teacher's table _____   b. Your desk _____

c. Notebook _____   d. Blackboard _____

Perimeter of a Rectangle

a. What do you know about a rectangle? _____
b. How many sides does a rectangle have? _____
c. How many of these are lengths and how many are breadths? _____
d. How would you find the distance around a rectangle? Give two methods.
   i. _____
   ii. _____

Here is a formula that you can use to find the perimeter of a rectangle. Since there are two equal lengths and two equal breadths, add one length and one breadth and multiply the total by 2.

So, the formula for **perimeter** (P) of a rectangle is (L + B) × 2.

Example

Here is a rectangle ABCD. Its length is 5 cm and breadth is 3 cm.

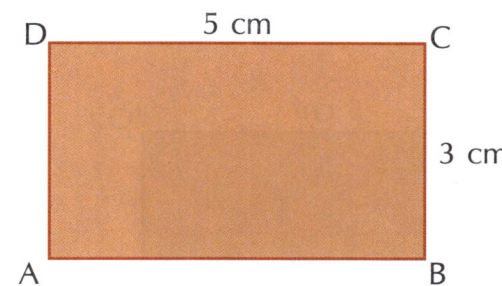

Since P = (L + B) × 2

So, P = (5 + 3) × 2 = 8 × 2 = 16 cm.

Exercise 2

Find the perimeter of the following rectangles by using the formula P = (L + B) × 2.

a.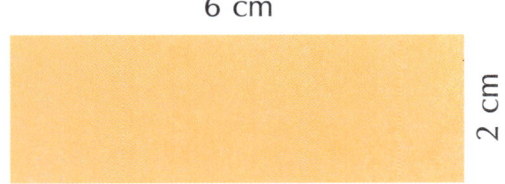

b.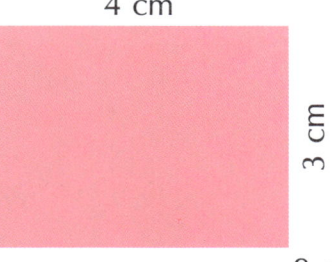

c.

d.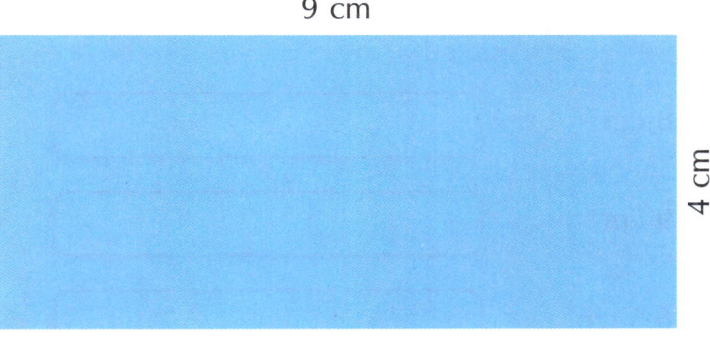

e.

Perimeter of a Square

a. What do you know about a square? _____

b. How many sides does a square have? _____

c. How many of these are lengths and how many are breadths? _____

d. How will you find the distance around a square? Give two ways.

   i. _____

   ii. _____

Here is a formula that you can use to find the perimeter of a square. Since all the four sides of a square are equal in length, multiply the length of one side by 4 to get the perimeter, leaving out 'B' which is used to refer breadth in rectangles.

So, the formula for perimeter (P) of a square is = side × 4.

Example Here is a square MNOP. Its each side is 5 cm.

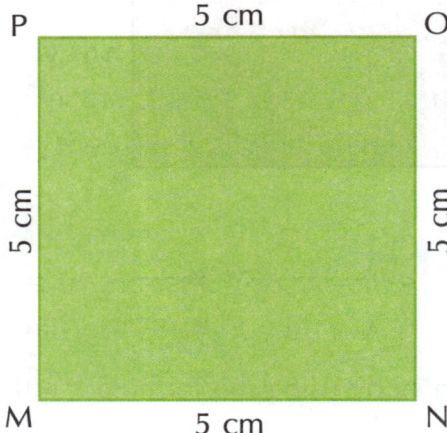

Since, perimeter = side × 4
Perimeter = 5 × 4 = 20 cm.

Exercise 3

Now, find the perimeter of the squares whose sides are given below. Use the above formula.

a. 8 cm _____   b. 7 cm _____

c. 9 cm _____   d. 6 cm _____

e. 6.5 cm _____   f. 3 cm _____

168

You have learnt to find the perimeter of regular shapes that have a rigid pattern. What about finding the perimeter of irregular shapes like this? Can any formula be applied?

Since this shape has more than four sides, you cannot have any definite formula. You have to measure each side separately and add them to find the perimeter.

Exercise 4

a. Find the perimeter (P) of the following irregular shapes.

i.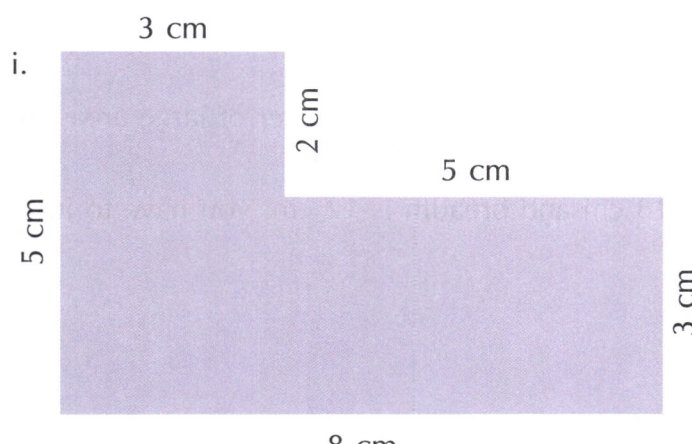

P = _____

ii.

P = _____

iii.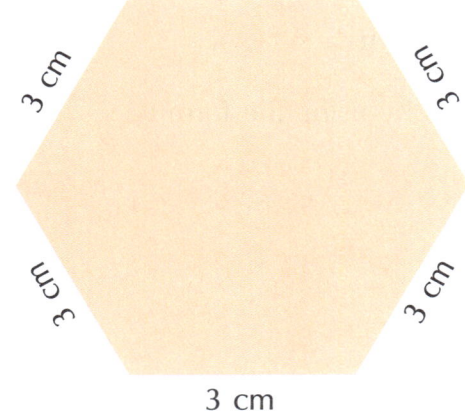

P = _____

iv.

P = _____

v.

P = _____

b. Find the perimeter of the following shapes after measuring them carefully in cm. Use the formula to find the perimeter wherever possible.

You cannot always use diagrams to calculate the perimeter. To find the perimeter of large areas like a playground where only measurements are given, only the formula can be used.

To find the perimeter of a rectangle whose length is 18 cm and breadth is 12 cm, you have to just use the formula.

P = (L + B) × 2

So, (18 + 12) × 2 = 30 × 2 = 60 cm.

Exercise 5

a. Find the perimeter of the following rectangles.

   i. L = 15 cm, B = 7 cm   ii. L = 21 cm, B = 3 cm

   iii. L = 18.5 cm, B = 13 cm   iv. L = 26 cm, B = 12.5 cm

   v. L = 124 cm, B = 44 cm   vi. L = 9 cm, B = 5.5 cm

b. In the same way, you can find the perimeter of bigger squares by using the formula. Find the perimeter of the squares with the following sides.

   i. 40 cm   ii. 82 cm   iii. 7.5 cm

   iv. 12.4 cm   v. 8.6 cm   vi. 5.8 cm

Area

You have now learnt to find the distance around closed shapes. How do you think we can find out how much space is occupied by that shape?

Look at this rectangle.

To find the space occupied by it, we need to fill it with something that fills it completely, without leaving gaps.

Exercise 6

Fill the inner space of the given shapes with different colours.

a.  b.  c.  d.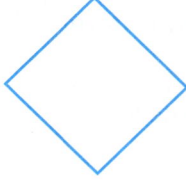

The distance around the boundary of a shape is called its **perimeter**. The space inside a shape is called its **area**. When you use something that fills the shape completely, you can count the number of pieces used and say that the area has so many pieces.

Look at the adjacent square. It has been filled with 1 cm square tiles and in each row there are 5 tiles. There are 5 rows altogether. So there are 5 × 5 = 25 square tiles that make up the area of this square.

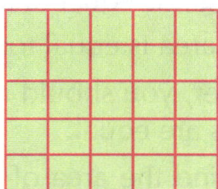

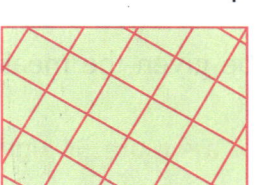

A shape like '◇' also fills up the space without leaving gaps, but it is difficult to estimate exactly how many have been used as all of them are not complete.

So, the area is generally measured by using only square units such as square cm, square m and square km, depending on the size of the object you are measuring. Since only square units are used, the answer is also given in square units. The area of the above square is equal to 25 square cm.

Exercise 7

Find out which unit of measurement you would use to find the area of the following. Match the two columns by colouring them alike.

Area of a postcard	millimetres
Area of a games field	centimetres
Area of a city	metres
Area of a stamp	kilometres

What do you think is the area of this rectangle?

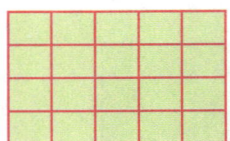

There are 4 rows of 5 squares each and 5 columns of 4 squares each. This means, 5 + 5 + 5 + 5 = 20 squares. So the area is equal to 20 square units.

Is there an easy way of finding this?

Yes. Instead of counting every box, you could multiply the number of rows by the number of columns, i.e.,

   5 × 4 = 20.

The columns form the length of the box and the rows form the width or the breadth of the box.

So, what do you think is the formula for finding area?

Area of a rectangle = Length × Breadth

The given rectangle has a perimeter of 24 m. Can you draw other rectangles with different dimensions but the same perimeter?

10 m

2 m

Now look at this square.

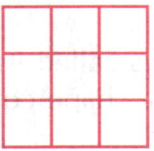

The length is equal to 3 units and the breadth is equal to 3 units.

So, the area is equal to 3 + 3 + 3 = 9 square units.

However, you should not use the words length and breadth when you are talking about squares because all sides are equal.

So, to find the area of a square, you will be given the measurement of a side and you have to multiply side × side, instead of length × breadth.

Area of a square = side × side

Here are a square and two rectangles. Fill each by drawing squares with sides equal to 1 cm inside them and find their areas by adding the squares. Then measure the length and breadth of the diagrams and multiply them together to see if you get the same answer.

Were the answers same?

Now, you should understand that you do not have to draw squares each time to find the area of a rectangle or a square. You can just multiply the length by breadth. In case of a square, it is side × side.

Exercise 8

Now find the area of the following squares and rectangles by using the correct formula.

a.
7 cm
3 cm

b.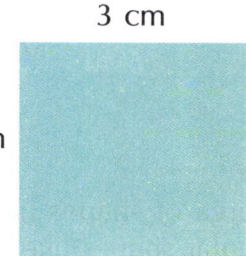
3 cm
3 cm

c.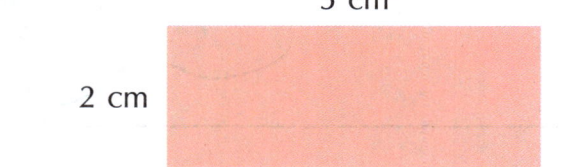
5 cm
2 cm

d.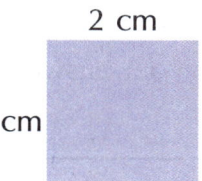
2 cm
2 cm

e.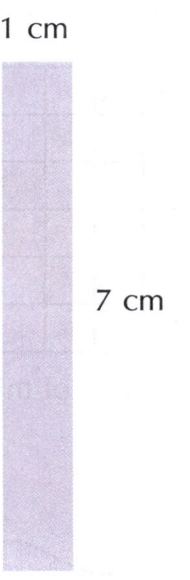
1 cm
7 cm

f.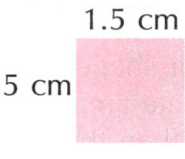
1.5 cm
1.5 cm

g.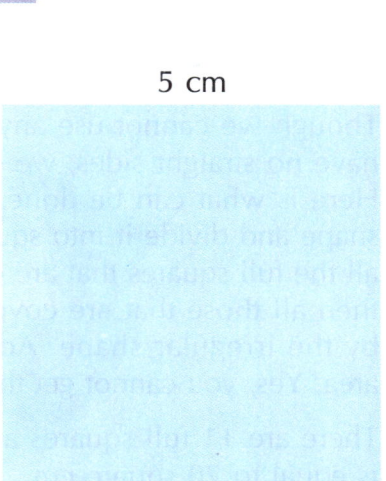
5 cm
8 cm

h.
3.5 cm
2.4 cm

Exercise 9

a. Find the area of the rectangles with the following dimensions by using the formula.

i. L = 12 cm, B = 5 cm

ii. L = 18 cm, B = 13 cm

iii. L = 16 cm, B = 2.5 cm

iv. L = 24 cm, B = 11 cm

v. L = 17.5 cm, B = 12.5 cm

vi. L = 16 cm, B = 4 cm

b. Find the area of the squares with the following dimensions by using the formula.

   i. Side = 12 cm   ii. Side = 2.7 cm   iii. Side = 4.6 cm

   iv. Side = 24 cm   v. Side = 31.4 cm   vi. Side = 5.1 cm

It is easy to find the area of shapes like rectangles and squares, but how do you think the areas of irregular shapes like this are found?

Do you think any formula can be applied? _____

Can you give reasons for your answer?

_____

_____

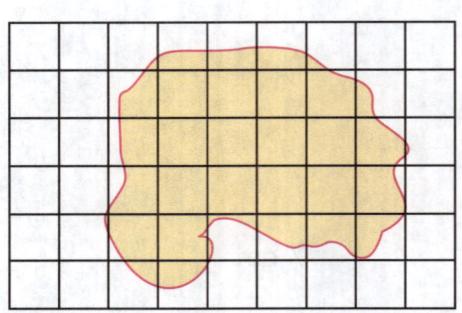

Though we cannot use any formula, because irregular shapes have no straight sides, we can still find the approximate area. Here is what can be done. Draw a rectangle bigger than the shape and divide it into squares of side 1 cm. Now, first count all the full squares that are enclosed by the irregular shape and then all those that are covered exactly half or more than half by the irregular shape. Add the two to get the approximate area. Yes, you cannot get the accurate area for irregular shapes.

There are 11 full squares and 9 squares that are more than half. So the approximate area of this shape is equal to 20 square cm.

Now by drawing 1 cm boxes on them, find the area of the following shapes.

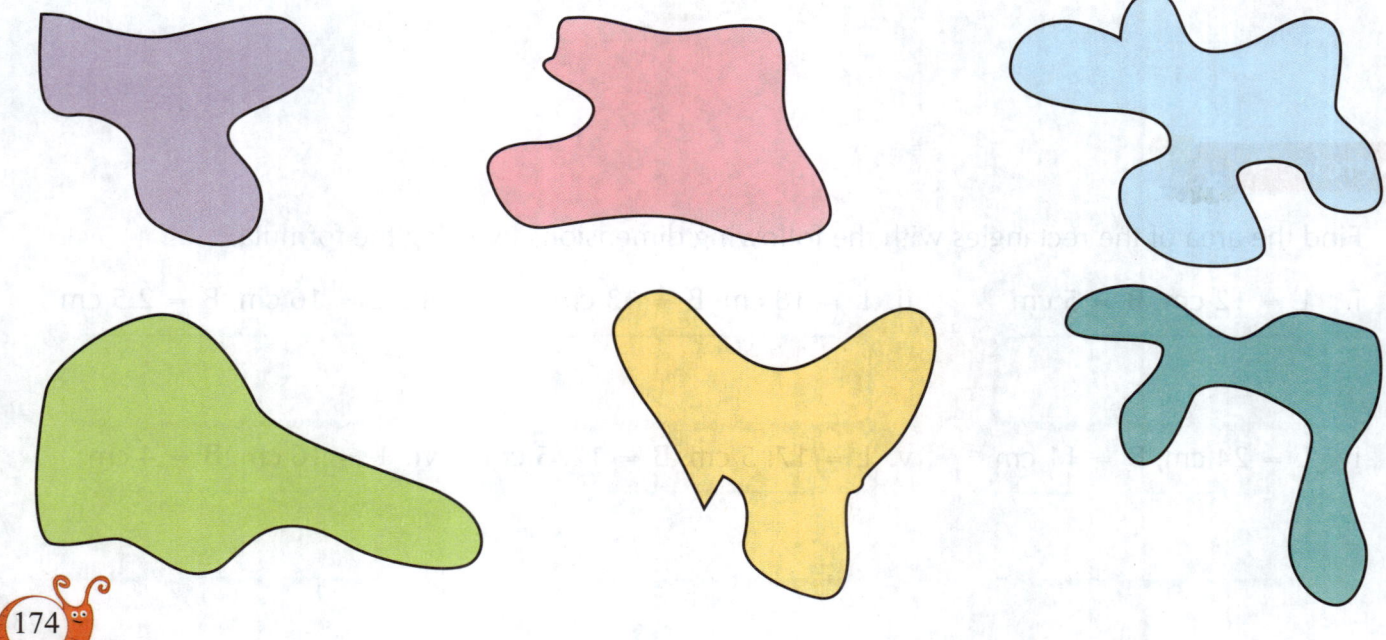

Exercise 10

Here are some irregular shapes drawn on a graph sheet, for your convenience. Find the approximate area of the shapes.

a.

b.

Remember
Every full square is equal to 1 unit.

c.

Remember
Every half or more than half squares is also counted as 1 unit.

d.

e.

Vocabulary Learnt

area   quadrilaterals   perimeter

irregular   space   breadth

approximate

Maths Lab Activity 2

Materials required
- Two pieces $\frac{1}{2}$ metre wool/threads
- Glue

Method (Note for the Teacher)

Ask the students to create any two irregular patterns on this square paper with the 2 half-metre threads. Each should be different in size and shape. Make sure that the two ends of the thread/wool do not overlap on finishing the shape.

Now find the area of the two shapes. You can only estimate the area of irregular shapes.

Remember

Count $\frac{1}{2}$ squares as one.

Remember

Leave out shape less than $\frac{1}{2}$.

Area of shape 1 = _____   Area of shape 2 = _____

15 Graphs

> **You know ...**
> - graphs are present in books and magazines.

A graph is a special kind of chart or picture containing a lot of information. Drawing graphs or locating points on a grid are some of the ways of showing the available information in a quick way, for one to read and interpret.

The plural of axis is axes.

Different Types of Graphs

There are many types of graphs.

| a. Pictograph | b. Bar graph | c. Line graph | d. Pie chart |

Pictographs

In a pictograph, lots of simple pictures are used to give information. Even when pictures are used as symbols, a key is provided to tell what quantity is represented by each symbol. Pictographs are used occasionally to represent less information, as they occupy a lot of space.

Example

If the graph is about 50 students in a class, you cannot be drawing 50 figures. So you need a key to it where one figure would mean 5 or 10 students.

Can you tell how many figures you would have to draw to show 50 students if one figure represented 10 students?

Exercise 1

Look at this pictograph.

Key: 1 fruit = 10 fruits

a. What does this graph represent?

b. What quantity is represented by each fruit?

c. Name the fruits in the shop.

d. Which is the most commonly found fruit?

e. Which two fruits are of equal quantity?

f. What numbers will you give along the 'Y axis' next to each fruit for this graph?

g. What is the total number of fruits in the shop?

h. How did you find the total number of fruits? Was it easy? Give one reason.

Exercise 2

Here is some information that you can use to make a pictograph. Make sure you use simple pictures or symbols that can be drawn to same size. Have a suitable key for the symbols. Give a name to the graph. Also, add the information about the graph on the two axes correctly.

Sally went to the terrace of her house. She looked around and saw 10 houses having slant roofs , 30 houses having dish antennas on the roofs , 5 houses having dish antennas , 10 houses having water tanks on top , 15 houses having roof gardens , 10 houses having a small room on top .

Now, record this information in a pictograph, so that Sally`s friends can learn all about the locality she lives in. Remember to give a key.

Bar Graph

A bar graph is another type of graph used for showing data or information in a quick way. A bar graph is also called a block or column graph because it is drawn by using vertical bars. Bar graphs are useful in comparing information. They are quite simple and easy to draw.

Exercise 3

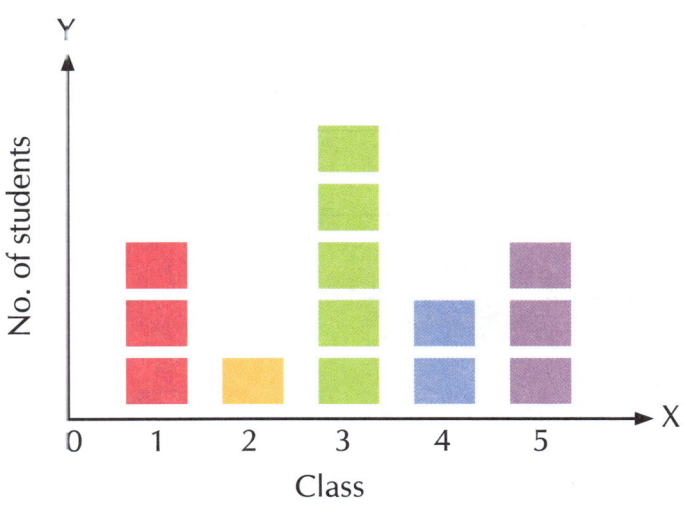

Key = is equal to 10 students.

This graph shows the number of students in a primary school. Each column shows the number of students in a given class.

The 'Y axis' shows the number of students in each class and the 'X axis' shows the names of the classes.

Now, answer the questions given below.

a. How many students are there in this school?
b. Which class has the highest number of students?
c. Which class has the least number of students?
d. Which two classes have the same number of students?

Exercise 4

The names of the dresses you have are shown along the 'X' axis and how many of each dress you have is represented along the 'Y' axis.

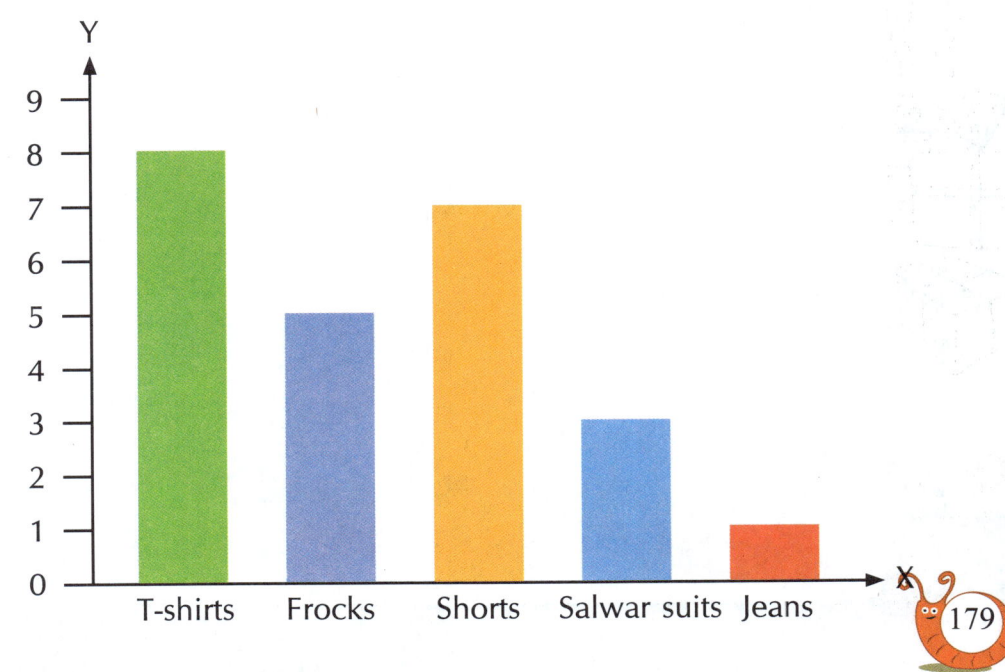

From this graph, you can find out the different kinds of dresses you have at a glance. It is also easy to say how many dresses you have without going to your room, opening your cupboard, pulling out all the dresses and counting them one by one. Can you write down five questions to gather information from this graph?

a. _____

b. _____

c. _____

d. _____

e. _____

Exercise 5

Now, use the information given below to make a bar graph.

Five friends, namely, Andrew, John, Suresh, Mukund and Harjeet, went for their friend's birthday party. They had lots of things to eat and plenty of games to play. But what they needed most was water as it was a very hot day. Andrew drank 16 glasses of water, John drank 10 glasses, Suresh had 12 glasses, Mukund had 8 glasses and Harjeet drank 10 glasses. Record how many glasses of water they drank by using a bar graph.

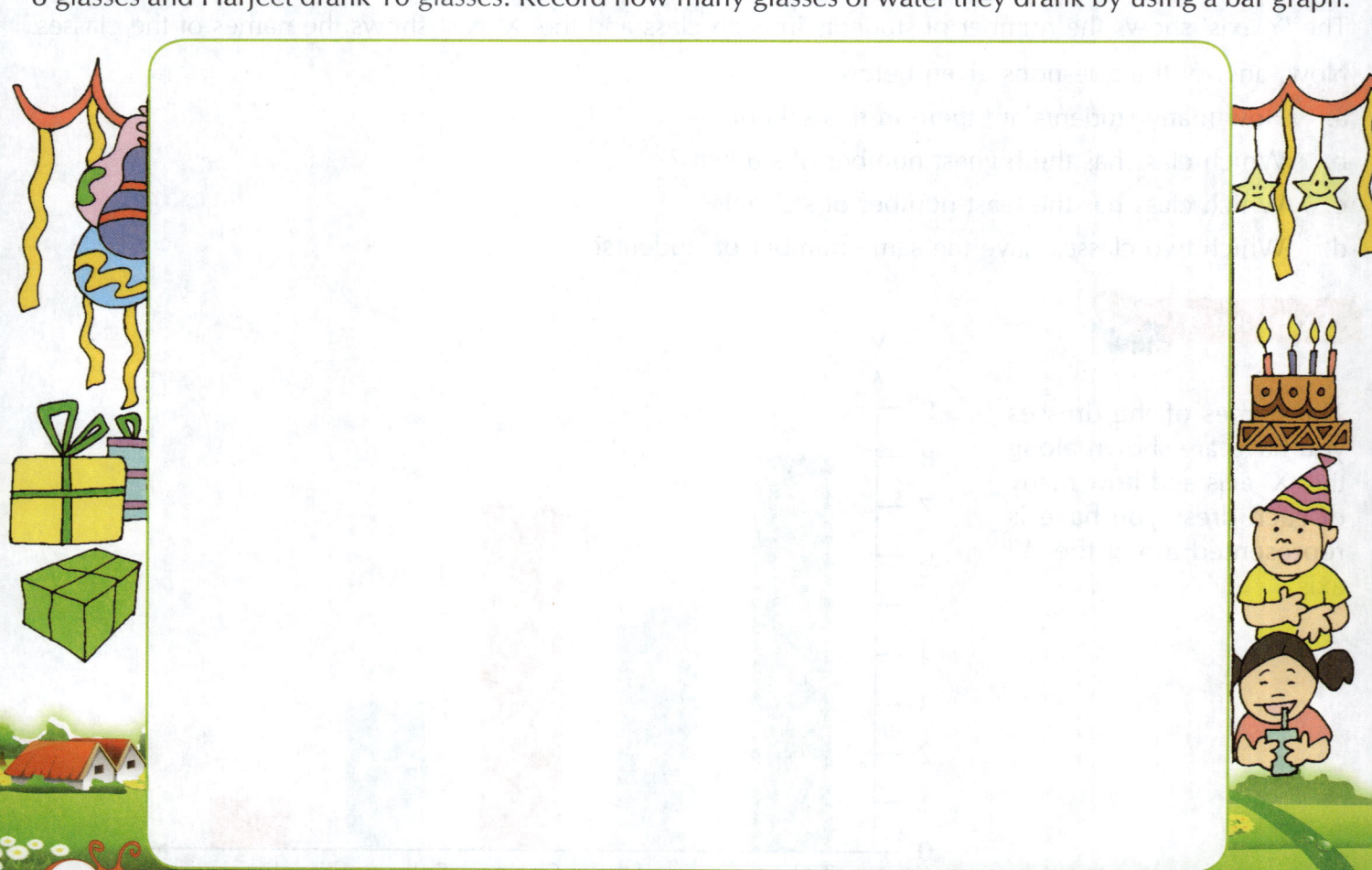

Line Graph

When a graph is drawn just with lines, instead of pictures or bars, we call it a **line graph**. Line graphs are used to show gradual changes in the information.

First you need the two axes. Then you need to write down what the graph is all about and write the information along the two axes. Now, find the coordinates of the two axes and mark a dot at their meeting point. After all the points have been marked, they should be joined to one another. By reading the line that goes up and down, we can find out the information presented on the graph. The line may just go up or down, and sometimes up and down.

Exercise 6

Look at this line graph. Answer the questions.

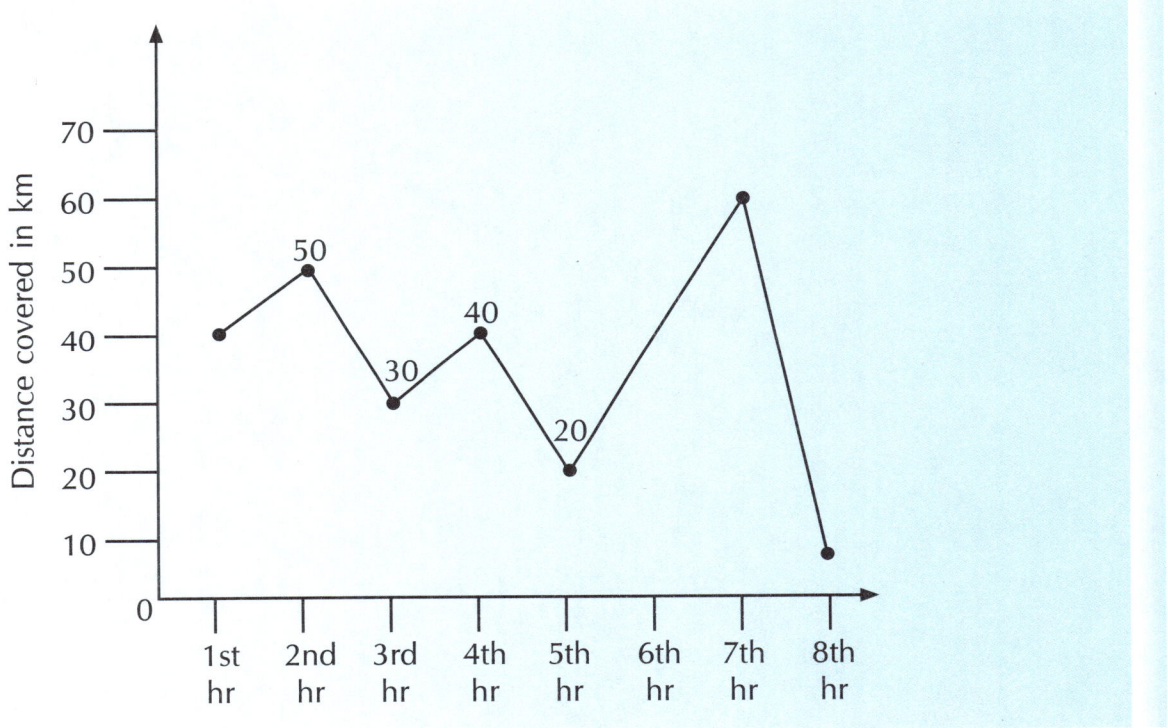

This line graph shows the distance covered by Alok when he made a trip in his car from Delhi to Shimla.

Try to answer the following questions.

a. How many hours did it take Alok to reach Shimla from Delhi? _____

b. In which hour did Alok travel the fastest? _____

c. What is the total distance from Delhi to Shimla? _____

d. Why do you think his speed reduced in the fifth hour? _____

e. If Alok left Delhi at 6 a.m., when do you think he would have reached Shimla? _____

f. Why do you think he covered only a short distance in the last hour? _____

Exercise 7

Now try to make a line graph to show the following information.

In the month of March, Raghu's teacher conducted five tests in preparation for his Board examinations. The following are his scores in the five tests – 45%, 60%, 45%, 80% and 95%. Can you draw a line graph to record his scores?

Pie Chart

Pie chart is a 'circular graph'. A circle is divided into the required number of parts to give the information. The parts are divided into different-sized sections, depending on the size of the information.

Exercise 8

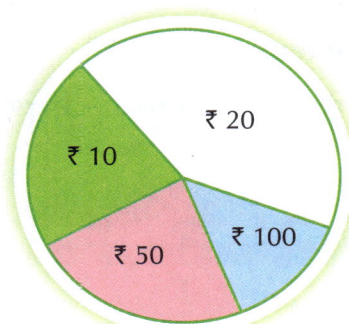

This pie chart is about the various tickets sold at an amusement park.

Just by looking at the pie chart, you can find a lot of information.

Answer the following.

a. Which is the costliest ticket? _____
b. Which is the cheapest ticket? _____
c. Which ticket was sold the most? _____
d. Which ticket was sold the least? _____
e. Can you think of a reason why more tickets of ₹ 20 were sold than those of ₹ 10?

_____
_____
_____

Exercise 9

Now draw a pie chart for the information given below.

Here is how Ramu spends his day usually.

Sleeping – 9 hours   At school – 6 hours
At play – 3 hours   Homework – 2 hours
Reading books – 1 hour Watching television – 2 hours
Time with parents – 1 hour

Make a pie chart to show this. Remember to first divide the circle into 24 parts as there are 24 hours in a day.

You can use this circle for your activity.

Fill each part with a different colour to make your pie chart look beautiful.

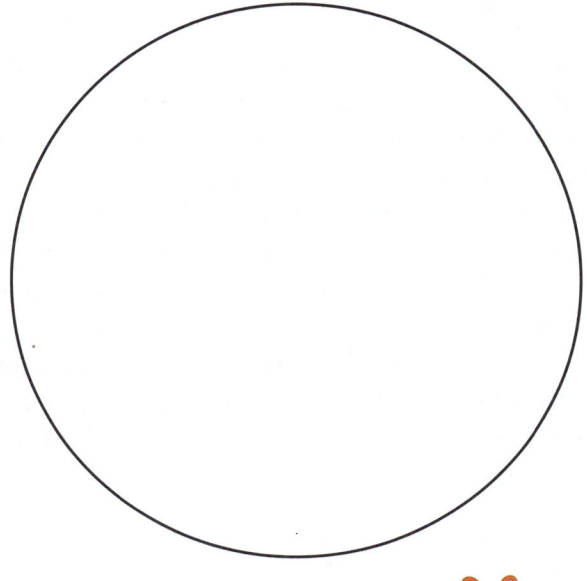

Vocabulary Learnt

locating   information   graph
interpret   data   pie chart
gather   axis   bars

Make a bar graph of your own for the story given below. Remember to give a title, and write the information both on the "Y" and "X" axes.

The class 4 students were very excited. They were going on a field trip to the zoo.

Their teacher gave them all the necessary instructions about how they should behave and stay as a group before they got off the bus at the zoo. After walking about 50 metres, they saw 3 huge baboons that were imitating the people around. It was funny to watch. Then they saw a cage with lions written on it. They were warned not to go too near. There were half a dozen lions, big and small. Some were walking up and down while some were growling. Probably they were hungry. Next they moved on to see some zebras. The children remembered their teacher telling them that no 2 zebras had the same type of stripes. So they wanted to check it out. But unfortunately there was just a lonely one grazing quietly.

Suddenly they were attracted by the loud call of the peacock. They turned around and found 5 of them, 3 white and 2 colourful. That was the first time they had seen a fully white peacock. It did not look that pretty they thought. Just then they saw the trio, ostriches running fast, chasing each other. It was an interesting sight. They would have for sure run faster if they had more space.

There were some squeaky noises from the tiger's cage. What a surprise! Quadruplets! Yes the tigress had just given birth but they could not see the mother. The babies were busy trying to push and climb on each other. They looked really cute. From far they could see the heads of some giraffes who were munching leaves from the branches of a tall tree. They thought that there were 6 of them. Since some of the children could not see them clearly, they went closer to check out. Actually there was 1 more that was not visible from far as it was not as tall as the others. So they had not spotted it. A pair of Rhinoceroses were lazing around in the dirty pond and they were fully covered by mud. The day was getting hotter. Some of them wanted to return as they were tired. So they started walking back. Just as they came closer to the exit gate, a dozen geese walked across majestically. So they stopped and gave way for them before coming out to board the bus. It was a great trip they thought even though they had not seen any bears, porcupines or elephants that are so common in zoos.

16 Money

> **You know ...**
> - about money
> - different denominations of coins and banknotes and their values
> - usage of money
> - how to convert different denominations.

You have already learnt about different denominations of coins and banknotes. Money is very important, as everything we use has some value and anything valuable cannot be procured free.

Money involves earning, spending and saving.

Maths Lab Activity 1

Materials required
- Scrapbook

Method (Note for the Teacher)
Ask the students to collect currency notes and coins of different countries. They can take the help of relatives and friends living abroad. Ask them to prepare a scrapbook based on the collection.

Exercise 1

Write **true** or **false**.

a. When work is done some money is earned.

b. All countries use the same currency.

c. Spending all your money leaves you with no saving.

d. When you buy some item, you get some money.

e. There is no need to look at the cost when you decide to buy an item.

f. Saving regularly helps to take care of sudden expenses.

Exercise 2

Different countries use different banknotes and coins. They also have different names. Here are pictures of few banknotes used in different countries. Find out their names. One has been done for you.

Name: Dollar
Country: United States of America

Name: _____
Country: United Kingdom

Name: _____
Country: Bangladesh

Name: _____
Country: United Arab Emirates

Name: _____
Country: Japan

Name: _____
Country: China

Conversion of Rupees and Paise
Converting rupees to paise

Example   ₹ 4.30
= 400 + 30 + 430 paise

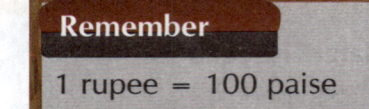

Remember

1 rupee = 100 paise

Exercise 3

Change to paise.

a. ₹ 8.50

b. ₹ 5.45

c. ₹ 6.45

d. ₹ 2.10

e. ₹ 2.15

f. ₹ 9.10

g. ₹ 8.80

h. ₹ 3.25

Converting paise to rupees and paise

Example
215 p
= 200 + 15
= ₹ 2 + 15 p   = ₹ 2.15

Remember
100 paise = 1 rupee

Exercise 4

Change to rupee and paise.

a. 335 p

b. 725 p

c. 645 p

d. 365 p

e. 410 p

f. 115 p

g. 720 p

h. 510 p

Converting rupees to 50 p coins

Example   ₹ 5.00
= 5 × 2 = 10
So 10 fifty paise coins make ₹ 5.00.

Remember
₹ 1 = two 50 paise coins
To change rupees to 50 p coins, multiply by 2.

Exercise 5

Change rupees to 50 paise coins.

a. ₹ 8.00

b. ₹ 9.00

c. ₹ 5.00

d. ₹ 6.00

e. ₹ 4.00

f. ₹ 1.00

g. ₹ 7.00

h. ₹ 2.00

MENTAL MATH

1. If Rohit spends ₹ 11.50 on a toy and ₹ 32.60 on a box of hand towels, how much does he spend all together?

2. If Mansi spends ₹ 14.50 for one bottle of Limca, and she needs 7 such bottles, how much will it cost her?

3. Shahnawaz went to the shop with ₹ 67.00 and spent ₹ 43.40. How much will be left with him?

4. When Joel went to buy a pair of shoes for ₹ 199.99, he was told that there was a discount of ₹ 18.50 on it. How much did he have to pay for the shoes?

5. Sheetal gets ₹ 15.00 as pocket money per week from her dad. If she spends ₹ 46.30 after 4 weeks, how much will be left with her?

Addition Involving Money

We add or subtract money the same way as we do with whole numbers. The point (dot) between numbers separates rupees from paise. So, when you add or subtract, remember to put the point.

Exercise 6

Add the following.

a.
   ₹ p
   25.40
   + 33.55

b.
   ₹ p
   34.90
   + 12.55

c.
   ₹ p
   14.55
   + 34.75

d.
   ₹ p
   24.10
   + 12.45

e.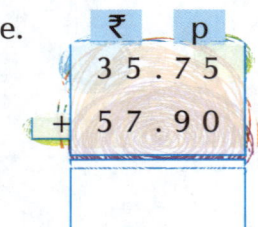
   ₹ p
   35.75
   + 57.90

f.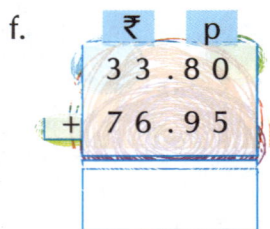
   ₹ p
   33.80
   + 76.95

g.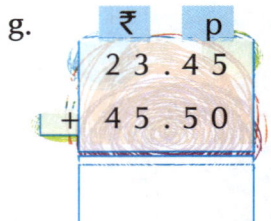
   ₹ p
   23.45
   + 45.50

h.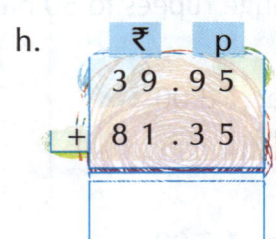
   ₹ p
   39.95
   + 81.35

i.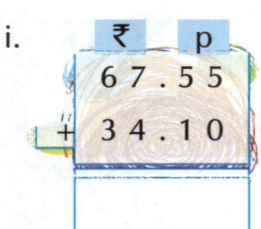
   ₹ p
   67.55
   + 34.10

j.
   ₹ p
   26.15
   + 71.55

k.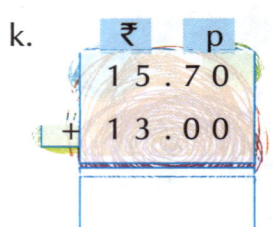
   ₹ p
   15.70
   + 13.00

l.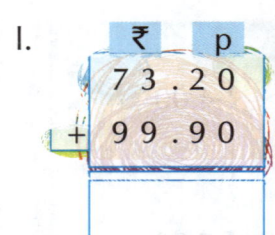
   ₹ p
   73.20
   + 99.90

Subtraction Involving Money

Exercise 7

Subtract the following.

a.
₹	p
63	40
− 45	50

b.
₹	p
39	90
− 21	35

c.
₹	p
67	55
− 34	10

d.
₹	p
26	15
− 11	25

e.
₹	p
15	70
− 13	00

f.
₹	p
73	20
− 56	90

g.
₹	p
34	70
− 15	50

h.
₹	p
56	40
− 21	75

i.
₹	p
58	20
− 24	10

j.
₹	p
62	45
− 10	70

k.
₹	p
65	40
− 12	80

l.
₹	p
93	70
− 66	15

Problem Solving

a. Gracy bought a diary for ₹ 8.25, a dictionary for ₹ 35.50 and a book mark for 50 paise. How much money did she spend in all?

b. Sarayu goes to a shop with ₹ 350 to buy a sari. The sari she chooses is priced ₹ 415.50. How much more money does she require to buy that sari?

c. Kasim bought a bar of chocolate for ₹ 15.00 and a packet of biscuits for ₹ 18.50. He gave ₹ 50 to the shopkeeper. How much money should he get back?

Exercise 7

Given below are some objects that you can buy from a bookstore. See their prices and answer the questions given on the next page.

₹ 2.50   ₹ 25.50   ₹ 3.50   ₹ 5.50

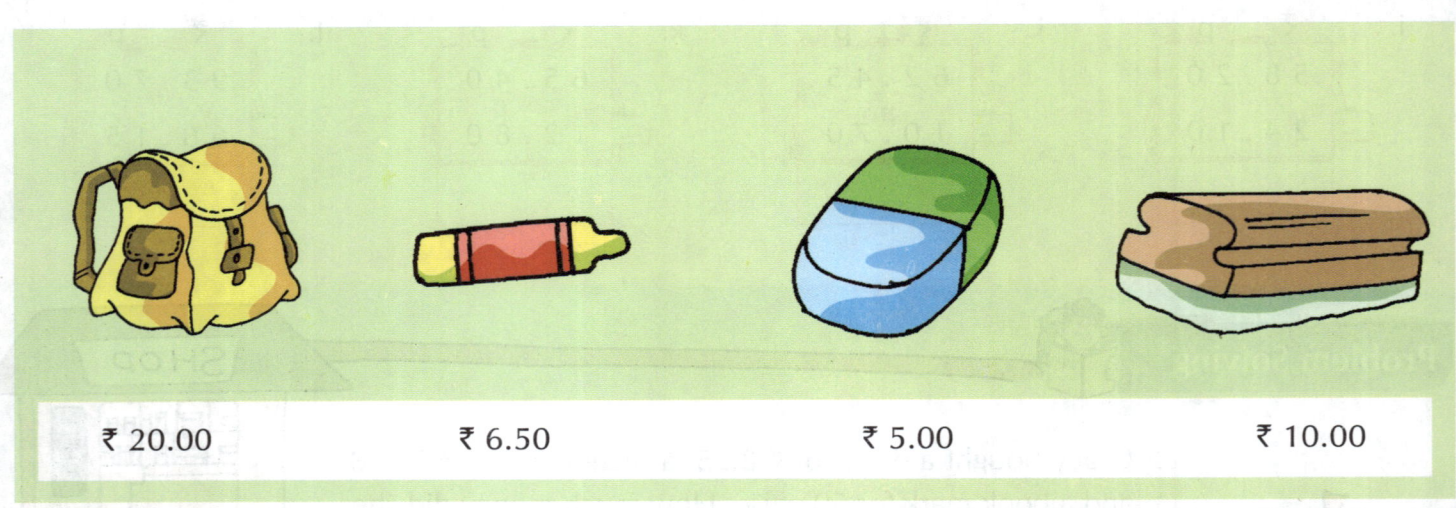

₹ 20.00   ₹ 6.50   ₹ 5.00   ₹ 10.00

₹ 12.50   ₹ 3.00   ₹ 84.50   ₹ 2.00

BOOKSTORE

a. If you go to a bookstore and you have to buy three things, which three will you choose? How much would you pay for them in all?

b. If you are interested in learning new words and you want to write them down, what are the three things you would buy? How much would you pay for them altogether?

c. You are selected for a drawing competition. Which are the things you would buy to take with you? Find their total cost.

d. You are now going to a higher class and your teacher says you cannot write with a pencil any more. What item would you buy from the shop to take to school? What is its cost?

e. Which item would you buy so that all the materials you buy for school use can be carried safely? What is its price?

f. You are doing a project on wild animals. Which item would you get from the bookstore so that you can gather a lot of information? What is its cost?

g. When you write down notes in your note pad, your writing goes crooked. What can you buy from the shop that will help you write in straight lines? What is its price?

h. Now write down a question based on the objects that you can buy from a bookstore.

Maths Lab Activity 2

Materials required
- Printouts of 500-rupee notes
- A set of questions on the note
- Paper
- Pencil

Method (Note for the Teacher)

Prepare a set of questions on 500-rupee notes (one has been shown below). Divide the students into groups. Give each group a printout of a 500-rupee note. Ask them to study the note carefully and answer the questions.

Some questions are given below.

a. What is the value of this note?

b. What are the two ways in which you can find out the value of this note?

c. There is a national emblem on the note. What is it called?

d. Whose face do you see here?

e. What do people call the person you see on the note?

f. What is the serial number on this note? (It is written twice.)

g. Who has signed this note?

h. What is the promise made by him on the note?

i. Which bank has printed this note?

j. How many languages have been used to write '500 rupees' on the reverse?

Summative Assessment 3
(For chapters 13 to 16)

1. Look at the calendar given below.

Sun	Mon	Tue	Wed	Thu	Fri	Sat
		1	2	3	4	5
6	7	8	9	10	11	12
13	14	15	16	17	18	19
20	21	22	23	24	25	26
27	28	29				

Now, answer the following questions:
   a. Which month is shown in this calendar?
   b. What date is the fifth Tuesday of this month?
   c. What date is the third Friday of this month?
   d. How many Saturdays are there in this month?
   e. Which is more — number of Sundays or Fridays?

2. Mark the time on the following clocks drawing minute and hour hands.

      3:15   4:50   6:35

3. Convert hours to minutes.
   a. 8 hr   b. 7 hr   c. 5 hr   d. 12 hr

4. Convert hours and minutes to minutes.
   a. 5 hr 13 min   b. 7 hr 23 min   c. 3 hr 39 min

5. Rony woke up at 6.00 a.m. and went jogging for 1 hr and 15 min. Then he did his homework for 1 hr and 25 min and left for school. At what time did he leave for school?

6. Find the perimeter of the following rectangles:
   a. Length = 8.5 cm   Breadth = 3 cm   b. Length = 9.5. cm   Breadth = 2.5 cm

7. Find the area of the following rectangles:
   a. Length = 6.4 cm   Breadth = 3.8 cm   b. Length = 7.7 cm   Breadth = 4.2 cm

8. Find the perimeter of the squares whose sides are given below.
   a. 3.4 cm   b. 7.2 cm   c. 5 cm   d. 8 cm

9. Find the area of the following squares:
   a. Side = 4.5 cm   b. Side = 7 cm   c. Side = 5.2 cm

10. Draw a line graph for the following information:

    Gokul went from Chennai to Trichi in 6 hours by car. He drove 50 km in the first hour, 40 km in the second hour, 35 km in the third hour, 40 km in the fourth hour, 45 km in the fifth hour and 55 km in the sixth hour and then reached Trichi.

    After drawing the graph, frame any 5 questions of your own for the graph.

11. How much more to make ₹ 3?
    a. 235 p b. 165 p c. 99 p d. 207 p

12. Akbar goes to a book shop with ₹ 150. The storybook he chooses is priced ₹ 217.25. How much more money does he need to buy that storybook?

13. Match by colouring alike.

    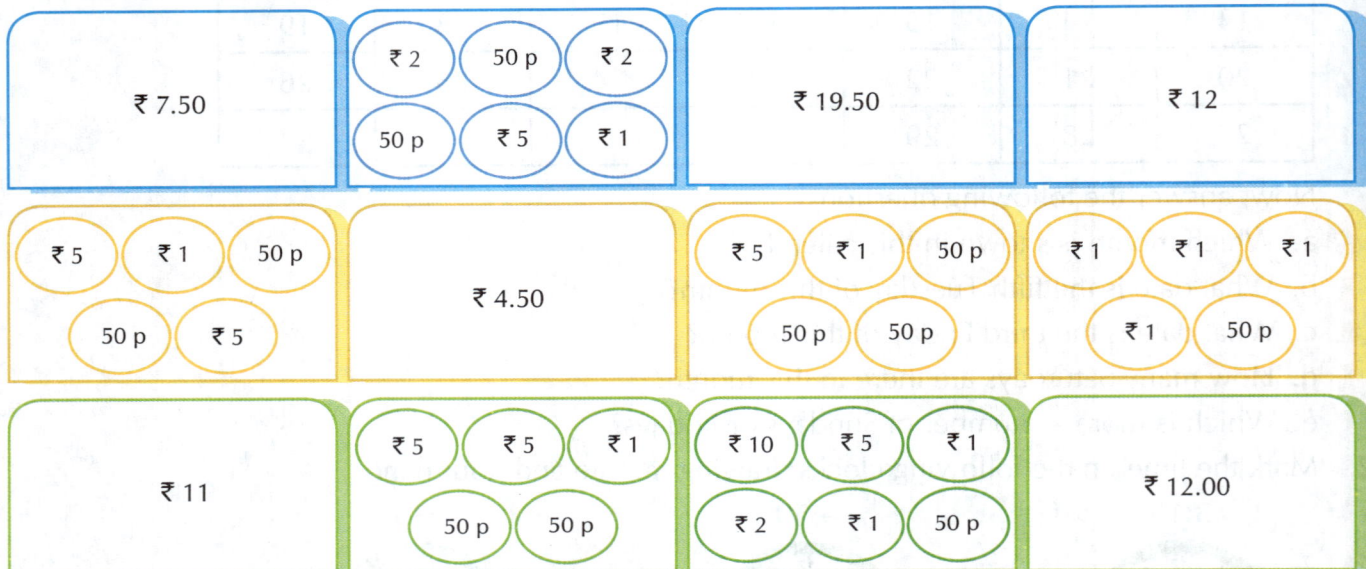

14. Add the following:

    a.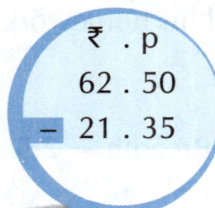

    ₹ . p
    32 . 50
    + 22 . 25

    b.
    ₹ . p
    53 . 30
    + 25 . 20

    c.
    ₹ . p
    97 . 40
    + 47 . 35

15. Subtract the following:

    a.
    ₹ . p
    62 . 50
    − 21 . 35

    b.
    ₹ . p
    98 . 10
    − 42 . 20

    c.
    ₹ . p
    82 . 25
    − 13 . 45

16. Change to rupees and paise.
    a. 133 p b. 826 p c. 939 p d. 225 p

17. Change to paise.
    a. ₹ 1.27 b. ₹ 4.30 c. ₹ 2.76 d. ₹ 880

Summative Assessment 4
(For chapters 1 to 16)

1. What is the 14th number after 129?
   a. 133
   b. 143
   c. 134
2. The smallest 5-digit number is
   a. 10000.
   b. 10001.
   c. 99999.
3. Four thousand one hundred two is
   a. 4210.
   b. 4120.
   c. 4102.
4. 36, 49, 184 is
   a. International numeral
   b. Roman numeral
   c. Hindu-Arabic numeral
5. (51 + 7) + (43 + 9) is
   a. Commutative property
   b. Distributive property
   c. Associative property
6. 7486 rounded to the nearest 100 is
   a. 7500.
   b. 7400.
   c. 7586.
7. 432 in Roman numeral is
   a. XXXXIIIII.
   b. CDXXXII.
   c. CCCCXXXII.
8. 7062 is divisible by
   a. 2 and 4.
   b. 3 and 4.
   c. 2, 3 and 6.
9. Twin prime numbers are
   a. 11 and 15.
   b. 11 and 13.
   c. 17 and 23.
10. Coprime numbers are
    a. 11 and 24.
    b. 11 and 99.
    c. 11 and 22.
11. Least common multiple of 75 and 30 is
    a. 105.
    b. 150.
    c. 155.
12. 56 is a multiple of
    a. 2, 3, 8, 14, 7, 28 and 56.
    b. 2, 4, 7, 8, 14, 28 and 56.
    c. 2, 3, 4, 7, 18, 28 and 56.
13. Which fraction has the largest denominator?
    a. $\dfrac{7}{21}$
    b. $\dfrac{8}{51}$
    c. $\dfrac{14}{36}$

14. What do you mean by perimeter and area?

15. Find perimeter of the following figures.

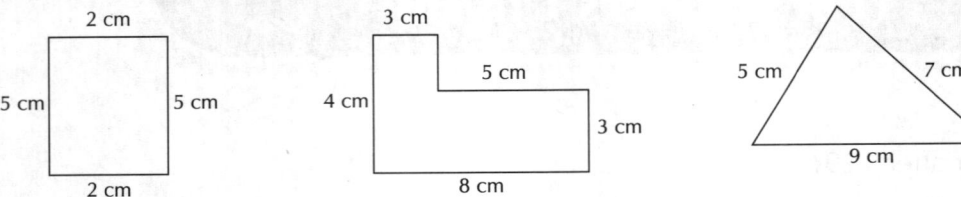

16. Find area of the following figures.

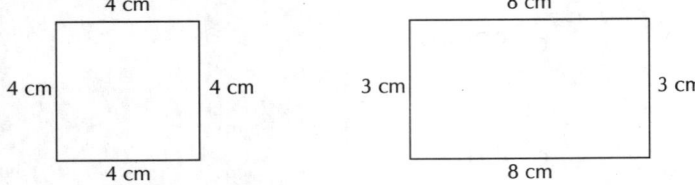

17. Name any 3 different kinds of graphs.

18. Draw a pictograph to show the following information.

    A man bought 5 apples, 8 bananas, 4 guavas and 10 oranges from a fruit market.

19. What is the cost of 8 pencils, if each pencil costs ₹ 2.50?

20. Preetam bought a ruler for ₹ 2.50, a book for ₹ 89.50, a pencil for ₹ 5.50, a box of crayons for ₹ 13 and an eraser for ₹ 2. How much did he spend in all?